AF898758

TOUCH

Previously published

SEE 2018

DOI: https://doi.org/10.16997/book12

TASTE 2018

DOI: https://doi.org/10.16997/book21

Forthcoming

SMELL

HEAR

Law and the Senses Series
The Westminster Law & Theory Lab

TOUCH

Edited by
Caterina Nirta
Danilo Mandic
Andrea Pavoni
Andreas Philippopoulos-Mihalopoulos

UNIVERSITY OF
WESTMINSTER
PRESS

Published by
University of Westminster Press
115 New Cavendish Street
London W1W 6UW
www.uwestminsterpress.co.uk

Text © the editors and several contributors 2020
First published 2020

Series cover concept: Hashemi-Nezhad Ltd.
Print and digital versions typeset by Siliconchips Services Ltd.

ISBN (Hardback): 978-1-912656-66-0
ISBN (Paperback): 978-1-912656-34-9
ISBN (PDF): 978-1-912656-35-6
ISBN (EPUB): 978-1-912656-36-3
ISBN (Kindle): 978-1-912656-37-0

DOI: https://doi.org/10.16997/book37

This work is licensed under the Creative Commons Attribution-NonCommercial-NoDerivatives 4.0 International License. To view a copy of this license, visit http://creativecommons.org/licenses/by-nc-nd/4.0/ or send a letter to Creative Commons, 444 Castro Street, Suite 900, Mountain View, California, 94041, USA. This license allows for copying and distributing the work, providing author attribution is clearly stated, that you are not using the material for commercial purposes, and that modified versions are not distributed.

The full text of this book has been peer-reviewed to ensure high academic standards. For full review policies, see: http://www.uwestminsterpress.co.uk/site/publish/

Suggested citation:
Nirta, C., Mandic, D., Pavoni, A. and Philippopoulos-Mihalopoulos, A. 2020 *Touch*. London: University of Westminster Press. DOI: https://doi.org/10.16997/book37. License: CC-BY-NC-ND 4.0

To read the free, open access version of this book online, visit https://doi.org/10.16997/book37 or scan this QR code with your mobile device:

Contents

Introduction

Caterina Nirta

Apart from touch … no other powers of sense-perception can exist: and this organ of touch is composed neither of the earth nor of any other of the elements … the animal cannot exist without the sense of touch.[1]

1. Law and the Senses

Philosophy tends to relegate senses to the realm of phenomenology and experience. By contrast, critical theory has gradually eroded the holy opposition between knowing and sensing to the extent that new speculative trends are now seeking to rebuild it. While the social sciences endeavour to frame sensing within socio-historical genealogies, scientific research draws deterministic connections between our sensing the world and the neurophysics hardware. At the same time, planetary modifications gesturing towards the seemingly unavoidable extinction of humanity suggest 'post' human ways

[1] Aristotle. 'De Anima' (435b XIII) translated by E. W. (c. 1870), 35.

of sensing, with novel technologies that enable us to understand things that escape human capacity to sense, thus widening up perception to inhuman scales and temporalities. Meanwhile, capitalism relentlessly crafts our sensorial immersion into hyperaesthetic atmospheres, mirrored by art's ongoing fetishisation of site-specific sensoriality.

Law is present in all this, and with a complexity that is yet to be addressed in the current sensorial turn in legal thinking.[2] In fact, law and the senses have been mostly explored through the usual *law vs. 'what escapes law'* framework, one that characterises many of the 'law *and…*' approaches (e.g. law and space, law and materiality etc.). In other words, the tendency in most cases has been that of remaining trapped within a phenomenological understanding of senses, oscillating between two sides (law vs. the senses) of an unquestioned opposition, occupying each of the sides of the partition without fully exploring its promising threshold.[3] This has generated a series of compelling but ultimately limited narratives. Namely, law is assumed to be the anaesthetic par excellence,

---

[2] We are not the first to deal with this. See Lionel Bently and Leo Flynn, eds., *Law and the Senses: Sensational Jurisprudence* (London: Pluto Press, 1996); Bernard J. Hibbitts, 'Coming to Our Senses: Communication and Legal Expression in Performance Cultures', *Emory Law Journal* 41, no. 4 (1992): 873–955. See also the ongoing project 'Law and the Regulation of the Senses: Explorations in Sensori-Legal Studies', coordinated by David Howes at the Centre for Sensory Studies, http://www.centreforsensorystudies.org/related-interest/law-and-the-regulation-of-the-senses-explorations-in-sensori-legal-studies.

[3] For a recent attempt in this direction see Sheryl Hamilton et al., eds., *Sensing Law* (Abingdon: Routledge, 2017).

constantly numbing the polymorphous realm of the sensorial in order to assert the rational domain of normativity. According to this narrative, the legal project is a systematic attempt to depurate law from any compromise with the sensible and its contingent imprecision. The *violence, coldness* and *alienation* of legal abstraction, and its systematic denial of the sensual spontaneity of life, are the de rigueur accusations against law, whose failure the critical thinker is quick to point out: senses are not amenable to legal machinations, they always escape law's cumbersome and joyless – to put it à la Spinoza – apparatus.

Hence the call to re-materialise, re-spatialise, re-sensitise law: to let law come to its senses, that is. Except that law has never been outside the senses. Its way of making sense of the world is always premised on its sensorial immersion in the world itself. This appreciation requires not only thinking law differently, but also thinking senses differently. This could open a path, we argue, towards exploring the sensoriality of law, both in the epistemological way in which law engages with, and indeed senses the world, as well as the ontological emergence of law from the sensorial continuum of the world itself. This series intends to pursue this path through four intersecting conceptual endeavours.

First, to disarticulate the sensorial from its reduction to the phenomenological, the subjective, the personal and the human dimension. This reductionism, which law is simultaneously responsible for and in denial of, underlies the majority of approaches dealing with law and the senses, and constitutes the unspoken fissure around which the two realms are split. Disarticulating the senses from their direct subjective and phenomenological relevance may enable them to appear as a gateway to a post-human and ecological understanding of the spatio-legal, thus repurposing them as a promising tool with which to investigate the materiality of law's relation to the world. At the same time, gesturing towards the inhuman dimensions of sensing that climatic catastrophes, technological innovations, and philosophical and artistic praxis hint at may allow us to think novel ways, subjects and objects of sensing, whose impact on questions of agency, responsibility and politics is paramount.

Second, to dismantle the law/senses separation by widening the fissure into a complex ontology, and thus revealing the necessary but ultimately insufficient critique of law's 'anaesthetising' enterprise. This entails challenging the taken-for-granted presupposition of the law as a systematic attempt to purify itself from any compromise with the sensible and its contingent frictions. This, in fact, is only a part of the story. Law is certainly an anaesthetising *project* aimed at manipulating, governing, and channelling the senses into precise categories, boundaries and definitions, protecting from and numbing the sensorial, the bodily, the libidinal. Yet law is also an emerging *process*, that is, a diffuse normativity emerging out of the intermingling of bodies and senses that constitutes our being-together, and as such is inseparable from it. The relation between law and the senses is not one of straightforward oppression or control of the latter by the former, but rather a surface on which sensorial law (law folding into senses) and legal senses (senses folding into law) are reciprocally affected, and on which surface each fold pursues its own mythology of origin, meaning, direction, teleology. The law-senses assemblage should be thus addressed by fully tackling the consequences of the unavoidable discrepancy between the de-sensitising project of legal control and the multi-sensorial process of legal emergence.

Third, and expanding on the foregoing observation: to expose the role of law in keeping this very dichotomy in place. This is effected by suggesting that beneath law itself lies unruly sensorial freedom; the law perpetuates a grand trick, an anarchic illusion apparently offering critique with an easy target (law's supposed denial of senses), which is only a decoy, however, in which critique all too easily ends up ensnared. Law's attempt to manipulate senses should not be underestimated or simplified. In a sense, law is constantly engaged in numbing the senses into common sense by manipulating, channelling and controlling the sensible; inserting properties and forbidding contacts; dissimulating violence, regulating sounds, defining taste. More precisely, law constructs its meaning (its sense, its direction) by orchestrating the senses in three ways. First, the law 'names' the senses, puts them into categories, thereby adding the moral weight of its sensorial judgement. Second, the law controls when senses should be kept apart and when blended, thus encouraging synaesthesia (coalesced sensorial modalities that encourage the attribution of one sensorial stimulation to another sense), or anaesthesia, depending on the way it adjusts its universal teleology to the particularity of the situation. In so doing, the law dissimulates the fact that these senses are blended or anaesthetised by something other than the individual herself. In other words, the law maintains an illusion of phenomenological perception and evaluation of senses, while on another level, the law works hard to build socio-political and cultural receptacles of sensorial taste construction that dissimulate the fact that the law is behind all this, deftly orchestrating both senses and its very own apparent absence of involvement. Finally, law elevates the phenomenology of senses to the corollary of the liberal individual's sense of personal freedom: what better exemplifies freedom than sensorial taste of food, colouring, odours, materials? The law manages to fool us by allowing us to think that we own our senses in full phenomenological immersion, while all along, the law inverts their 'sense', by constructing their origin and facilitating a fake causality from senses to atmosphere, rather than from the legally constructed, preconscious atmosphere *in which* senses come to be perceived as individually owned.[4] Understanding this complex interplay of intervention and disappearance obviously requires much more than simply assuming senses as a dynamic excess to law's static numbness. As much as overestimating it, underestimating law is a perilous mistake.

Fourth, to envisage an approach to law beyond these strictures, unfolding alternative strategies and methodologies to which law attuned to *its* senses may open up. We do not simply wish to push legal thinking beyond its comfortable socio-legal and critical methods. This series rather intends to pursue a constructive endeavour, namely ushering law into a different mode of dealing with

[4] Andreas Philippopoulos-Mihalopoulos. 'Atmospheres of Law: Senses, Affects, Lawscapes'. *Emotion, Space and Society* 7 (2013): 35-44.

the world: one which is tentative, tempting, reflexive and uncertain, a mode of sensing, that is, which sanctions the impossibility for law to avoid its own materiality. This requires emphasising at the same time both the posthuman and the inhuman quality of law, and understanding its relations to senses accordingly. On one level, in fact, law emerges out of the coming together of human and nonhuman bodies, spaces and times. On another level, law pretends to address a purely rational and disembodied, inhuman subject, namely a fully institutionalised subject whose 'humanity' is constructed to the extent that it is useful to the institution. Both dimensions are crucial. The first suggests that law is not a socio-cultural construct that is superimposed over inert matter, but a normativity made of flesh and stones, thought and water streams, cosmic and everyday interaction, human and nonhuman sensing: a way in which the 'world' is organised. The second points to the fact that law is a force of abstraction and, insofar as abstract, plays a generative role in creating and giving consistency to identity, relations, spaces and worlds.[5] Thinking the posthuman and inhuman dimension of senses thus permits rethinking law's sensorial engagement and entanglement with the world, at the same time gesturing towards different ways to use legal abstraction, beyond the absolutisation or dismissal of the senses.

[5] Derek P. McCormack. 'Geography and Abstraction: Towards an Affirmative Critique', *Progress in Human Geography* 3, no. 6 (2012): 717–718.

2. Touch

In *The Story of My Life*, Helen Keller writes: 'I did nothing but explore with my hands and learn the name of every object that I touched; and the more I handled things and learned their names and uses, the more joyous and confident grew my sense of kinship with the rest of the world'.[6] Deaf and blind, taken by the hand of her teacher, Helen learns to sense the world through touch: 'as the cool stream gushed over one hand, she spelled into the other the word water, first slowly, then rapidly. I stood still, my whole attention fixed upon the motions of her fingers. Suddenly I felt a misty consciousness as of something forgotten – a thrill of returning thought; and somehow the mystery of language was revealed to me. I knew then that 'w-a-t-e-r' meant the wonderful cool something that was flowing over my hand. That living word awakened my soul, gave it light, hope, joy, set it free! There were barriers, still, but barriers that could in time be swept away'.[7] Touch is for Helen the way in which she experiences and learns about the world; touching becomes seeing, it is visceral, as she builds meaning, creates languages, forms thoughts and learns about herself in relation to her surroundings, what her body is capable of. Helen can only see because she can touch, and it is through touching that she is able to situate herself in the world, find her localised presence and activate her *sensing*.

The intimate connection between seeing and touch comes from afar: this was already suggested by Aristotle

[6] Helen Keller. *The Story of My Life* (New York: Signet Books, 2010), 37.
[7] Ibid 35.

who located touch within the realm of seeing, an integrated function in the act of perceiving. In *De Anima* he writes that seeing is a kind of touching, the work of the soul that makes itself felt through the body. This 'localised sensation', which happens through touch and is oriented towards the localisation of one's body, generates a double perception in a way that seeing does not: the sensation of touch lingers when the touching object has ceased to touch and activates sensing while it is simultaneously sensed. In doing this, touch is constitutional of the body. Husserl writes, 'I do not see myself, my body, the way I touch myself',[8] and what he means is that the eye can be touched and it can too touch, but its touch can only provide a relational sensation, not the 'double sensation'[9] of touch which, while it senses, is intent on constituting the body.

Revisiting the list of five senses compiled by Democritus, Aristotle for the first time attributes psychical functions to *sensing*. He distinguishes between, on the one hand, touch as direct contact and, on the other, touch as perception, that psychic ability of the soul (placed by Aristotle in the centre of being)[10] to establish contact with

[8] Edmund Husserl. *Ideas Pertaining to a Pure Phenomenology and to a Phenomenological Philosophy. Studies in the Phenomenology of Constitution*, Book II (Dordrecht: Kluwer Academic Publishers, 1989), 155.

[9] Jacques Derrida. *On Touching – Jean-Luc Nancy* (Stanford: Stanford University Press, 2000), 172.

[10] Aristotle. *On Sense*, 439a 1: '[...] the soul [is] resident in these parts of the body.'; Aristotle. *On the Soul*, 420b 28. Cited In Józef Bremer, S. J. 'Truth, Reality and Religion New Perspectives In Metaphysics'. *Forum Philosophicum*, 16, no. 1 (2011), 74.

an object. In this sensorial framework made of intangible and transitory relations, touch, more than other senses, carries the material *potentia* of the body and makes itself essential in establishing a body. Keller finds herself and the world around her through it. Touch incarnates both the physical and metaphysical in its ability to express the determination of being as matter and of 'thought that thinks itself'.[11] This sets it apart from the other senses.

For Aristotle, a 'well developed sense of touch is essential to a humans intelligence'[12] and underscores being as the principle of life, while the other senses exist 'for the sake of well-being'.[13] This hierarchy, though mutable, as Aristotle himself also knew, given that his ideas on the senses and sensorial perception continued to change until the end of his life, is determined by the immediacy of touch: sight, smell and hearing happen at a distance from the main organ and do not require contact; touch and taste need contiguity.[14] To manifest itself, touch relies on a precise and active bodily/physical involvement that other senses do not require.

To hear, to smell or to see preserve an involuntariness that touch bypasses altogether: the space where senses, still virtual, can pause before they are activated into sensations – that shift from hear to listen, from see to look – touch does not possess at all. To touch is *already* to

---

11 Aristotle. *Metaphysics,* in 2 volumes, trans. Tredennick and Armstrong (Loeb Classical Library: Harvard University Press: 1072b), 17.

12 Aristotle. *De Anima*, Op. cit. 9, modified translation.

13 Ibid., 13.

14 Pascal Massie. 'Touching, Thinking, Being: The Sense of Touch in Aristotle's *De Anima* and Its Implications', *Minerva – An Internet Journal of Philosophy*, 17 (2013), 79.

be active, to make a decision, to move forward, to invite and instigate, and to put oneself in a position of vulnerability. It is action that awaits an unknown counteraction.

Jacques Derrida writes, 'each gesture of the other toward me obligates me to respond by sacrificing the other of the other, his or her (or its) other gesture, or the absence thereof, but also the other other and, finally, all the other others'.[15] This relational understanding of the body – when touching I experience something through the edges of my body – pushes me to surpass my limits and to confront the finite nature of myself as fleshed out by the presence – outside of myself – of the object I reach out to touch. I overcome my own self and take a leap beyond what I know. I get to know my difference through the consciousness of my finite body in relation to what it touches. Similarly, to touch oneself – to direct touch to oneself – poses the same set of challenges: it means to become aware of one's limits, to sense oneself as a limited unity dependent on and restricted by the relationship – the touch – with my hand. Aristotle had already claimed something analogous in *De Anima* when he wrote that 'the distinction between myself and others is fundamentally born right here from the sense of touch!'.[16] It is precisely the experience of being *exposed* to something outside oneself and to accept the limitations of one's body through the act of touching that makes touch a sense *of* the world, namely an outwards sense, one that exists only insofar as it can reach out of itself, to that

---

[15] Jacques Derrida. *On the Name* (Stanford University Press, 1995), 68.
[16] Aristotle. *De Anima*, 9.

which it does not know. In the movement of touching, extending and differentiating, the body remains closed, impenetrable: when it touches another body, it presents itself to the other, but the encounter remains a moment of acknowledgement of each other's secret: 'the other is secret because he is other'.[17]

Tactile sacrifice goes hand in hand with the violence of touch: touch embodies the original violence of being brought to life, a continuous violence that moves the skin of animate beings from enclosures of wraparound protection to the irredeemable violence of the touch of the world, with its other air, its other bodies and its other laws. This gives touch a specific spatiality, a *where*, a 'being in the world' that pre-exists sensing (sensibility) which, just an instant later, is activated by the touched object which in its turn touches back. This shift is crucial: the epistemology of touch presents us with an inevitable negotiation between inner-system and the environment, between touching and being-touched, which are, as Sartre writes, 'two essentially different orders of reality … two species of phenomena which it is useless to try to reunite … in the fact that they are radically distinct, and they exist on two incommunicable levels'.[18] For Sartre, the body-as-subject that touches and the body-as-object that is touched belong to two totally separate spheres. Neither negotiation nor tension of any kind ever takes place between the two. Rather, it is a split in bodily perception,

---

[17] Jacques Derrida. *On Touching – Jean-Luc Nancy*, trans. C. Irizarry. (Stanford: Stanford University Press, 2005), 107.

[18] Jean-Paul Sartre. *Being and Nothingness* (New York: Washington Square Press 1966), 402–403.

for the touched object is not contemplated in the act of touching, 'my body for-me'.[19] Therefore, for Sartre, to touch oneself is equivalent to touching another body. The variable is contingency, the skin, namely the real locus of corporeality, sole testimony of my presence which 'reveals my body to my consciousness'.[20]

Maurice Merleau-Ponty's view on the other hand rejects Sartre's unidirectional vision and suggests that touch is a *unitary* and *reversible* movement: 'my body touched and my body touching: there is overlapping and encroachment'.[21] The movements may not coincide, the organ that touches may be clumsy, the touch awkward, de-centred, its touch 'opens my body in two',[22] but this discrepancy is essential to perception. In fact, it determines perception. As Martin C. Dillon suggests, the distance given by that non-coincidence is what confirms that perceiving something is not the same as being that thing.[23] This difference, however, is not to be understood as dualism. It is rather unified by the body that both touches and is touched. It is precisely in this difference within identity that Merleau-Ponty's ontology of touch lies: to be oneself whilst being of the world; my body 'takes its place among the things it touches, is in a sense one of them, opens finally upon a tangible being of which it is a part'.[24] As

[19] Ibid., 434.

[20] Ibid., 338.

[21] Maurice Merleau-Ponty. *The Visible and the Invisible*. (Evanston: Northwestern University Press, 1969), 123.

[22] Ibid.

[23] Martin C. Dillon. *Merleau-Ponty's Ontology* (Bloomington: Indiana University Press, 1988), 159.

[24] Merleau-Ponty. *The Visible and the Invisible*, 133.

my hand touches and is touched, it perceives two or more distinct sensations. It is a 'double touch', a 'reversibility' of touch that contains simultaneously the sense of being touched. The distance between I and the object I touch disappears in this moment of unity where, through touch, self and other are joined together in their difference.

This double and reversible sensation which can only originate in the body, makes touch's ontology essential to the very sensibility of the body. It is a form of self-awareness of the body that senses and, at the same time, becomes the guarantee of *the body proper* and its inextricable corporeality. For Merleau-Ponty, tactility is situated within the body and localised through sensing. So, unlike Sartre, as I shake a hand, the break between my body and the body of the other determines two separate bodily experiences, although my body – 'I remain on the side of my body'[25] – re-conducts this reversibility back into the only point of view of which I am capable, that is enabled by my flesh.

There is yet another vulnerability that sets touch apart from the other senses. Although it has the privilege of immediacy, the object that it touches and by which it is touched is indefinite, changeable, obscure, always the result of the internal and external movement of perception and of the skin. We could even argue that touch is the most active of the senses because it activates the potentiality of the organ that touches and by which it is touched. Yet it is also the most ambiguous and unpredictable

---

25 Ibid., 194.

because it relies on the impulse that it receives back from the touched object.

3. Law and Touch

If we take seriously the above suggestion that touch is an act of poking into the unknown – a provocation in its original meaning of *pro vocare*, to call forth, to summon, to challenge – and being open to what touches us back, then it would be safe to assume that the law does not and cannot touch. In fact, the law's primary impulse is precisely the opposite: to pull back, to sedate, to calm down, to normalise, to join extremities, to smooth excesses. The dialectics of the law, which aims at the perfect balance between permission and restriction, create a field of tranquillity, whether real or only perceived, where action is controlled and the real is imagined, planned and often staged. Here, reaction is a threat to the juridical order. To touch is to alter this order by introducing a new element between the various bodies involved and thus voiding their exclusivity. To touch is 'a violent opening'[26] 'into the realm of unknowability',[27] an act of non-symbolic exposure that endangers rather than preserves.

Can we then say that the law does not touch? Or could it be that touch, just as all the other senses, is an institutionalised affect, fully emerging within the law and contributing to its conative abilities? Is it not more accurate to say

---

[26] Jacques Derrida. *Of Grammatology*. (Baltimore: John Hopkins University Press, 2005), 139.

[27] Erin Manning. *Politics of Touch: Sense, Movement, Sovereignty*. (Minneapolis: University of Minnesota Press, 2006), 56.

that the law pretends not to touch? Law's temporality and the representativeness it nurtures are open to constant negotiation, reinterpretation and reformulation: morals, values and traditions change, and the representational quality of the law is called to catch up with those changes or anticipate them. This makes its imprint vacuous, weak and extremely dependent on a necessary sense of collectiveness through which individuals can *feel* represented and protected. This *do ut des* relationship, a pact of trust and duty of care, preserves the game of roles between the law and individuals but it also *depotentialises* its expression. Touch eludes representation; it comes directly from being and goes straight back into being. However, as Pascal Massie suggests, the absence of another body in its activation (for example, the eye and the visible object) does not mean that touch eludes mediation; rather, 'even in the experience of intimate closeness, mediation remains'.[28] This is explained by Aristotle through locating the organ of touch within the body: the object we see preserves a distance from the organ of sight, while touch occurs in the depths of our own flesh, making its sensations instant and immediate (but not unmediated). This instantaneity further distinguishes touch from all the other senses in that it prompts it constantly to renew itself, to seek new surfaces, to diversify its intensity and to touch again. This is the temporality of touch. Touch vanishes at the very moment of contact and can only return in different forms: 'at the point where I make contact with

[28] Massie. 'Touching, Thinking, Being', 80.

the world, I am already dead'.[29] The temporality of touch paralyses the law, unequipped to synthetise the dynamism of such movement. If senses are a 'multiplicity of potential connections',[30] touch is the movement of desire that only exists in a state of perpetual emergence.

Touch's temporality comes with a spatiality, as mentioned above. Nancy, for example, distinguishes between the spatiality of touch determined by its contiguity which limits it to *mere* contact, and the time of touch, which he understands as the *passibility* to sense, namely a mode of being susceptible to touching.[31] The distinction between contact and touch, space and time – the former enters the other, reaches beyond its impenetrability, the latter *merely* touches that which does not offer itself to be *entered* – is what Derrida observes in relation to the law. The force of law is built on a fundamental and necessary misunderstanding: when one seeks to touch the law, the law moves further away, makes itself inaccessible and does not allow itself to be touched. Like contact, the law touches and simultaneously forbids touch, making itself inaccessible:

> Perhaps the law is always a law of tact. This law's law finds itself there, before anything. There is this law, and it is this law itself, the law of law. One cannot imagine what a law would be in general without something like tact: one must touch without touching.

[29] Mark C. Taylor. *Hiding*. (Chicago: Chicago University Press 1997), 13.

[30] Brian Massumi. *Parables for the Virtual-Movement, Affect, Sensation*. (Durham: Duke University Press, 2002), 93.

[31] 'The world is passible to sense, it is this passibility because it first comes to be in accordance with this' Jean-Luc Nancy, *The Sense of the World*, trans. J. Librett. (Minneapolis: Minnesota University Press), 67.

> In touching, touching is forbidden: do not touch or tamper with the thing itself, do not touch on what there is to touch. Do not touch what remains to be touched, first of all law itself—which is the untouchable, *before* all the ritual prohibitions that this or that religion or culture may impose on touching.[32]

Tact, more than touch, then, best captures what the law does and the capacity of its action. Touch is always a voluntary and active movement, an invitation, an action and reaction. Tact is a self-controlled, self-declared, 'anticipated-in-advance'[33] declaration of intent. Tact has the quality to mediate, to smooth over the excessiveness, the *differential*, to find the proper, most appropriate forms of dealing with the self and others. In other words: to conform. Tact, like law, preserves *intact* a fundamental formality – *a form* – that touch refuses altogether, a 'certain politeness'[34] that holds us back from being exposed to the surprise of life. Interestingly, in a medical study on physiology of 1835, Fletcher describes the distinction between touch and tact as follows:

> The perception of which constitutes Touch … is in all the superior classes of animals the Dermoid Tissue, and the nerves which convey it are the Sensiferous portions of the Trigemini, and of all the Regular nerves which are distributed upon the surface of the body. The stimulus to this irritation is the contact of palpable material substances in general, and it is necessary, at least in man, for its full perception … It will now be understood what is meant by the

32 Jacques Derrida, *On Touching – Jean-Luc Nancy*, 66.
33 Manning. *Politics of Touch*, 135.
34 Derrida. *On Touching*, 68.

> distinction between Touch and Tact – the former term being used to signify the sensation which is communicated by the Sensiferous nerves thrown into a state of tension … - and the latter that sensation which is communicated by the same nerves in state of relaxation. Touch, therefore, … is voluntary, active and necessary … while tact, which is quite involuntary and passive, maintains the organs employed … in the same condition. [35]

Though rudimentary, this medical tract indicates the privileged role of touch, 'the only sense where Man excels every other class of animals',[36] in the active reception and manifestation of bodily sensations. Importantly, touch is attributed a primordial position in the biology of the body and all those energies that constitute a body. If touch powers the body, tact is overpowered by the body.

Tact happens the moment before touch storms into the unknown and reaches beyond. It is the 'touch without touching'[37]: tact can emerge from the field of touch, but only operates in a condition of security, while touch is always tactless. Tact's intentions are always declared in advance, 'attempting to put senses in their place, even as I continue to reach towards the untouchability of the senses as senses, asking of my body that it expand, prosthetically, towards a concept of the senses that signifies not the biological body but the body's imminent excesses'.[38]

---

[35] John Fletcher. *Rudiments of Physiology in Three Parts.* (London: Longman, 1835), 66–67.

[36] Ibid., 67.

[37] Derrida. *On Touching*, 66.

[38] Manning. *Politics of Touch,* 135–136.

Paradoxically, in its restless pursuit of conformity, tact too nurtures an out-of-the-body dimension in its necessity to bypass specificity and nurture an artificial fit-all model that inevitably rejects human *being*. Perhaps the most notable difference between tact and touch is that touch, unlike tact, exists in traction with the body, that is, it claims its relevance through an act of belongingness to the body. Here lies the posthuman contingency (from *cum*, 'together with'; and *tangere*, 'to touch') of touch, that is, the materiality of human and nonhuman, of being together in ways that exceed both the 'security' of tact and the intentionality of touch, rather pointing to an ontological contiguity which is promisingly, but also disturbingly, contagious (again, from *cum* and *tangere*). It is this contagion that the tactful apparatus of law seeks to invalidate. This does not happen by way of negation, but rather by neutralising the potential inner conflict of that con-tact. In this sense, tact appears to be pointing to an inhuman, abstract disembodiment, the inhuman projection of reality that law nurtures in its pretence to touch tactfully. Tact, unlike touch, appears to exist despite the body.

The contraposition is evident: the law's primary impulse is to bind together in the name of a widely shared, or at least widely recognised and often imposed, ideal of social existence. This is not to say that the law refuses pluralism or change, but these are always negotiated according to the parameters and tools within its capacity. This capacity can be, perhaps simplistically, understood as normativity, the means by which the law keeps itself alive, the force that touches without touching, that 'abstains from touching on what it touches'[39]. According to Derrida, this *a priori* notion that characterises tactile experiences determines the law's untouchability. More specifically, the law's function is to create experiential identification and simulate a sense of representation where individuals can find correspondence. Touch, by contrast, as Massumi writes, is a movement that:

> strikes the body first, directly and unmediatedly. It passes transformatively through the flesh before being instantiated in subject-positions subsumed by a system of power. Its immediate effect is a differing. It must be made a reproduction. The body, fresh in the throes of expression, incarnates not an already-formed system but a change.[40]

Arguably, the law's interest is precisely the opposite. Namely, to render the individual compliant with the promoted order, and to interject itself between the body and its erring. And yet, at the same time, by always and unavoidably belonging to the contingent materiality of the world, law touches (untactfully) and is exposed in return to the touch, and contagion, of other bodies, spaces and times.

In fact, can we not describe law as a haptic norm which embodies the material weight of law itself, namely its being always already 'rooted in the direct and immediate action and reaction of bodies, long before any normative abstract scheme'?[41] This is what Deleuze suggests when

---

[39] Derrida. *On Touching*, 67.

[40] Brian Massumi ed. *A Shock to Thought – Expression After Deleuze and Guattari.* (London and New York: Routledge, 2002), xvii.

[41] Andrea Brighenti. 'Did We Really Get Rid of Commands? Thoughts on a Theme from Elias Canetti'. *Law and Critique,* 17, no. 1 (2006), 49.

he writes that 'law weighs with all its might, even before its object is known, and without ever its object becoming exactly known.'[42] It is a tangible presence in the here-and-now that is consistent with the peculiar temporality of touch, an eventful and contingent temporality, that is, that law must somehow process and tame. We could suggest this as the material touch of law, that is, the way law always already touches and penetrates the world way before elaborating its own tactful image.

In this vein, this volume of *Law and the Senses* attempts to illuminate and reconsider the complex and interflowing relations and contradictions between the tactful intrusion of the law and the untactful movement of touch. Each contribution unveils a multi-faceted new dimension to the *force of touch,* its ability to form, deform and reform what it touches. In unique ways, each recognises the trans-corporeality touch has to traverse the boundaries on the body and entangle other bodies and spaces, thus challenging the very notion of corporeal integrity and human *being.*

Naomi Segal's touch is a paradox – touch which does not touch: the most proximate of senses, conditioned by its impossibility to overcome the distance between pleasure and taboos on bodily contact. Her account exposes the risks of bodily contact while at the same time exploring the desire to shorten that distance to embrace touch and its violence. We are faced with a cyclical impossibility which cannot be avoided, yet we are compelled to search for new ways of overcoming it. Segal identifies modes

---

[42] Gilles Deleuze. *The Logic of Sense* (London: Continuum, 2004), 59.

of desire and impossibility in a series of European texts from the late nineteenth and early twentieth century and reflects on the inevitable conflict that stems from this negotiation. Hers is an exploration into forms of distanced proximation where desire, in a posthuman era, is mediated between deconstruction as well as creation, touching and not-touching.

Jan Hogan's piece explores the space between urban and natural environments and how the sense of touch becomes the cohesive force through which different landscapes meet and initiate a dialogue. Her ethnographic account of walking a trail, The Track, surrounded by wildness on an island in the Southern Ocean, exposes the author to sensorial discoveries where touch is not simply the gesture of the body, but expands *across* the body and becomes memory, breath and the vehicle through which it situates itself within the unpredictability of space, time and matter. Through a series of photographs of the Truganini Track on the edge of Hobart, Tasmania, Hogan reveals the endless possibilities for space to exist, expand and contaminate its ever-changing boundaries outside the representation of normativity. Here, touch challenges the relationship between humans and the environment.

Moritz von Stetten offers an intriguing analysis of the discourse around brain surgery and brain stimulation. He suggests that no other mental health therapies have ever met equal levels of collective criticism and sense of distrust in mental care providers, which have contributed to increasing the sense of stigma attached to these techniques. In spite of this, research in the field of brain stimulation is as strong as ever: from the production of new and always less invasive antidepressants, to innovation in brain surgery. This contribution uses the neurological framework to argue that brain stimulation practices rely on *regimes of touch*, an articulation of normative experiences and affects that alter the *sensing* of the body. Here von Stetten draws from the phenomenological tradition of Helmuth Plessner, Maurice Merleau-Ponty, Thomas Fuchs and Gesa Lindemann to argue that the corporeality of the body is made of subjectivity and objectivity, and that the *Leib* (living body) has to come to terms with its carnality as well as with its consciousness. From here, this chapter embarks on a fascinating reading of severe depression and how brain stimulation as a medical technique promotes an understanding of the human body, its vulnerability and sense of touch that is counter to the phenomenological concept of *Leib*. Touch is mutilated, as therapeutic practices fail to negotiate with the contingency of the body that suffers and seeks help and the body that receives that request that offers help.

Erin Manning's contribution looks at synaesthesia as a sublime experience where touch becomes the spacetime in which the body abandons itself and is at the same time revealed to itself, surpassing the gravity of its deficiency through the experience of multi-sensing. There is an interesting distinction between interaction and relation: the former is a human-centred type of emotion that responds to social norms and feeds from a normative environment structured on mutual recognition and acceptance. The latter is an overflow of sensations and multi-sensing experiences that cannot be contained within a body-schema. It is best described as *overfeeling* and is so intensely entwined with the phenomena of the world that its sole mode of expression is relational, beyond the limits and conventions of interaction, towards a 'continuum of perception'. Through a self-reflective analysis of her own artistic practice, Manning suggests that the normative interactions that constitute empathy are unable to account for the complexity of multi-sensing. Similarly, consciousness acts as a watchdog that calibrates the boundaries of normativity, and reduces, when it does not nullify, the unexpressed, yet present, primordial force of our senses. Here, touch becomes a nonhuman, beyond human rather, mode of being in the world.

Remaining in the realm of nonhuman experience, Nicole Nyffenegger's contribution is a fascinating exploration through the ways in which illicit touch can violate the skin and transgress the limits of the body, in the attempt to appropriate and reframe what is usually considered moral, ethical or legal. To Nyffenegger, traces of illicitness are found in the marks of abused and marked skin with which, she says, our culture brims. This contribution conveys the corporeal gravity of marked skin through the use of powerful symbols which, we discover, become literal materiality, artefacts, autobiographical accounts, traces of stratified real life which, today, relived through different people and contexts, document the punitive, macabre at times, and dehumanising *force of touch* which, in appropriating those narratives, histories and bodies, constructs hierarchies, establishes relevance and reproduces norms.

We close this issue of *Law and the Senses* with two artist contributions: the first, by B. A. Zanditon, presents a self-reflective account of her artistic practice through which she looks at the rigidity of institutional power in relation to the instinctual character of her work. To what extent does normativity manipulate art? In the attempt to answer this question, Zanditon explores the hegemony of the eye over touch in contemporary artistic representation and reflects on the difficulties she encounters making rubbings, an artistic practice that strongly relies on touch and the ability touch has to discern textures, materials, surfaces, so often ignored or dismissed by the eye.

The exploration of textures, nuances and materials is also central in Tolis Totolas' contribution. Here, what we have is the photographic reproduction of the complex stratifications hidden within urban environments. These often provoke conflict, contradictions and trigger sensorial memories that can form a spatio-temporal archive through which we navigate space. In the ever-changing chaos of this sensory arena and the over-stimulation resulting from fast-paced technologies, touch, more than other senses, has had to reform itself to remain relevant. This collection of photographs probes the central role of touch in the process of recognising and establishing new relations conducive to a functional and modern society.

References

Aristotle. *Metaphysics* in 2 volumes. Cambridge, MA: Harvard University Press, 1072b.

Bently, Lionel and Leo Flynn, eds. *Law and the Senses: Sensational Jurisprudence*. London: Pluto Press, 1996.

Bremer, Józef. 'Aristotle on Touch'. *Truth, Reality and Religion New Perspectives In Metaphysics: Forum Philosophicum* 16, no. 1 (2011): 73–87.

Brighenti, Andrea. 'Did We Really Get Rid of Commands? Thoughts on a Theme from Elias Canetti', *Law and Critique*, 17, no. 1 (2006): 47–71.

Deleuze, Gilles. *The Logic of Sense*. London: Continuum, 2004.

Derrida, Jacques. *On the Name*. Stanford: Stanford University Press, 1995.

Derrida, Jacques. *On Touching – Jean-Luc Nancy*. Stanford: Stanford University Press, 2000.

Derrida, Jacques. *Of Grammatology*. Translated by Gayatri Spivak. Baltimore: John Hopkins University Press, 2005.

Dillon, Martin C. *Merleau-Ponty's Ontology*. Bloomington: Indiana University Press, 1988.

Everson, Stephen. *Aristotle on Perception*. Oxford: Oxford University Press, 1997.

Fletcher, John M.D.F. R.C.S.E. *Rudiments of Physiology in Three Parts*. London: Longman, 1835.

Husserl, Edmund. *Ideas Pertaining to a Pure Phenomenology and to a Phenomenological Philosophy. Studies in the Phenomenology of Constitution*, Book II. Dordrecht: Kluwer Academic Publishers, 1989.

Keller, Helen. *The Story of My Life*. New York: Signet Books, 2010.

Manning, Erin. *Politics of Touch: Sense, Movement, Sovereignty*. Minneapolis: University of Minnesota Press, 2006.

Massie, Pascal. 'Touching, Thinking, Being: The Sense of Touch in Aristotle's *De anima* and Its Implications' *Minerva – An Internet Journal of Philosophy* 17 (2013): 47–101.

Massumi, Brian. *Parables for the Virtual: Movement, Affect, Sensation*. Duke University Press, 2002.

Massumi, Brian, ed. *A Shock to Thought – Expression After Deleuze and Guattari*. London and New York: Routledge, 2002.

Merleau-Ponty, Maurice. *The Visible and the Invisible*. Evanston: Northwestern University Press, 1969.

Nancy, Jean-Luc. *The Sense of the World*. Translated by J.Librett. Minneapolis: University of Minnesota Press, 67.

McCormack, Dereck P. 'Geography and Abstraction: Towards an Affirmative Critique', *Progress in Human Geography* 3, no. 6 (2012): 777–798.

Philippopoulos-Mihalopoulos, Andreas. 'Atmospheres of Law: Senses, Affects, Lawscapes.' *Emotion, Space and Society* 7 (2013): 35–44.

Sartre, Jean-Paul. *Being and Nothingness*. Translated by Hazel Barnes. New York: Washington Square Press, 1966.

Taylor, Mark C. *Hiding*. Chicago: Chicago University Press, 1997.

Touching and Not Touching: The Indirections of Desire

Naomi Segal

L'amour, tel qu'il existe dans la Société,
n'est que l'échange de deux fantaisies
et le contact de deux épidermes.
(Chamfort 1796)[1]

Love, as it exists in Society,
is nothing more than the exchange of two fantasies
and the contact of two epidermises.

NOTES

NB All translations from French and German, unless otherwise noted, are my own. Poetry citations are given in both original and translation. Citations without page number are from the last-referred page. Sections of this material are adapted from my book *Consensuality* (2009).

[1] This epigraph, the 359th of Chamfort's *Maximes et pensées* (1923) [1796], is a familiar notion in French culture; it is cited, for example, by Sartre in his discussion of the caress, Jean-Paul Sartre, *L'Être et le néant* (Paris: Gallimard, 1943), 130; André Gide, *Corydon* (Paris: Gallimard, 1993 [1911, 1922, 1924]), 61; and Didier Anzieu, *Le Moi-peau* (Paris: Dunod, 1995 [1985]), 32); NB henceforth, all quotations from Anzieu's *Le Moi-peau* are taken from my translation: Didier Anzieu, *The Skin-Ego*, tr. Naomi Segal, London: Karnac, 2016; this reference, 10–11.

Of all the senses, touch is the most proximate. To touch is to be close enough to encounter something with one's skin – fingertips or body surface. Yet the desire to touch is conditioned, like all desire, by modes of distance. The wish to overcome distance, to embrace or touch, is stimulated by its impossibility. This essay looks at modes of negotiating or exploiting the indirections of touch. My set of literary examples are in a variety of genres, languages and tones, yet all challenge the possibility of touching, for despite a sustained fantasy of reaching – zooming and hovering – there is no actual stopping-point. In the final sections, contemporary technologies introduce new expediencies of 'the progressive cyborgization of humanity' which,[2] in different ways, replace the violent or loving touch of the hand.

Before we look at how touch is impossible, however, we need to consider, in relation to the context of law, how it is forbidden. In *The Skin-Ego* (*Le Moi-peau* 1995 [1985]), Didier Anzieu observes that a key turning-point in every child's development is the taboo on touching, which separates the subject from its own and other bodies, and not only precedes but makes possible the oedipal taboo that marks the entry into social relations. If, as Chamfort tells us, love in society is essentially the exchange of fantasies, how might these fantasies prevent rather than enable the contact of the skin?

---

[2] Chris Hables Gray. In Joanna Zylinska, ed., *The Cyborg Experiments*, London & New York: Continuum, 2002, 181.

Touching the Senses

First, let us set the scene. How do we understand the senses, and where is the place of touch in their spectrum? Most human beings have five senses, more or less. Everyday experience is 'multisensual',[3] and 'the senses are not merely passive receptors of particular kinds of environmental stimuli but are actively involved in the structuring of that information'. I say more or less five, for the history and geography of the senses show that while that total is traditional, it is often disputed, not only for the sake of precision but because of a general feeling that there must be something else.

> We have five senses in which we glory and which we recognise and celebrate, senses that constitute the sensible world for us. But there are other senses – secret senses, sixth senses, if you will – equally vital, but unrecognised, and unlauded. These senses, unconscious, automatic, had to be discovered. Historically, indeed, their discovery came late: what the Victorians vaguely called 'muscle sense' – the awareness of the relative position of trunk and limbs, derived from receptors in the joints and tendons – was only really defined (and named 'proprioception') in the 1890s. And the complex mechanisms and controls by which our bodies are properly aligned and balanced in space – these have only been defined in our own century and still hold many mysteries.[4]

---

[3] Paul Rodaway. *Sensuous Geographies* (London & New York: Routledge, 1997), 4.

[4] Oliver Sacks. *The Man Who Mistook his Wife for a Hat* (London: Picador, 1986 [1985]), 68.

One suggestion lists ten basic senses, including four varieties of touch plus two of orientation.[5] Others searching for the proverbial sixth sense cite extra-sensory perception,[6] desire,[7] proprioception defined as 'our totally intuitive sense of our own bodies',[8] or more rarefied abilities like that of the skilled wine-taster. Different cultures have more or fewer senses, or lay stress on different aspects. Of three non-literate societies cited by Constance Classen, 'each has a very distinct way of making sense of the world: the Tzotzil accord primacy to heat in their cosmology, the Ongee to odour, and the Desana to colour'.[9] Words for sensing are also variable, and often clustered: 'the Hausa have one word for hearing, smelling, tasting and touching, understanding and emotional feeling';[10] French too, of course, uses one word (*sentir*) for smelling and for both physical and emotional feeling.

However many senses we wish to number, it is interesting that, until recently, they were discussed only in order to be distinguished and separated. Since Aristotle, the senses have been placed in a hierarchical order, dependent either on proximity to the thing sensed or on the difference between human and animal. Thus 'touch (and thereby

---

5 See Rodaway. *Sensuous Geographies*, 28.

6 See David Howes, ed. *The Varieties of Sensory Experience* (Toronto, Buffalo, London: University of Toronto Press, 1991), 258, 290.

7 Michel Serres. *Les cinq sens* (Paris: Grasset, 1985), 57–60.

8 Gabriel Josipovici. *Touch* (New Haven & London: Yale University Press, 1996), 110.

9 Constance Classen. 'McLuhan in the Rainforest: The Sensory Worlds of Oral Cultures', in *The Empire of the Senses*, ed. David Howes (Oxford & New York: Berg, 2005), 148.

10 Ian Ritchie. 'Fusion of the Faculties: A Study of the Language of the Senses in Hausaland', in Howes, *Varieties*, 194.

taste) was found in all animals and so became the lowliest sense [... Aristotle] posed a hierarchical order of the senses, from most to least valuable: vision-hearing-smell-taste -touch'.[11] Even if animals showed more skills than us with certain senses, theirs were intrinsically the inferior ones. This hierarchy slides into the other, for the last three of these are the 'proximity' or 'intimate senses',[12] devalued because they are deemed the furthest from thought, imagination and memory. As I have remarked elsewhere, these three senses are also the ones in which the nuances of active and passive perception are linguistically the least differentiated. If for sight and hearing we have three verbs:

> I look at the picture, I see the moon, I look tired,
> I listen to the music, I hear thunder, I sound interested,

for smell, taste, and touch, one verb has to stand in for all these functions:

> I smell a rose, I smell burning, I smell funny,
> I taste the soup, I taste a trace of cinnamon, it tastes bitter,
> I feel the velvet, I feel the sun on my face, I feel pretty.

But this could be a reason for suggesting that, far from being more blunt, the words we use for the proximate senses 'do more work, convey more variation, carry more weight'.[13]

---

[11] David Howes, ed. *Empire of the Senses: The Sensual Culture Reader* (Oxford & New York: Berg, 2005), 61.

[12] Rodaway. *Sensuous Geographies*, 26.

[13] Naomi Segal. 'L'échange de deux fantaisies et le contact de deux épidermes': skin and desire', in *Sensual Reading*, eds. Michael Syrotinski and Ian Maclachlan (Lewisburg and London: Associated University Presses, 2001), 18.

However undifferentiated language seems to think them, recent theory has turned back to these less favoured senses because, actually, they are better at imagining (Baudelaire), remembering (Proust) and of course loving.

Contemporary theory sees the senses as a multiplicity – hence the use of terms like 'sensorium [...] sense ratio'[14] or 'sensotypes'.[15] To McLuhan sensing is a 'kaleidoscope',[16] to Serres 'knots' or 'an island',[17] to Howes synaesthesia, the latter defined as a way of 'short-circuiting the five sense model'.[18] It is the meeting of senses and sensations that most preoccupies current thinking: the 'pluri-sensorial',[19] 'combinatory',[20] 'multidirectional [...] intersensoriality'[21] – or, as Didier Anzieu calls it, 'consensuality'.[22] And, as the rest of this essay will explore, the multiplicity of the senses is most richly focused in the sense of touch.[23] Curiously, whichever way one looks at the lists of senses, touch is almost always found at one end.

---

14 Marshall McLuhan. 'Inside the Five Sense Sensorium', in Howes, *Empire*, 43–52.

15 Mallory Wober. 'The Sensotype Hypothesis', in Howes, *Varieties*, 33.

16 Cited in Howes. *Varieties*, 167.

17 Serres. *Les Cinq Sens*, 51–52.

18 Howes. *Empire*, 292.

19 Howes. *Varieties*, 6.

20 Ibid., 167.

21 Howes. *Empire*, 12.

22 Anzieu. *Le Moi-peau*, 127 *et passim*; see also Naomi Segal, *Consensuality: Didier Anzieu, Gender and the Sense of Touch* (Amsterdam and New York: Rodopi, 2009).

23 See Serres, *Les Cinq Sens*, 82-84; Rodaway, *Sensuous Geographies*, 28, 44–54; Laura U. Marks, *Touch* (Minneapolis & London: University of Minnesota Press, 2002, p. xiii); and A. Morton Heller and William Schiff, *The Psychology of Touch*. (Hillsdale, Hove & London: Lawrence Erlbaum, 1991, 1-3).

> In the evolution of the senses the sense of touch was undoubtedly the first to come into being. Touch is the parent of our eyes, ears, nose, and mouth. It is the sense which became differentiated into the others, a fact that seems to be recognized in the age-old evaluation of touch as 'the mother of the senses'.[24]

Among the three histories of feral children discussed by Constance Classen, Victor's faculties were ranked thus: "The sense of smell is first and most perfected; taste is second, or rather these senses are but one; vision occupies the position of third importance, hearing the fourth, and touch the last",[25] whereas Kaspar Hauser 'had an almost supernatural sense of touch. The touch of humans and animals gave him a sensation of heat or cold, at times so strong that he felt as if he had received a blow'.[26] More generally, 'the senses of *Homo sapiens* develop in a definite sequence, as (1) tactile, (2) auditory, and (3) visual. As the child approaches adolescence the order of precedence becomes reversed, as (1) visual, (2) auditory, and (3) tactile'.[27] Indeed in infant development, of humans as well as animals, the stimulation of this sense is so crucial that 'when the need for touch remains unsatisfied, abnormal behaviour will result'[28] – 'children need touch for survival'.[29]

---

[24] Ashley Montagu. *Touching: The Human Significance of the Skin* (New York: Harper & Row, 1986 [1971]), 3.

[25] Pierre-Joseph Bonnaterre, cited by Constance Classen in 'The Sensory Orders of "Wild Children"', in Howes, *Varieties* (1991), 49.

[26] Ibid., 54.

[27] Montagu.*Touching*, 314-315.

[28] Ibid., 46.

[29] Tiffany Field. *Touch* (Cambridge: MIT Press, 2003[2001]), 5

The work of Didier Anzieu, and in particular his magisterial *Le Moi-peau* [*The Skin-Ego*], is a psychoanalytic examination of the significance of both physical and psychical touch in creating and maintaining a sense of self in the form of a 'Skin-ego'. In relation to the senses, he notes:

> The skin is a surface containing pouches and cavities in which the sense organs – other than those of touch, which are set in the epidermis itself – are housed. The Skin-ego is a psychical surface which links together sensations of various kinds and makes them stand out as figures against the original background of the tactile wrapping: this is the *intersensorial* function of the Skin-ego, which leads to the formation of a 'common sense' (the *sensorium commune* of medieval philosophy) whose basic reference point is always the sense of touch.[30]

Of course 'the human sensorium [...] never exists in a natural state. Humans are social beings, and just as human nature itself is a product of culture, so is the human sensorium'.[31] In infants, the first version of this social interaction is the whole complex of holding, massage, breastfeeding understood as 'reciprocal interstimulation'[32] provided by the mother or primary caregiver.[33] This is never only one-sided: among the Wolof of Senegal, 'when a visitor arrives, male or female, often before any word is exchanged, he or she is handed a baby. This ges-

---

[30] Anzieu. *The Skin-Ego*, 112.

[31] Howes. *Empire*, 3.

[32] Montagu. *Touching*, 43.

[33] See also Winnicott's theory of maternal 'holding', D. W. Winnicott. 'The Theory of the Parent-Infant Relationship', in *The Maturational Processes and the Facilitating Environment* (London: Karnac, 1962 [1960]): 37–55; and Anzieu, *The Skin-Ego*, 39 *et passim*.

ture is intended to "mediate" the relation between adults'.[34] Touch is 'a kind of communication between person and world, a corporeal situation rather than a cognitive positioning [...] Touch is direct and intimate, and perhaps the most truthful sense';[35] it is the sense we use to test the material reality of a thing by direct bodily perception.[36] If, then, 'the history of the senses has been, essentially, the history of their objectification',[37] the 'history of touch is, essentially, a history of resisting objectification'.[38]

The Taboo on Touching

If touch, as the most intimate of the senses, everywhere seeks survival in subjective reality-testing or love, this quest is rarely fulfilled, or rarely for long. An infant's reality is its mother's arms, breast or caress, but once we grow up we enter the less safe world of Chamfort's social exchange. And growing up begins, even before the laws of Oedipus, with what Anzieu calls the taboo on touching.

> The oedipal prohibition (you must not marry your mother; you must not kill your father) is derived metonymically from the prohibition on touching. The taboo on touching prepares the ground for the oedipal taboo by providing it with a presexual foundation. In psychoanalytic treatment it becomes possible to understand at what particular cost – through what difficulties, failures, counter-cathexes

---

[34] Howes. *Varieties*, 184.

[35] Rodaway. *Sensuous Geographies*, 44.

[36] Josipovici. *Touch*, 2, 29.

[37] Carla Mazzio. 'The Senses Divided: Organs, Objects, and Media in Early Modern England', in Howes, *Empire*, 85.

[38] Ibid., 86.

> or hypercathexes – this derivation has been effected in each case.[39]

But these laws cut more than one way. Familial prohibitions on touch rely on four dualities: 'Every prohibition is dual in nature. It is a system of tensions between opposing poles; these tensions in the psyche develop force-fields which inhibit some functions and cause others to change their form'. The first duality refers to both sexuality and aggression:

> It channels the pressure of the drives, defines their bodily sources, reorganises their objects and aims, and structures the relations between the two major families of drives. It is clear how this applies to the oedipal taboo. The taboo on touching is similarly-concerned with the two basic drives: do not touch inanimate objects in case you break them or they hurt you; do not use excessive force against parts of your own or other people's bodies (this prohibition aims to protect the child against aggression, whether its own or that of other people); do not constantly touch your body or other people's bodies in the areas sensitive to pleasure, for you will be overwhelmed with an excitation you are incapable of understanding or satisfying (this prohibition aims to protect the child against its own and other people's sexuality). In both cases, the taboo on touching puts the child on its guard against an excess of excitation and its consequence, the surging of the drive.
>
> In the taboo on touching, sexuality and aggression are not differentiated structurally: they are both expressions of instinctual violence in general. The incest taboo, on the other hand, distinguishes between

[39] Anzieu. *The Skin-Ego*, 159.

> them and places them in a relation of inverse symmetry rather than similarity.

How does this taboo, made up of prohibitions and interdictions, take the form of a law? – through repetition, internalisation, and because it creates or consolidates the child's necessary understanding of the difference between inside and outside.

This, the second duality, 'has a double face, one turned outwards (which receives, accommodates and filters the interdictions communicated by other people) and one turned towards inner reality (which deals with the representational and affective representatives of instinctual currents)'.[40] Like the Skin-ego, it creates a psychical boundary.

> The earliest interdictions related to touch that are imposed on a child serve the principle of self-preservation: don't put your hand in the fire, don't touch knives or the rubbish or medicines, for this would put your body, or even your life, in danger. Their correlatives are prescriptions of touch such as: don't let go of my hand when you're leaning out of the window or crossing the road. Interdictions refer to external dangers while prohibitions refer to internal ones. Both assume that the child already understands the distinction between inside and outside – without this the taboo makes no sense – and the taboo itself reinforces that distinction. Any prohibition is an interface separating two areas of psychical space, each with its own psychical qualities. The prohibition on touching separates the area of the familiar, which is protected and protective, from the area of the unfamiliar, which is disturbing and dangerous. [...] The

[40] Ibid., 160.

> taboo on touching helps to differentiate orders of reality that are confused in the early tactile body-to-body experience of infancy: your body is different from other bodies; space exists independently of the objects that populate it; animate objects behave differently from inanimate objects.[41]

To continue the pathway from the taboo on touching to the social, oedipal taboo, Anzieu observes how the latter both inverts and develops the former. Both taboos exist to create the operations of exceptions – which, however, are always underlaid with inhibition.

> The oedipal taboo reverses what is learned from the taboo on touching: whatever is familiar (in the original sense of familial) becomes dangerous in relation to the dual instinctual investments of love and hatred: danger resides now in the twin risks of incest and parricide (or fratricide) and the price to be paid is castration anxiety. On the other hand, under certain conditions, the little boy will have the right – even the duty – to do battle against men outside his family, clan and nation, and to choose a wife from outside his family.[42]

The third duality – the two-phase construction of prohibitions – and the fourth – the fact that the taboos affect equally the child and the adult disciplining it – need not detain us here. The key point is that after the blissful, painful demands of primary infancy meet the block of early separation the hardest thing about the joy of touching is how it might be safely rediscovered. To conclude

---

41 Ibid., 160–161.

42 Ibid., 161.

Anzieu's discussion, I return to its opening. How, he asks, is the taboo ever to be overridden?

> According to the modes of organisation of the psychical economy, what are the effects of tactile stimulation – narcissistic restoration, erogenous excitation or traumatic violence? What comprises the play of tactile interactions in primary communication? In what kinds of case might it be thinkable or even necessary to bring back that play, and in what kinds might it be useless or even harmful? What stimulating or inhibiting consequences for later sexual life arise from the success or failure of the psychical apparatus to create a Skin-ego for itself and then overcome it in favour of a thinking Ego? Why is it that today's psychoanalytic theory tends to lose sight too often of the Freudian (and clinical) finding that psychical life is grounded in sensory qualities? These are the interrelated questions that arise from the necessity of recognising the taboo on touching.[43]

Images of Non-Touch: Getting Inside the Body of the Other

Let us move now from psychoanalytic theory to a series of instances of the desire to touch and how it is inhibited. These are extended metaphors of the way in which 'psychical life is grounded in sensory qualities'. Like dreams that aim at the fulfilment of wishes but in the end swerve off and forego them, these glimpses at the life of fantasy illustrate how we curb desire and what then becomes of it.

---

[43] Ibid., 150.

My first example of the impossibility of touch – a fantasy which, perhaps, can itself never be shared in any direct sense – is the fantasy of being inside the skin of another human being. When Gide looked at a photo of Pierre Herbart, a handsome young friend of Cocteau's whom he met in 1927, he said 'I really think he has the physique that I would most like to inhabit'.[44] We need to distinguish this idea of entry inside the other from a notion of sexual penetration. In the instances that follow, the skin or external appearance of another is not so much the *object* as the *context* for desire, the imagined pleasure of being rather than having. This is the desire to live as another person, don their appearance, in order to do something we cannot imagine doing any other way.[45] Here, for example, is a governess finding herself literally in the shoes of her admired employer:

> A strange thing about those shoes was the way in which, when she was wearing them, Mrs. Brock, who was a heavy treader by nature, planted her feet and walked with the same long steps as Lady Grizel, and stood in the same careless, rather flighty way. A lovely sort of fantasy possessed Mrs. Brock as she moved in this new pretty way, this confident way.

---

[44] Maria Van Rysselberghe. *Les Cahiers de la Petite Dame. Cahiers André Gide* vol 5 (Paris: Gallimard, 1974), 205.

[45] Three 1990s films focus on this structure: Andrew Niccol's *Gattaca* (1997), Anthony Minghella's *The Talented Mr Ripley* (1999), and Spike Jonze's *Being John Malkovich* (1999). In the first two, a male figure takes on the bodily existence of another for reasons of combined envy and desire; coincidentally or not, the other man is played in both cases by Jude Law. The more complex structure of *Malkovich* sees three people (as well as many others) entering the 'Malkovich body'.

> Part of herself became Lady Grizel – she absorbed Lady Grizel and breathed her out into the air around herself, and the air around was a far less lonely place in consequence.[46]

It is not always such a pleasant fantasy. Flaubert sent Louise Colet a letter in April 1853, in the early stages of writing *Madame Bovary*, where he complained of the feeling that he was being drawn inside characters he resented:

> *Saint Antoine* did not cost me a quarter of the intellectual tension that *Bovary* demands. It was an outlet; I had nothing but pleasure in the writing, and the eighteen months I spent in writing its 500 pages were the most deeply voluptuous of my whole life. Consider then, every minute I am having to get under *skins* that are antipathetic to me.[47]

Gratifying authorship, in this image, is an orgasmic outpouring; painful authorship forces Flaubert to look out from inside the skin of hateful characters. I have explored elsewhere what this seems to mean to Flaubert, and how the intense involvement with characters whose despicable nature is to be somewhat like himself creates the particular demands of an aesthetic of 'objectivity' both within and across the gender divide.[48]

---

[46] Molly Keane. *Good Behaviour* (London: Virago, 2001 [1981]), 20–21.

[47] Gustave Flaubert. *Correspondance II*, ed. J. Bruneau (Paris: Gallimard, 1980 [1853]), 297; see also André Gide, *Journal 1887–1925*, ed. Éric Marty (Paris: Gallimard, 1996), 1245; and Naomi Segal, *André Gide: Pederasty and Pedagogy* (Oxford: Oxford University Press, 1998), 118–120.

[48] Naomi Segal. *The Adulteress's Child: Authorship and Desire in the Nineteenth-Century Novel* (Cambridge: Polity, 1992), 115–122.

In similar vein, Anzieu cites Jean Starobinski: 'Flaubert represents in the body of Emma sensations he has felt himself; and he feels in his own body the sensations he has represented in the carnal subjectivity of Emma'.[49] More generally,

> A text is a *chef-d'œuvre* when, out of what his life has left unused and unknown to him [*sic*], the writer creates a work in which the hyper-reality of evocations and the uncanny familiarity of their consequences gives the reader the feeling of entering a dream or living a hallucination which represents, localized at the margin of his own body, an other part of himself.[50]

We shall return in a moment to the fantasy of authorship (especially in Flaubert) embodied in the image of the figure hovering on high, forbearing to come close enough to his – whether the author is a man or not, this is a masculine fantasy[51] – characters and fictional world to represent any fantasy of touching.

The assumption of a false self can prove, like a second skin, difficult to slough off again. Thus Musset's eponymous Lorenzaccio, after years of acting the part of companion in corruption to the duke his cousin whom he wishes to assassinate, recognises with despair that 'vice used to be a garment – now it has become stuck to my

49 Didier Anzieu. *Le Corps de l'œuvre* (Paris: Gallimard, 1981), 119.

50 Ibid., 225.

51 Here and elsewhere I distinguish strictly between *gender* (masculinity/femininity, whether located in a body sexed male or female) and *sex*, which is that identification of bodily differentiation by XX and XY or vagina/penis, etc. As social as both these ideas may be, they are differently social.

skin'.[52] The original purpose that motivated disguise is no longer there 'inside' the gestures and actions he has aped too well – indeed, this mimicry seems to prove that he never can have been the innocent he thought. An act of futile and suicidal murder is, after this realisation, 'all that remains of my virtue'.[53]

Whether motivated by 'virtue', curiosity or a more sinister end, the desire that assumes the costume of another's identity will, like Lorenzaccio's, find the garment hard to remove – like the psychical tearing of the early fantasy of a 'common skin' with the mother.[54]

For we need to think about what that desire to get inside a beloved person actually is: it may appear to be the ultimate reaching and touching, but this never happens. What is it we imagine getting to when we 'get there'? The protagonist of Sartre's story 'Intimité' [Intimacy] complains about the incompleteness of her husband's love:

> He loves me, but he doesn't love my guts, if you showed him my appendix in a jar, he wouldn't even recognize it, he's always groping me but if you put the jar right in his hands he wouldn't feel anything inside himself, he wouldn't think 'that's hers', you should love everything about a person, their oesophagus and their liver and their intestines.[55]

Is there in fact a contradiction between wishing to get into the other and imagining what we would find there?

52 Alfred de Musset. *Lorenzaccio* (Paris: Bordas, 1976 [1834]), 118.
53 Ibid., 119.
54 Anzieu. *The Skin-Ego*, 44–48 *et passim*.
55 Jean-Paul Sartre. *Le Mur* (Paris: Gallimard, 1939), 107.

> Maybe people don't love those bits because they're not used to them, if they saw them the way they see our hands and arms maybe they'd love them; in that case, starfish must love each other better than we do, they stretch out on the beach when it's sunny and pull their stomach out to take the air, and everyone can see it.[56]

A similar idea about the 'insides', though in a more sadistic tone, underlies David Cronenberg's *Dead Ringers* (1988). It is, of course, possible by such techniques as X-ray, ultrasound, MRI or CAT scans – or, more impressively by the motion-picture use of endoscopy – to 'see inside' our own or other people's bodies (on the normal ignorance of the inside of one's own body, see Fisher, Leder, Jacques-Alain Miller).[57] But, though twenty-first-century biotechnological advances have raised the stakes, as my final section will show, this imagery of what Paul Virilio calls the third, '*transplantation revolution*' is not so very new.[58] In 1996, artist Mona Hatoum made the video *Corps étranger* [*Foreign body*], which moves from a caressive journey across the surface of her skin to take the viewpoint of an endoscopic camera inserted, in turn, into her throat and cervix and revealing her oesophagus, intestines and other viscera. However, as Laura Marks

---

[56] Ibid., 108.

[57] Seymour Fisher. *Body Consciousness* (Glasgow: Fontana/Collins, 1976 [1973]); Drew Leder, *The Absent Body* (Chicago and London: University of Chicago Press, 1990); and Jacques-Alain Miller, 'Extimité', trans. Françoise Massardier-Kenney, in *Lacanian Theory of Discourse*, eds. Mark Bracher *et al.* (New York and London: New York University Press, 1994): 74–87.

[58] Paul Virilio. *Open Sky*, trans. Julie Rose (London & New York: Verso, 1997 [1995]), 51.

points out: 'The question of identification in this tape is perplexing [...] Hatoum can "afford" to treat her body as an object; the effect of this work would be quite different if it were performed with any body but her own.'[59] A comic version of the intra-body story can be found in the form of a promiscuous gift in Robbie Williams' music video *Rock DJ* (2000), where the tattooed and muscular star, singing on an island-stage encircled by skating or ogling models, fails to interest the girl [Lauren Gold] even after removing the last garment, so he takes his striptease to its logical conclusion by ripping off skin, guts and buttocks and finally, rocking still, duets with her in just his bones. A traditionally tragic one is the obsession of Musset, whose Lorenzaccio we have already seen lamenting the impossibility of separating mask from flesh, with reaching below the surface to expose inner corruption. In an image from the opening scene of *La Confession d'un enfant du siècle* [*The Confession of a Child of the Century*] (1836), the protagonist discovers his adored mistress's infidelity by peeping under a table-cloth; disillusioned, he embarks on a period of debauchery and observes:

> The fatal idea that truth is nakedness was in my head now all the time. I said to myself: the social world calls its face-powder virtue, its rosary religion, its trailing cloak propriety. Honour and morality are its two chambermaids; in its wine it laps up the tears of the poor in spirit who believe in it; it walks with lowered eyes while the sun is high; goes to church, parties and meetings; and in the evening, it undoes

[59] Laura U. Marks. *The Skin of the Film* (Durham and London: Duke University Press, 2000), 190.

> its robe and reveals a naked bacchante with the feet of a goat.
>
> But talking like this just made me loathe myself; for I sensed that if the body is underneath the clothing, the skeleton is underneath the body.[60]

Nakedness may seem to be 'a lure to intimacy and proximity',[61] but the inside or underside, the real nakedness of self or other, is nothing but more body, unknown but surely incapable of speaking a final truth. There is no 'ground' of love, just as there is no ground of truth. Or if there is, as Anzieu reminds us, it belongs to the surface, not to the depth:

> Ever since the Renaissance, western thought has been obsessed with one epistemological notion: the idea that we acquire knowledge by breaking through an outer shell to reach an inner nucleus or kernel. This notion is now exhausted, after having achieved some successes and also created many serious dangers – after all, it was *nuclear* physics that led scientists and the military to the point of atomic explosions. As early as the nineteenth century, neurophysiology called a halt to this, though it was not much noticed at the time. The brain is in fact the upper and frontal section of the encephalon; the cortex – the word means bark or shell in Latin and entered the vocabulary of anatomy in 1907 – denotes the outer layer of grey matter that caps the white matter. We are faced with a paradox: the centre is situated at the periphery. [...] what if thought were as much a matter of the skin as of the brain? and what if the

[60] Alfred de Musset. *La Confession d'un enfant du siècle* (Paris: Gallimard, 1973 [1836]), 111–112.

[61] Elizabeth Grosz. 'Naked', in *The Prosthetic Impulse,* eds. Marquard Smith and Joanne Morra (Cambridge, MIT Press, 2006), 194.

> Ego, now defined as the Skin-ego, had the structure of a wrapping?[62]

Images of Non-Touch: Zooming and Hovering

In my next section I want to follow the process of a double fantasy of *not* reaching that elusive and frustrating 'inside'. This is the fantasy, common in nineteenth-century French poetry – but not only there – of zooming and hovering. These two movements or positions, however contrary they may look or feel, form a single continuous gesture, the motion-above that is flight. One example is Baudelaire's poem 'Élévation', in which, in a series of vivid images of movement, the poet imagines his 'spirit' leaping up away from the earth and speeding 'avec une indicible et mâle volupté' [with an ineffable, virile delight] towards 'les champs lumineux et sereins' [bright serene fields]. But in the last two lines, motion is suddenly replaced by another spatial relation. Happy is he:

> – Qui plane sur la vie et comprend sans effort
> Le langage des fleurs et des choses muettes ![63]

> – who hovers over life and understands with ease
> the language of flowers and silent things!

Birds and other flying things are a central passion of Romantic poets: Hugo's verses are full of swans, doves, butterflies, eagles and other avatars of the poetic 'songeur

---

[62] Anzieu. *The Skin-Ego*, 9–10.

[63] Charles Baudelaire. *Les Fleurs du mal*, in *Œuvres complètes*, ed. Marcel Ruff (Paris: Seuil, 1968 [1857]), 46.

ailé' [winged dreamer][64] or his loved ones. In Baudelaire they are the counterfactual aspect of a fascination with claustrophobia that focuses on the lowering skies and tide of roofs of 1850s Paris. For this reason, as we see in all these poems, flying never reaches a goal. Vast skies are framed in the city by windows or balconies, and swans paddle in dust; over the ocean, albatrosses soar only to be snared and mocked; even the last voyage of death cannot be imagined except as anti-climax: 'La toile était levée et j'attendais encore' [the curtain had gone up, and I was still waiting].[65]

The excitement of the poem is, rather, in the repetition of take-off – what Leo Bersani calls 'a kind of vertical leap of consciousness'[66] – that is rehearsed in a cluster of prepositions or verbs of precipitation. Zooming as a fantasy cannot be separated from the moment of departing from the ground. Birds take off by generating enough airflow to create lift or dropping onto an existing gust of wind. Aeroplanes build up speed by taxiing, again relying on headwind or high-lift devices to set up the first upward motion. Dumbo proves he is no ordinary elephant by becoming the staple of drunken imaginings. Freud identifies the dream or fantasy of flying as a typical phenomenon, especially in children:

---

64 Victor Hugo. *Les Contemplations*, ed. Léon Cellier (Paris: Garnier, 1969 [1856]), 339.

65 Charles Baudelaire. 'Le rêve d'un curieux' [The dream of a curious man], in *Œuvres complètes*, 122.

66 Leo Bersani. *Baudelaire and Freud* (Los Angeles and London: University of California Press, 1977), 24.

> why do so many people dream of being able to fly? The answer that psychoanalysis gives is that to fly or be a bird is only a disguise for another wish, […] a longing to be capable of sexual performance. […] Whenever children feel in the course of their sexual researches that in the province which is so mysterious but nevertheless so important there is something wonderful of which adults are capable but which they are forbidden to know of and do, they are filled with a violent wish to be able to do it, and they dream of it in the form of flying, or they prepare this disguise of their wish to be used in later flying dreams. Thus aviation, too, which in our days is at last achieving its aim, has infantile erotic roots.[67]

And Kafka's 'Wunsch, Indianer zu werden' [Wishing to be a Red Indian] (1913) traces in a single breathless if-only sentence a centaur-like zooming that loses spurs, reins, ground and, by the fifth line, even the horse. Something of the same fantasy surely underlies Anzieu's 1992 description of himself: 'I have formed with my superego a couple united in the way a horseman is with his mount – and I don't know exactly which of us was the man and which the horse'.[68] As in Kafka, the imagined unity of two such different creatures out of their more complex inter-

[67] Sigmund Freud. 'Leonardo da Vinci and a memory of his childhood' [Eine Kindheitserinnerung des Leonardo da Vinci], trans. James Strachey, in *The Pelican Freud Library* vol. 14, eds. James Strachey and Angela Richards (Harmondsworth: Penguin, 1985 [1910]), 219–220; for a difference between this motif in the two sexes, see Sigmund Freud, *The Interpretation of Dreams* [*Die Traumdeutung*], trans. James Strachey, in *The Pelican Freud Library* vol. 4, eds. James Strachey and Angela Richards (Harmondsworth: Penguin, 1985 [1910]), 516–518.

[68] Françoise Parot and Marc Richelle, eds. *Psychologues de langue française* (Paris: PUF, 1992), 257.

dependence as master and servant – elsewhere, Anzieu calls the horse, like free association, 'man's most noble conquest'[69] – actually means that one of the two must disappear. There is here a defiant endorsement of the castration complex that I will return to.

In his analysis of the creative process, *Le Corps de l'œuvre* [*The Body of the Art-work*] (1981), Anzieu identifies creativity as 'the illusion of lightness',[70] and 'take-off' or 'lift-off' [*décollage*] as its essential first stage: this is what transforms creativity, a predisposition, into creation, an activity: 'most creative individuals are never creators; what makes the difference, as Proust says of Bergotte, is the take-off'.[71]

The wish to zoom is, as 'Élévation' shows, not an aim towards a goal. Once Anzieu gets on to the five stages of creation, he leaves *décollage* behind. But in this study of what purport to be the bodily sources of creativity, we can see how intensively (and traditionally) he sites the possibility of creation in a model of the male body. Thus even if the 'anchoring' of word or code in the body or emotions is one of the feminine aspects of creation, as is the sense of 'being penetrated by a strong idea or by a project she feels as firm inside her' (!),[72] these exceptions only serve to confirm the essential masculinity of the creator. Indeed take-off in this theory is something akin to the moment

[69] Didier Anzieu. *Contes à rebours* (Les Belles Lettres-Archimbaud, 1995 [1975]), 7.

[70] Didier Anzieu. *Le Corps de l'œuvre* (Paris: Gallimard, 1981), 12.

[71] Ibid., 17–18.

[72] Ibid., 86.

when the foetus, female by default in its earliest stages, receives the hormone that makes it male:

> why does an individual, whom one knew to be gifted, whether he thought this of himself or not, suddenly or at the end of a long incubation, begin to write, paint, compose, find formulae, and in this way have an impact on readers, spectators, listeners or visitors? Why does he fly forth while others remain on the ground?[73]

The fantasy of flying is gratuitous, purposeless, either an act of sheer undirected joy or the premise for something else. (In this, we can contrast it with the weighted, awaited object of Rilke's poem 'Der Ball', which rises in order to fall.)[74] To soar like Superman is a simple phallic image – but take-off is a rather more complicated one. As the metaphors from Baudelaire, Kafka and Anzieu suggest, the desire to fly forth is a wish to gain by losing. It is all about positive separation, but – as the terms show in both French and English – it is also a risk of ungluing or unscrewing, of removing, of being separated.[75] If what can

---

[73] Ibid., 18.

[74] Rainer Maria Rilke. *Neue Gedichte* and *Der Neuen Gedichte anderer Teil* (Frankfurt: Insel, 1974 [1907, 1908]), 158–159.

[75] I am grateful to a number of correspondents on *francofil* who answered my query in January 2006 about the term 'décoller' having the underlying meaning of 'ungluing'; in this transitive form, it dates back to 1382, but the intransitive form used by Proust and Anzieu was introduced ca. 1910. Edward Forman noted: 'I remember from old war movies that the speed you have to reach before taking off in a plane is referred to in English as the "unstick speed"'. The most extreme version of this unsticking is escape velocity, the speed required, in physics, to take an object out of the orbit of its source gravitational field. A composition of that name by Benjamin Wallfisch was premiered on 2 September in the 2006 BBC Proms.

fly is the phallus rather than the man, who is he when he is no longer anything but his desire to desire? The boyish bravado – 'I'm youth, I'm joy [...] I'm a little bird that has broken out of the egg', cries Peter Pan when challenged by Hook[76] – that dreams of sexuality in the form of flying is dealing with the fear of castration by a kind of preemption; but then what becomes of the self that feared?

This explains, I think, the Baudelairean insistence that 'les vrais voyageurs sont ceux-là seuls qui partent / Pour partir' [the only true travellers are those who leave for the sake of leaving]:[77] the fantasy of soaring or zooming is simply the fantasy of taking off without any next stage. Or rather, what it leads to is a corollary that is also almost directly its obverse. Let us now examine the second fantasy of sexual desire: that of hovering. If we return to the ending of 'Élévation' where the poet, once on high, uses his position to drift overhead understanding the language of silent things, we find that Baudelaire's term is 'planer', to hover or glide. Anzieu's term, borrowed from Proust, is 'survoler': to fly above. Both images describe a relationship of stable superiority, a God's-eye view, conferring knowledge rather than pleasure, an ability that Baudelaire suggests is something like hearing the unvoiced speech of the inanimate (flowers as *bijoux indiscrets* born to blush unseen?) but which Victor Hugo and others would present as reading the world as a book – even though as writers they have created the thing they read.

---

[76] J. M. Barrie. *Peter Pan and Wendy* (London: Pavilion, 1988 [1911]), 135.

[77] Baudelaire. 'Le voyage', *Les Fleurs du Mal*, in *Œuvres complètes*, 123.

As fantasies, authorship and hovering are closely allied, then. They both confer a divine privilege – but over something that is only *fantasised* to have preexisted the leap. In a letter of 1852, after all, Flaubert defines the presence of the author in the text as being 'like God in the universe: everywhere present and nowhere visible'.[78] It is the logical corollary of his distaste for entering 'under' his characters' skin. Of course, our image of what it might be like to be God is drastically conditioned by our longing, unseeing viewpoint 'from below', and it is this tyranny of the unseen divinity that the aspiring author longs to assume. The author-fantasy is a wish to be immortal *vis-à-vis* a toyshop of mortal objects we can scorn and ironise – characters, readers, pottering about far below.

In fact, of course, the ones who actually are immortal (since they have never lived) are the characters: Flaubert's compulsion to ironise stupid Emma or Charles is surely an expedient based on envy. These infants of his wishful mastery are actually the easiest things in the world to master – impossible not to master. But they are also attempts at mastering readership (Emma embodies this, since she lives and dies by reading), and readers are much harder to control. The wish to be immortal, which the children of our imagination do not even have to form, so inconceivable is it for them to die, is something that only flesh-and-blood people can have, and they have it by seeking virtual readers who will agree to make them virtual writers. Nothing could, perhaps, seem further from

[78] Flaubert. *Correspondance,* 16.

the body that makes it possible to have desires at all. But that would be misleading.

Like Anzieu, Sartre uses the term 'survol' [flying over/overflying] in describing how Flaubert in fantasy rises up above the rest of the human race who have made him feel abjectly despised: after climbing in fantasy to the top of a high tower from which giant-like position he can despise everyone, there is a sort of rush of motion and 'whether he has been snatched up from the earth or the futile planet has dropped by itself into the abuses of space-time infinity, the fact is that he finds himself *in the air*'.[79] Or again, 'all of a sudden, panting and sacred, he rises up above his torturers, above Nero himself: how small they look, these instruments of his glory. He hovers and looks down, from the ether, at the rag he has left behind in their hands'.[80] The rag, like the skin of flayed Marsyas, is the bodily thing left after the fantasy has disembodied him. But we should not forget that it is the bodily thing that produces the fantasies.

Here is another, less human but also less agonised version of hovering. Leconte de Lisle (1818-1894), whose poems are suffused with a fulsome remembrance of Réunion, the Indian Ocean island where he spent his youth, writes of jungle scenes in which the apparent peace of sleep contains the coiled menace of animal violence: far-off lions or elephants slumber in the noonday heat, a tiger

---

[79] Jean-Paul Sartre. *L'Idiot de la famille: Gustave Flaubert de 1821 à 1857* vol 2 (Paris: Gallimard, 1971), 1185.

[80] Ibid., 1177.

'falls asleep, its belly in the air, and dilates its claws';[81] and the jaguar dreams, a proper Freudian *avant la lettre*, that it is plunging 'its streaming nails / Into the flesh of terrified, bellowing bulls'.[82] His birds are nobler: his albatross, unlike Coleridge's or Baudelaire's (and contrast the vulnerable swans of Mallarmé or Rilke: some poets like their zoology classically uncomplicated) does not plunge to earth but 'tranquil amidst the terror' of a violent storm on high,[83] 'approaches, passes and disappears majestically'. It is in 'Le Sommeil du condor' ['The sleep of the condor'], however, that the full fantasy of hovering – the coexistence of extreme power with extreme stillness – is clearest.

The condor is a member of the vulture family. It is supposed to have various peculiarities: to be able to go for long periods without feeding and to flush pink when emotional; but the aspect that has made most impact, and was noted by Darwin, is its ability to hover for long periods without apparently flapping its wings. Leconte de Lisle's poem begins, like Baudelaire's, with vivid prepositions of flight, and then observes 'Le vaste Oiseau, tout plein d'une morne indolence'[84] [the vast Bird, filled with gloomy indolence] gazing down upon the map-like panorama of America. As night rolls in like a tide from the east, it waits 'comme un spectre, seul, au front du pic altier' [alone,

[81] Charles-Marie-René Leconte de Lisle. *Œuvres,* vol 2: *Poèmes barbares*, ed. Edgard Pich (Paris: Société d'édition « Les belles lettres », 1976 [1889]), 175.

[82] Ibid., 185.

[83] Charles-Marie-René Leconte de Lisle. *Œuvres,* vol 3: *Poèmes tragiques ; derniers poèmes*, ed. Edgard Pich (Paris: Société d'édition « Les belles lettres », 1977 [1884, 1886]), 67.

[84] Ibid., 166.

like a ghost, atop the lofty peak], until at last the darkness covers it. Then,

> Il râle son plaisir, il agite sa plume,
> Il érige son cou musculeux et pelé,
> Il s'élève en fouettant l'âpre neige des Andes,
> Dans un cri rauque il monte où n'atteint pas le vent,
> Et, loin du globe noir, loin de l'astre vivant,
> Il dort dans l'air glacé, les ailes toutes grandes.[85]

> He groans out his pleasure, shakes his plumage,
> erects his muscular, hairless neck,
> and soars up, whipping the acrid snow of the Andes;
> with a hoarse cry, he rises to where the wind cannot reach
> and, far above the black globe, high above the living star,
> he sleeps in the icy air, his great wings outstretched.

This is, of course, a fantasy of phallic absoluteness: permanently tense, permanently relaxed – the ballet of male desire. But, as we have already observed, the ideal relies on failure: not simply on the logical impossibility of this fusion of extremes, but also on a different, psychical impossibility. In relation to Baudelaire's sudden switch from zooming to hovering, Leo Bersani observes:

> The emergence of an erotic esthetic will also involve the eroticizing of knowledge. But in early poems such as 'Élévation' and 'La Beauté', the sexual imagery is merely juxtaposed with the epistemological claims. In 'Élévation', the description of the poet's spirit plunging beyond the confines of the 'starry spheres' suggests sexual penetration […], but this erotic 'rising up' seems to have no effect on the nature of the poet's comprehension of 'the language of

[85] Ibid., 167.

> flowers and of silent things'. An effortless serene understanding is unaffected by the erotic energy of the leap into understanding.[86]

My own view is that these contraries are disconnected in a rather different way. The erotics of the flying fantasy is three-fold. If we trace it in reverse, the end-point of hovering stands both for the *survol* of superior knowledge, control from on high, and for the erectile tension that has become a sort of immortality or grace. Before this, the effort of desire is expressed in the fantasy of zooming, reaching-towards. Before even this, the initial movement is a taking-off, the initiative of excitement that lifts. Each one of these actions is, separately and together, a tracking-forth of the excitement of castration. Like 'escape velocity', the most extreme and deathly version, or the aimless aim of going into space of Vincent, the protagonist of *Gattaca*, they are all fantasies of distance. To rephrase this in terms of laws: he cannot command (know) where he desires, and he cannot desire and know in a single movement: desire is inevitably failure.

In Anzieu's citation from Proust, the relation of take-off to hovering that represents Bergotte's creativity is a sort of zigzag: 'In order to travel in the air, it is not the most powerful automobile that is needed but one which is capable, by sheer ascensional force, of ceasing to run on the ground and cutting across the line of its horizontal speed with the vertical'.[87] Bergotte's talent may be nothing very

---

[86] Bersani. *Baudelaire and Freud*, 25.

[87] Marcel Proust. *A l'ombre des jeunes filles en fleurs. A la recherche du temps perdu*, vol 1, ed. Pierre Clarac and André Ferré (Paris: Gallimard, 1954 [1918]), 554.

special in itself, despised by family friends in Rolls Royces, but it has this capacity: 'from inside his modest machine which had at last 'taken off', he hovered above them [*les survolait*]'.[88] Carefully examined, the first motion is horizontal, the second vertical, the third again horizontal, but no longer moving forward, for the relation of superiority is not directional but static. It is all about separation. This knowledge is, *pace* Bersani, still erotic, but an erotics of distance, coolness born out of heat.

Penthouses and Drones: 'Power Without Vulnerability'

The whole point of the fantasy of hovering is its inability to touch. The fact that it must not come to an end means that it is, effectively, all end.

Two further kinds of example suggest themselves. The first is our contemporary relation to verticality – 'being above' – in one kind of static position: the fascination with high buildings and how it is to live or stand in them. A couple of centuries ago, the contrasts of urban living were the opposite. In Balzac's *Le Père Goriot* (1835), the eponymous protagonist demonstrates his gradual loss of income and status by moving ever further up the floors of the *pension* Vauquer, having settled into the smallest, least appealing top-floor apartment by the start of the novel. Anyone who has lived in a Paris *chambre de bonne* knows what this feels like. In Baudelaire, being in the eaves with a balcony view over Paris means he can see or imagine or

---

[88] Ibid., 555; cited in Anzieu, *Le Corps de l'œuvre*, 17.

both, 'par-delà des vagues de toits' [beyond a sea of roofs], characters he can pretend to pity in a burst of poetic projective identification.[89] In this, as in much else (not least his fascination with urban weather), Baudelaire's writing marks the late Romantic turning-point that inverts 'bohemian' abjection into creative pride.

In our day the highest place in a city-centre building is more likely to be a penthouse, the badge of wealth rather than poverty. High-rise has two different meanings, as – to take London as an example this time – the unloved social housing of the 1960s is discarded in favour of the Gherkin or the Shard.[90] But the topography of urban life has two vocabularies. Walking through the cityscape may be represented in one way in Baudelaire's or Benjamin's *flâneur*,[91] in another in the peregrinations of Breton and

---

[89] Baudelaire. 'Les Fenêtres' [Windows], *Petits poèmes en prose*, in *Œuvres complètes*, 174.

[90] This change is argued, for example, in Stephen Graham, 'Luxified Skies: How Vertical Urban Housing Became an Elite Preserve', *City* 19, no. 5 (2015): 618–645. The risks of vertical social housing were starkly demonstrated by the Grenfell Tower disaster of June 2017, see Andrew O'Hagan, 'The Tower', *London Review of Books* 7 June 2018, https://www.lrb.co.uk/v40/n11/andrew-ohagan/the-tower; yet many residents of Grenfell had appreciated the combination of verticality and home explored by Richard Baxter in 'The High-Rise Home: Verticality as Practice in London', *International Journal of Urban and Regional Research* 41, no. 2: 334–352.

[91] Baudelaire's essay 'Le peintre de la vie moderne' [The painter of modern life] first appeared in 1863 but the idea of the *flâneur* harks back to Paul Gavarni's sketch of 1842 and Edgar Allan Poe's tale 'The Man of the Crowd' of 1840; in 1903 Georg Simmel picked up the image in his 'Die Großstadt und das Geistesleben' [The Metropolis and Mental Life] and Walter Benjamin developed the Baudelairean version of Paris in his *Passagen-werk* [Arcades Project] in the 1920s and 1930s.

Aragon in the 1920s or the *situationnistes* forty years later,[92] and in a third way in the last half of the twentieth century in the theoretical writings of Roland Barthes and Michel de Certeau.[93] In all these versions, it is not so much a question of the adventures of the urban wanderer as of the textuality of spatial movement. Thus Certeau writes of walkers 'whose bodies follow the downstrokes and cross-strokes of an urban "text" which they write but cannot read'.[94] The walker traces shapes – but far above his or her puny movements, the tourist looking down from on high (Certeau was writing in 1980 from the 110th floor of the World Trade Center) possesses a New York that is a 'city composed of paroxysmal places in monumental reliefs. The spectator can read in it a universe that is taking off

[92] See Louis Aragon, *Le Paysan de Paris* [*The Paris Peasant*] (1926); André Breton, *Nadja* (1928); and Guy Debord, *La Société du spectacle* [*The Society of the Spectacle*] (1967).

[93] The text of Barthes' 'Sémiologie et urbanisme' [Semiology and the urban] was a lecture given in Naples in 1967 and first published in 1971; Certeau's 'Marcher dans la ville' [Walking in the city] first appeared in *L'Invention du quotidien* [*The Practice of Everyday Life*] vol 1, in 1980.

[94] Michel de Certeau. 'Marcher dans la ville' [Walking in the city], in *L'Invention du quotidien* [*The Practice of Everyday Life*] vol 1, ed. Luce Giard (Paris: Gallimard, 1990 [1980]), 141. Certeau goes on to give a brief history of this fantasy of living on high at the 'top' of a city, from medieval maps to Manhattan. Of course this fantasy goes back to antiquity, and aspirations to build and stand high have been associated with overweening ambition from Babel to Ibsen's *The Master Builder* (1892), just as the verticality of gaze or aim are analysed in such texts as Foucault's *Surveiller et punir* (1975) and Peter Sloterdijk's *Du mußt dein Leben ändern* (2009). In *Consensuality*, I mark the importance of the positioning of Princess Diana at the meeting-point of the upward and downward gaze: 'a double-facing skin between the feudal and the modern modes of the exercise of power' (118).

into the air'.[95] The walker writes, the viewer from above reads; one traces and is traceable, Dedalus creating the labyrinth, while the other becomes 'a voyeur',[96] or more precisely 'a god's eye'. He concludes (whether thinking directly of Flaubert or not): 'to be nothing but this point of vision, that is the fiction of knowledge'.

Hovering is intrinsically different from standing or living on high, however. I have characterised it as castratory because, ultimately, the bird or machine hovers alone isolated from its point of origin; there is not even a tightrope suspended in the air as, terrifyingly, in the recolonisation of the Twin Towers in Robert Zemeckis's *Man on Wire* (2015). This version of looking-down is always 'commanding'. The obvious corollary of the condor – that patient predator – is the modern bomber-plane. Its association with death may be suicidal, like that of Yeats's Irish airman in 1919, driven on high by 'a lonely impulse of delight',[97] very similar to that of Saint-Exupéry's heroes experiencing 'the mysterious labour of a living flesh';[98] or it may be homicidal like that of Marinetti, who writes in *The Battle of Tripoli* (1912) of the pleasure of bombing without needing to dirty his hands. But ultimately it goes out beyond the flesh, representing the extreme 'clean' violence of the *survol*: brains without bodies.[99] In 1921, with remarkable prescience, Marinetti wrote of the possibility – like Kafka's

95 Certeau, 'Marcher dans la ville', 139.

96 Ibid., 140.

97 William Butler Yeats, *W. B. Yeats: The Poems*, ed. Daniel Albright (London: Dent, 1990), 184.

98 Antoine de Saint-Exupéry. *Vol de nuit* (Paris: Gallimard, 1931), 23.

99 See Martin Jay, *Downcast Eyes* (London, Berkeley & Los Angeles: University of California Press, 1993). 90, 213, 387.

Red Indian fantasy – of the violence of hovering imagined at the furthest extreme from bodily presence:

> Phantom-aeroplanes laden with bombs and without pilots, remote-controlled by a 'shepherd' aeroplane. Phantom-planes without pilots which will explode with their bombs, which can also be guided from the ground by an electric control-panel. We will have aerial torpedoes. One day we will have electric war.[100]

As I hope I have shown, anticipating the tactics of today's aerial bombardment, and the very reverse of our contemporary suicide bombers, these masculine fantasies of desire are both self-separation and separation from the other. Consummation, it seems, is neither sought nor achieved; but there is no loss either, because the 'other' – land viewed from above, flowers and other silent things – is actually much too far away to be heard, seen or touched. This is the fantasy of the drone: violence without sacrifice; or rather, a body without a sense of touch.

In a remarkable article on the recent film *Eye in the Sky* (dir. Gavin Hood, 2015), Derek Gregory writes:

> As soon as the Wright brothers demonstrated the possibility of human flight, others were busy imagining flying machines with nobody on board. In 1910 the engineer Raymond Phillips captivated crowds in the London Hippodrome with a remotely controlled airship that floated out over the stalls and, when he pressed a switch, released hundreds of paper birds on to the heads of the audience below. When he built the real thing, he promised, the birds would

[100] Filippo Tommaso Marinetti. *L'Alcova di acciaio* [*The Steel Alcove*] (Milan: Serra e Riva, 1985 [1921]), 121.

> be replaced with bombs. Sitting safely in London he could attack Paris or Berlin.[101]

But, Gregory warns:

> Remoteness [...] is an elastic measure. Human beings have been killing each other at ever greater distances since the invention of the dart, the spear and the slingshot. The invention of firearms wrought another transformation in the range of military violence. And yet today, in a world shrunk by the very technologies that have made the drone possible, the use of these remote platforms seems to turn distance back into a moral absolute.

He cites a veteran of Bomber Command saying: 'The good thing about being in an aeroplane at war is that you never touch the enemy. [...] You never see the whites of their eyes'. Similarly, the pride of the US Air Force is in having weapons that endow it with 'power without vulnerability'. This is a logical corollary to the converse pride of the suicide bomber for whom the willingness to die through killing (or kill through dying) is an internalised ethical demand. Yet ethics creep back in because not touching here is dependent upon seeing – not the whites of their eyes, but an eerily silent, grainy image of people moving on the ground, up on a screen in which the bright production values of videogame are absent but the manipulative possibilities seem the same.

Why is the protagonist of *Eye in the Sky* a woman (Col. Katherine Powell, played by Helen Mirren)? Because

---

[101] Derek Gregory. 'How a Hollywood film reveals the reality of drone warfare', *The Observer*, 9 April 2016, 33.

questions about the morality of not-touching need to be asked and by implication these are questions of gender (not sex, gender). In another possible antidote to the fantasies of masculinity embodied in zooming and hovering, I want to cite a BBC Radio 4 broadcast of 29 November 2015, 'Twenty-first century war poet'. In this 'first-person' programme, airforce veteran and poet Lynn Hill describes her experience of working with drones. 'The plane is physically in those countries [but] you can pretty much operate a drone from anywhere and they chose Las Vegas'. She goes on to explore the situation she found herself in: 'whatever faults you have as a person, the drone programme intensified it [...] sometimes I didn't care and then I felt guity that I didn't care, and I wanted to care [...]; I was depressed [...] "they serve up poison like entrees at Blueberry Hill: I'll have the crazy, with a side of numb, please"'.

As far as the body is concerned, Hill speaks of the drone operators as sharing 'this removal from war' yet, in relation to the remote black-and-white image of a soldier falling, of being able to 'taste it and hear it'. Part of her reaction to the guilt and craziness is grammatical: how names are used in the military, how people avoid the complicity of the pronoun 'we'; she sometimes refers to herself in the masculine (as 'a good airman or a bad airman'), though in reasserting her humanity she moves from the masculine to the universal: responding to the usual definition of a drone as 'an unmanned aircraft' she says: 'No, no – I'm the man behind the drone [...] I'm the human: I have feelings, I have fears, I have opinions, I have thoughts, and if I'm flawed, the drone is flawed, but if I'm moral and ethical, then the drone is going to be moral and ethical'. But the main bodily imagery she uses is tied to her femaleness: 'I've been living with the war inside of me all this time [...] it sits with me and it grows'; and then, in a connected fluid image of 'contamination': 'I ask myself questions, like how telling these stories are [*sic*] keeping the experiences alive in me: I wondered if when I gave birth or breastfed my baby, was I pouring into her the war that still lives in me'?

Teletactility, or 'Intimacy Without Proximity'

'Teletactility' is a term cited by Claudia Benthien from Stahl Stenslie;[102] 'tactile telepresence' is Paul Virilio's term;[103] another commonly found is 'telehaptics'. They all mean touching at a distance, or 'relationships of immediate proximity giving way to remote interrelationships'.[104] These terms first arose in the 1990s, and are uttered in varying tones of excitement or horror. For the rise of the posthuman – though a complete surprise to my doctor when I told her I was working on it yesterday – is by now a familiar trope in cultural and political theory.[105]

---

[102] Claudia Benthien. *Skin* (New York: Columbia University Press, 2002 [1999]), 221–234; she cites Stahl Stenslie, 'Vernetzung des Fleisches', *Die Zukunft des Körpers I, Kunstforum* 132: 178–187.

[103] Virilio. *Open Sky*, 105; see also 10, 39, 45, 105 *et passim*.

[104] Ibid., 19.

[105] The term 'posthuman/ism' carries with it, of course, all the positive and negative ambivalences of 'human/ism'; it also overlaps somewhat with 'transhuman/ism', which is itself weighted with the many uses of the prefix 'trans'. For discussions of the difference, see Joanna Zylinska, ed.,*The Cyborg Experiments* (London & New York: Continuum, 2002), 107.

Not everyone looks cheerfully to a world in which we 'have in common a sustained commitment to work out the implications of posthumanism for our shared understandings of the human subject and of humanity as a whole' or in which we should be able to realise 'the cybernetic dream of creating a world in which humans and intelligent machines can both feel at home'.[106] The notion is as divisive as every new step in our way of conceiving ourselves. Some theorists get lost in the 'ecstatic pronouncements and delirious dreams' of a state of being in which the body is obsolete or even erased, in which the 'cyborg myth is about transgressed boundaries, potent fusions and dangerous possibilities'.[107] Apart from increasingly familiar developments in biotechnology, genetics and robotics (which I shall return to below), such dangerous possibilities are most consistently represented in the performance art of Stelarc:

> I'm much more interested in what happens between states, between people – not so much at the boundary but *between* boundaries and to question what constitutes boundaries, to undermine them altogether. [...] [Virilio] sees the skin as a boundary. On the one side is the bounded self and on the other there is the world. He found it very disconcerting when I started inserting electronic objects,

---

106 Respectively: Rosi Braidotti. *The Posthuman* (Cambridge: Polity 2013) 46; and N. Katherine Hayles. *How We Became Posthuman* (Chicago & London: University of Chicago Press, 1999), 239.

107 Respectively: Hayles. *How We Became Posthuman*, 193; Donna Haraway. 'A Cyborg Manifesto' (1984) reprinted in Haraway, *Simians, Cyborgs and Women* (London: Free Association Books, 1991), 154.

> like STOMACH SCULPTURE, into the body.[108] The point where technology invades the body is the point where hysteria is usually generated.[109]

The revolutionary dissolution of boundaries or 'edges', and the fixity of the skin as a guardian of the inside/outside dynamic of the self, understood as both a material and a psychical entity, is much exaggerated by the advocates of posthumanism, however. The idea of the skin has never been one of impermeability, as witness Anzieu's 'double face', Paul Schilder's body image, Freud's mystic writing-pad or discussions of sweat and other indices of porosity in the cultural histories of Benthien, Jablonski or Connor.[110]

But Stelarc makes a larger claim for one of his other art experiments:

> A hollow body is a host body. So in this way the body is not simply a site for a psyche but becomes a host for a sculpture.[111] In the performance FRACTAL FLESH for Telepolis, people in other places could remotely access and actuate a body. People at the Pompidou Centre in Paris, the Media Lab in Helsinki and the Doors of Perception Conference in Amsterdam were connected to my body, located in Luxembourg. We

---

[108] Stelarc's habit of referring to his body as 'the body' is noted by four different writers, in Hayles, *How We Became Posthuman,* 51, 59, 87, 187. Obviously it is not casual, but could be seen as much as an aggrandisement as an anonymisation of his self.

[109] Stelarc, interviewed in Hayles, *How We Became Posthuman*, 117.

[110] For 'edges', see Smith and Morra, *The Prosthetic Impulse*, 3, 6. For other discussions, see Benthien, *Skin*, 37–43; Nina Jablonski, *Skin* (Berkeley, Los Angeles & London: University of California Press, 2006), 39; and Steven Connor, *The Book of Skin* (London: Reaktion, 2004), 21–22.

[111] On the spatial context of sculptures, see Segal, *Consensuality*, 125–141.

> had video screens at either end, so I could always see the face of the person who was programming my body movements, and they in turn could always see the results of their choreography. These images were always superimposed so we could see each other. That created a kind of intimacy without proximity and it gave you the sense of being 'possessed' by that remote agent.[112]

'Possessed' is a good word: as we see below in a quotation from Sartre, it was much used by men for a kind of proximity without intimacy, the fantasy of 'possessing' a woman – always a paradox, since it was their body part that took the risk of a temporary stay inside her boundaries. It still commonly refers to ghosts and should by rights refer to foetuses: the thing inside another thing, like an occupying army or Freud's all-purpose, mistranslated concept of *besetzen*. Here it suggests a momentary but powerful suspension of autonomy on the part of the artist. What it surely does not suggest is intimacy.

Let us return to where this essay began – the sense of touch, and its place at the extreme of the senses. Steven Connor refers to touch as a 'mastersense' and Tiffany Field calls it 'the mother of the senses'.[113] In these two images, we see first the hands that deploy and manipulate and second the hands that care and caress. In the world of the posthuman, what does each of these become? – prosthetics and cybersex.

The prosthetic use of technology is not simple 'enhancement', as disability researchers in a range of fields have

---

[112] Stelarc, interviewed in Hayles, *How We Became Posthuman*, 119.

[113] Connor. *The Book*, 185; Field. *Touch*, 76.

eloquently argued. Vivian Sobchack is impatient with the ubiquity of a metaphor that she lives with in material earnest, and contradicts Marquard Smith's assertion that 'the discourse of prosthesis [...] can be located in [...] the deeply ideological subject of "passing"', by describing how she often reveals 'as a marvel what the prosthetic leg is cosmetically supposed to hide (that I have a prosthetic leg)' because she takes pride in how gracefully it enables her to 'get about [her] world with a minimum of prosthetic thought'.[114]

In a less nuanced debate we are all cyborgs endowed with prostheses: indeed the Gordian knot of the posthuman is often sliced with the observation that technology can be equated with culture,[115] for it is what assists the body in fulfilling its 'natural' existential projects. Stelarc summarises: 'Technology is not simply external. **Technology is what defines being human**. It's not an antagonistic alien sort of object, it's part of our human nature. It constructs our human nature'.[116] This goes as far back as Aristotle, and enters neo-modernity with Mar-

---

[114] Marquard Smith. 'The Vulnerable Articulate' in *The Prosthetic Impulse,* eds. Marquard Smith and Joanne Morra (Cambridge MA & London: MIT Press, 2006), 50; Vivian Sobchak, 'A Leg to Stand On: Prosthetics, Metaphor and Materiality', in *The Prosthetic Impulse,* eds. Marquard Smith and Joanne Morra (Cambridge MA & London: MIT Press, 2006), 33, 38.

[115] See also Julie Clarke, 'The Human/Not-Human in the work of Orlan and Stelarc', in *The Cyborg Experiments*, ed. Joanna Zylinska (London & New York: Continuum, 2002), 37–38; Neil Badmington, ed., *Posthumanism* (Basingstoke: Palgrave Macmillan, 2000).

[116] Stelarc, cited in Gary Hall, *Para-Site*, in *The Cyborg Experiments*, ed. Joanna Zylinska (London & New York: Continuum, 2002), 139, emphases Stelarc's.

shall McLuhan's 'extensions of man'.[117] Thus even if, at times, 'our machines are disturbingly lively, and we ourselves frighteningly inert', it is also true that 'bodies and technologies function in a self-feeding relation where transformations in the one produce transformations in the other, which in turn feed back on both'.[118] And our contemporary 'transplantation revolution' has married a general envy of pregnancy to a continuing fascination with other kinds of hybridity and grafting – the 'intruder' heart that interpolates the donor's feelings,[119] the criminal's hands attached to the concert-pianist's wrists, Frankenstein's rough sewing of body parts – we are never short of opportunities for the uncanny. On the other hand … robotics has invented appendages that are more like the sentient fingertips than they are themselves. Stelarc describes an ambidextrous hand whose fingers and thumb bend both ways and thus offer left and right capabilities simultaneously, or an extended arm which has 11-degree manipulation: each finger splits open to produce further fingers which can lift and grip.[120] The MIT robot 'Cog' can turn a crank or swing a pendulum, and other early robots take the analogy with human touch much further:

---

[117] Cited in Zylinska, *The Cyborg Experiments*, 1–3.

[118] Respectively: Haraway. *Simians, Cyborgs and Women*, 152; and Grosz. *Naked*, 188.

[119] The epithet refers to Nancy's 'l'intrus', but the donor's feelings are picked up from a 2016-2017 Spanish TV series called *Pulsaciones* (translated as *Lifeline*).

[120] Stelarc, in 'Zombies, Cyborgs and Chimeras', Youtube video, 2014, https://www.youtube.com/watch?v=TqtiM1hK6lU.

> Tactile sensors are devices attached in various ways to robotic grippers, to aid in the grasping and manipulation of objects. These sensors are specifically designed to calibrate accurately the force of the robotic device's grasp so that, for example, the machine uses enough force to pick up and move an object without crushing it in the process. [...] This way of conceptualising touch is derived from scientific understandings of the skin. [...] In fact, function (tactility) and materiality are inextricably linked in this understanding of touch, so that sensing requires a skin-like materiality to enable a skin-like quality of touch.[121]

When Hans Moravec imagined his 'robot bush' in the 1980s, he described its structure:

> Noting both the power and the limitations of human hands, Moravec invents his robot bush as an extraordinarily dexterous entity. He moves from a general account of the robot's capacities to an 'actual design', describing the robot's structure as a 'large branch that splits into four smaller ones, each half the scale' (Moravec 1988: 104). This branching and splitting extends to twenty levels, from an initial meter-long trunk that is ten centimeters in diameter. The aptly named 'bush' ends in a trillion tiny 'leaves'.[122]

Not only does it enjoy 'skin-like qualities' but it far exceeds them, for this robot can '"see" through touch': 'if our bush puts its fingers on a photograph, it will "see" the image

[121] Claudia Castañeda. 'Robotic skin: The Future of Touch?', in *Thinking Through the Skin*, eds. Sara Ahmed & Jackie Stacey (London & New York: Routledge, 2001), 226. In this and the next two quotations, Castañeda is citing Hans Moravec's *Mind Children* (Cambridge, MA: Harvard University Press, 1988), 105.

[122] Castañeda. 'Robotic skin', 225.

in immense detail simply by feeling the height variations of the developed silver on the paper. It could watch a movie by walking its fingers along the film as it screened by at high speed'.[123] Thus might touch and sight, the two extremities of the sense-spectrum, bizarrely meet.

But what of care and the caress? We have already glimpsed the power of maternal holding and tending; let us proceed into adulthood. In the work of Sartre and Merleau-Ponty we discover two passages in which the caress exemplifies the psychology of the self-other encounter. For Sartre in *L'Être et le néant* (1943) desire is always that of a body for another body, through which both discover themselves as flesh:

> Everyone is disappointed by that famous saying: '[love is] the contact of two epidermises'. Love is not meant to be mere contact; it seems that only man can reduce it to a contact, and when that happens it loses its true meaning. The caress is not a simple floating touch [*effleurement*]: it is a *fashioning*. When I caress another person, I bring forth [*fais naître*] their flesh by my caress, with my fingers. The caress is that set of rituals that *incarnates* the other. […] The caress creates the other as flesh both for me and for themselves. [… It] reveals the flesh by divesting the body of its action, splitting it off from the possibilities that surround it […]
>
> In the caress what caresses the other is not my body as a synthetic form in action, but my fleshly body which creates the flesh of the other. By means of pleasure, the caress is able to create the body of the other both for them and for myself as a *touched* passivity, in the sense that my body becomes flesh in

[123] Ibid., 227.

> order to touch their body with its own passivity – in caressing itself against it rather than caressing it. This is why the gestures of lovemaking have a languor that one might almost call studied: it is not so much that we *take hold of* [*prendre*] a part of the other's body but that we *bring* our own body up against the body of the other. Not so much pushing or touching, in an active sense, but *placing up against* [*poser contre*]. [...] By *realizing* the other's incarnation, the caress uncovers my own incarnation to me. [...] I make the other person taste my flesh through their own flesh in order to make them feel themselves being flesh. In this way *possession* is revealed as a *double reciprocal incarnation*.[124]

Here, sexual desire brings the body to the fore in a way that its everyday existence, a means of enacting projects in the world, cannot. It creates two selves of flesh. It does this because of the peculiar 'impenetrability' of the other's body, the caress being closer than an *effleurement* but further off than a penetration: a placing-up-against that slides briefly along the smoothness of the other's otherness. Unlike the appropriativeness of knowledge, sport or art, however, desire creates, through the caress that makes them flesh, an encounter of two bodied freedoms. What I want when I love, according to Sartre, is to be 'the object by whose proxy the world exists for another; in another sense, I am the world. Instead of being a *this* standing out against a background of world, I am the object-background against which the world stands out'.[125]

---

[124] Jean-Paul Sartre. *L'Être et le néant* (Paris: Gallimard, 1943), 430–431.

[125] Ibid., 409–410.

In Merleau-Ponty's posthumously published notes collected as *Le visible et l'invisible* (1964), in the essay on 'Interlacing – the chiasm', we find a striking paragraph inserted in the middle of a discussion of the 'solipsistic illusion' of the bodied subject:[126]

> For the first time, the body no longer couples with the world, it intertwines with another body, applying itself carefully to it with its whole expanse, tirelessly sculpting with its hands the strange statue which, in its turn, gives everything it receives, cut off from the world and its aims, occupied with the sole fascination of floating in Being together with another life, making itself the outside of its inside and the inside of its outside. And then at once, movement, touch and vision, applied to the other and to themselves, head back to their source and, in the patient, silent work of desire, commence the paradox of expression.[127]

In the 'careful' image of the statue, this scene echoes something of Sartre's concept of the caress making the self and other into flesh, but turns it aesthetic. The key term is 's'appliquer', which appears both in reference to the person of the lover working on the 'strange statue' of the other's life and also to the senses working among themselves. The ending of this passage seems just about to point forward to a development of the 'paradox of expression' – but it never happens, the argument at that point turning elsewhere. What this paradox might be, though, is an *active* relation of consensuality that would supplement Sartre's passive one.

126 Maurice Merleau-Ponty. *Le Visible et l'Invisible* (Paris : Gallimard, 1964), 186.

127 Ibid., 187.

Bearing in mind these notions of what the direct caress is, let us turn to the indirection of cybersex. Virilio inserts it into his theory of 'the law of least action', as '*the couple that was the driving force* of history [...] entering divergence mode',[128] and identifies it as a new version of the *survol* or safe sex:

> As with the nozzle on the jet engine of a machine capable of breaking the sound barrier, everything comes together in long-distance love, thanks to the power of ejecting others, to this ability to ward off their immediate proximity, to 'get off on' distance and make headway in sensual pleasure the way jet propulsion propels the jet. So, just as the supersonic aircraft's take-off enables it to *overfly* Mother Earth and the geography of the continents, so the 'remote manipulation' of jet-propelled love allows partners to *overcome* their reciprocal proximity without risk of contamination, the electro-magnetic prophylactic outdoing by a long shot – and how! – the fragile protection of the condom.[129]

Another way of thinking about cybersex is by analogy with the idea of the 'haptics' of cinema. This concept looks not at 'technologies that attempt to reproduce the sense of smell (for example, Odorama) or touch (for example, the Power Glove) – in effect, movement-image strategies for evoking smell and touch – [but at] how audiovisual media evoke these other senses within their own constraints'.[130] It works against the dominance of vision as the primary filmic sense, not by pretending to overcome or supersede

---

[128] Virilio. *Open Sky*, 111, 108.
[129] Ibid., 104.
[130] Marks. *The Skin of the Film*, 131.

it but by examining what it does other than present or represent things to our eyes. Cybersex is similarly, perforce, a mediation and thus a perversion or inversion of touch.

As such it potentially creates 'new kinds of tactile experience', abolishing the 'distinction between near and far senses'.[131] But how could this work? Benthien cites Stahl Stenslie's description of his *Cyber SM-Projekt* of 1993:

> The communications system places the emphasis on the conveyance and the reception of a sensual contact. If I touch my own body, I am at the same time also touching the other participant. [...] Above all, I have to do to myself what I want the other person to feel. This turns my own body into a self-referential object of communication. There is no possibility of forgetting oneself or of hiding behind the actions one is performing. If I touch my genitals, the other person will notice that I am touching them. Such a one-on-one transfer of stimuli creates a direct, immediate, almost intimate form of communication.[132]

Almost intimate? Benthien questions the collapse of touch into 'communication': 'the entire setup rests on the idea of pushing a button or using a keyboard, except that now it is the body itself that is used in this way';[133] but I would like to raise a different problem, one implied by her use of the generic definite article favoured by Stelarc, and which precisely hides its presumptions in and behind an apparent anonymity – 'the' body. Of course there is no

---

[131] Benthien. *Skin*, 223, paraphrasing Derrick de Kerckhove, 'Touch versus Vision', in *Die Aktualität des Ästhetischen*, ed. Wolfgang Welsch (Munich: Fink, 1993).

[132] Ibid., 224.

[133] Ibid., 226.

'the body'; and the sexualised body is precisely animated in its potential for difference. This difference does not depend on morphological specifics of sex/gender or anything else, but it does depend on you being not-me. If I have breasts and a clitoris and I touch those and you feel this touch on your chest and penis, in what sense are we feeling the same thing? The fascinating implication of this version of cybersex is that there is no longer any heterosexuality – or there is only heterosexuality, and thus no homosexuality. How can I 'incarnate the other' if I am no longer caressing 'another person'?

This is illustrated more powerfully in the discussion by Lisa Cartwright and Brian Goldfarb of a scene in 'Burning Chrome', a story by William Gibson published in 1986, which 'reflects some of the desires that drove researchers to introduce sensitivity to prosthetic and paralyzed limbs': the protagonist Jack has a prosthetic arm whose covering is 'a medium of sensual pleasure. [...] Through this skin prosthesis, the meaning of feeling slips from the sense of touch to affect, emotion, and communicated sentiment'.[134] The story refers to a real-life invention by prosthetic engineer John Sabolich called the 'Sense-of-Feel' [SOF] system. The SOF 'draws on memories of 'warm feeling' (love) communicated through hand-to-hand contact';[135] to do this it requires training:

---

[134] Both these quotations: Lisa Cartwright and Brian Goldfarb. 'On the Subject of Neural and Sensory Prostheses', in *The Prosthetic Impulse,* eds. Marquard Smith and Joanne Morra (Cambridge MA & London: MIT Press, 2006): 125–154, 128.

[135] Ibid., 131.

Abstraction is an important part of this process. Temperature sensation is delivered in isolation from other types or qualities of sensations that are conducted through touch – such as texture, tickle, itch, numbness, position sense, and pressure (pressure is delivered to the Sense-of-Feel prosthesis not by thermophiles but through electrodes). Sensations are parsed in this system. Touch in itself is reduced to the abstraction of one of its aspects, temperature, which is in return reduced to warmth as a synecdoche of the 'feeling', a euphemism for love.

Cartwright and Goldfarb take these observations a step further:

> We might ask, what does the Sense-of-Feel hand feel like to the wife of the Sabolich client? Had she learned to incorporate the mechanical prosthesis into their relationship as fetish? Is this new prosthesis a model that offers the surface texture of flesh to her hand, and will Sabolich design a model that can also communicate warmth back to her hand on contact? Might the simulation of warmth involve mechanisms for stimulating blood flow to the surface of the 'skin' on stimulation so that the hand can radiate the meaning of warmth? We might also ask how important it is that this example relies on the beloved as the object that communicates 'warmth' to the sensory hand. Can the client discern between different degrees of physical and semiotic intensity – say, between the warmth of love and the heat of anger or between the heat of a body and that of a burning flame?[136]

They rightly, and startlingly, describe these as 'hypothetical questions about fleshing out what it means for a

[136] Ibid., 132.

partner to be incorporated as a prosthetic of feeling'. And indeed, where else do we find such a searching inclusion of the object of the desiring touch as themselves a subject? Not in either of the albeit touching quotations I have given above from Sartre and Merleau-Ponty – and certainly not in the disappointing version of the caress found in the writings of Lévinas.[137] Does being the object of desire always make us a prosthetic to the other? Is touch, in other words, never reciprocal after all?

Virilio talks of 'the coming insemination of *emotional prostheses*', Badmington of '*cyborg envy*'; but Paula Rabonowitz warns us that 'posthumans always lie'.[138] As long as we have bodies that seek intimacy as well as autonomy, we will, it seems, never be naked.

References

Ahmed, Sara and Jackie Stacey, eds. *Thinking Through the Skin*. London & New York: Routledge, 2001.

Anzieu, Didier. *Le Corps de l'œuvre*. Paris: Gallimard, 1981.

Anzieu, Didier. *Contes à Rebours*. Les Belles Lettres-Archimbaud, 1995 [1975].

Anzieu, Didier. *Le Moi-peau*. Paris: Dunod, 1995 [1985].

Anzieu, Didier. *The Skin-Ego*, tr. Naomi Segal. London: Karnac, 2016.

---

[137] See the discussion in Segal, *Consensuality*, 184–187.

[138] Virilio. *Open Sky*, 95. Neil Badmington. 'Posthumanist (Com)Promises: Diffracting Donna Haraway's Cyborg Through Marge Piercy's *Body of Glass*', in *Posthumanism*, ed. Neil Badmington (Basingstoke: Palgrave Macmillan, 2000), 85; Paula Rabinowitz. 'Soft Fictions and Intimate Documents: Can Feminism be Posthuman?', in *Posthumanism*, ed. Neil Badmington (Basingstoke: Palgrave Macmillan, 2000), 44.

Badmington, Neil, ed. *Posthumanism*. Basingstoke: Palgrave Macmillan, 2000.
Barrie, J. M. *Peter Pan and Wendy*. London: Pavilion, 1988 [1911].
Baudelaire, Charles. *Les Fleurs du mal*, in *Œuvres complètes*, ed. Marcel Ruff. Paris: Seuil, 1968 [1857]: 40–131.
Baxi, Upendra. *Human Rights in a Posthuman World*. Oxford: Oxford University Press, 2009 [2007]
Baxter, Richard. 'The High-Rise Home: Verticality as Practice in London'. *International Journal of Urban and Regional Research* 41, no. 2 (2017): 334–352.
Benthien, Claudia. *Skin*, tr. Thomas Dunlap. New York: Columbia University Press, 2002 [1999].
Bersani, Leo. *Baudelaire and Freud*. Berkeley, Los Angeles and London: University of California Press, 1977.
Braidotti, Rosi. *The Posthuman*. Cambridge: Polity, 2013.
Cartwright, Lisa and Brian Goldfarb. 'On the Subject of Neural and Sensory Prostheses'. In *The Prosthetic Impulse*, edited by Marquard Smith and Joanne Morra. Cambridge, MA & London: MIT Press, 2006: 125–154.
Castañeda, Claudia. 'Robotic Skin: The Future of Touch?'. In *Thinking through the Skin*, edited by Sara Ahmed and Jackie Stacey. London & New York: Routledge, 2001.
Certeau, Michel de. 'Marches dans la ville' 1980. In *L'Invention du quotidien* [*The Practice of Everyday Life*] vol 1, edited by Luce Giard. Paris: Gallimard, 1990.
Chamfort, Sébastien-Roch Nicolas. *Maximes et pensées*. Paris: Éditions G. Crès, 1923 [1796].
Classen, Constance. 'The Sensory Orders of "Wild Children"'. In *The Varieties of Sensory Experience*, edited by David Howes. Toronto, Buffalo, London: University of Toronto Press: 1991, 47–60.
Classen, Constance. 'McLuhan in the Rainforest: The Sensory Worlds of Oral Cultures'. In *The Empire of the Senses*, edited by David Howes. Oxford & New York: Berg: 2005: 147–163.
Connor, Steven. *The Book of Skin*. London: Reaktion, 2004.

Field, Tiffany. *Touch*. Cambridge, MA: MIT Press, 2003 [2001].
Fisher, Seymour. *Body Consciousness*. Glasgow: Fontana/Collins 1976[1973].
Flaubert, Gustave. *Correspondance II*, edited by Jean Bruneau. Paris: Gallimard, 1980 [1853].
Freud, Sigmund. 'Femininity' [Die Weiblichkeit]. Translated by James Strachey. In *The Pelican Freud Library* vol 2, edited by James Strachey and Angela Richards. Harmondsworth: Penguin, 1973 [1933], 144–169.
Freud, Sigmund. 'Leonardo da Vinci and a memory of his childhood' [Eine Kindheitserinnerung des Leonardo da Vinci], translated by James Strachey. In *The Pelican Freud Library* vol 14, edited by James Strachey and Angela Richards. Harmondsworth: Penguin, 1985 [1910]: 143–231.
Freud, Sigmund. *The Interpretation of Dreams* [*Die Traumdeutung*], translated by. James Strachey. In *The Pelican Freud Library* vol 4, edited by James Strachey and Angela Richards. Harmondsworth: Penguin, 1976 [1900].
Gide, André. *Corydon*. Paris: Gallimard, 1993 [1911, 1922, 1924].
Gide, André. *Journal 1887–1925*, edited by Éric Marty. Paris: Gallimard, 1996.
Graham, Stephen. 'Luxified Skies: How Vertical Urban Housing Became an Elite Preserve'. *City* 19, no. 5 (2015): 618–645.
Gregory, Derek. 'How a Hollywood film reveals the reality of drone warfare', *The Observer*, 9 April 2016.
Grosz, Elizabeth. 'Naked'. In *The Prosthetic Impulse*, edited by Marquard Smith and Joanne Morra. Cambridge, MA & London: MIT Press, 2006: 187–202.
Hables Gray, Chris. 'In Defence of Prefigurative Art: The Aesthetics and Ethics of Orlan and Stelarc'. In *The Cyborg Experiments*, edited by Joanna Zylinska. London & New York: Continuum, 2002: 181–192.
Haraway, Donna. *Simians, Cyborgs and Women*, London: Free Association Books, 1991.
Haraway, Donna. *When Species Meet*. Minneapolis & London: University of Minnesota Press, 2008.

Hayles, N. Katherine. *How We Became Posthuman*. Chicago & London: University of Chicago Press, 1999.

Heller Morton A. and William Schiff. *The Psychology of Touch*. Hillsdale, NJ, Hove & London: Lawrence Erlbaum, 1991.

Hill, Lynn. 'Twenty-first century war poet'. BBC Radio 4, 29 November 2015.

Howes David, ed. *The Varieties of Sensory Experience*. Toronto, Buffalo, London: University of Toronto Press, 1991.

Howes David, ed. *Empire of the Senses: the Sensual Culture Reader*. Oxford & New York: Berg, 2005.

Hugo, Victor. *Les Contemplations*, edited by Léon Cellier. Paris: Garnier, 1969 [1856].

Jablonski, Nina G. *Skin*. Berkeley, Los Angeles & London: University of California Press, 2006.

Jay, Martin. *Downcast Eyes*. London, Berkeley & Los Angeles: University of California Press, 1993.

Josipovici, Gabriel. *Touch*. New Haven & London: Yale University Press, 1996.

Keane, Molly. *Good Behaviour*. London: Virago, 2001 [1981].

Kerckhove, Derrick de. 'Touch versus Vision'. In *Die Aktualität des Ästhetischen*, edited by Wolfgang Welsch. Munich: Fink, 1993: 137–168.

Laqueur, Thomas. *Making Sex*. Cambridge, MA: Harvard University Press, 1990.

Leconte de Lisle, Charles-Marie-René. *Œuvres*, vol 2: *Poèmes barbares*, ed. Edgard Pich. Paris: Société d'édition « Les belles lettres », 1976 [1889].

Leconte de Lisle, Charles-Marie-René, *Œuvres*, vol 3: *Poèmes tragiques ; derniers poèmes*, ed. Edgard Pich. Paris: Société d'édition « Les belles lettres », 1977 [1884, 1886].

Leder, Drew. *The Absent Body*. Chicago and London: University of Chicago Press, 1990.

Marinetti, Filippo Tommaso. *L'Alcova di acciaio* [*The Steel Alcove*]. Milan: Serra e Riva, 1985 [1921].

Marinetti, Filippo Tommaso. *The Battle of Tripoli [La Bataille de Tripoli]*. Milan: Futuristo di Poesia, 1912.

Marks, Laura U. *The Skin of the Film*. Durham and London: Duke University Press, 2000.

Mazzio, Carla. 'The Senses Divided: Organs, Objects, and Media in Early Modern England'. In *The Empire of the Senses*, edited by David Howes. Oxford & New York: Berg, 2005: 85–105.

McLuhan, Marshall. 'Inside the Five Sense Sensorium'. In *The Empire of the Senses*, edited by David Howes. Oxford & New York: Berg, 2005: 43–52.

Merleau-Ponty, Maurice. *Le visible et l'invisible*. Paris: Gallimard, 1964.

Miller, Jacques-Alain. 'Extimité', Translated by Françoise Massardier-Kenney. In *Lacanian Theory of Discourse: Subject, Structure, and Society*, edited by Mark Bracher, Marshall W. Alcorn, Ronald J. Corthell and Françoise Massardier-Kenney. New York and London: New York University Press, 1994, 74–87.

Montagu, Ashley. *Touching: The Human Significance of the Skin*. New York: Harper & Row, 1986 [1971].

Moravec, Hans. *Mind Children*. Cambridge, MA: Harvard University Press, 1988.

de Musset, Alfred. *La Confession d'un enfant du siècle*. Paris: Gallimard, 1973 [1836].

Musset, Alfred de. *Lorenzaccio*. Paris: Bordas, 1976 [1834].

Nancy, Jean-Luc. *L'Intrus*. Paris: Galilée, 2000.

O'Hagan, Andrew. 'The Tower', *London Review of Books*, 7 June 2018: https://www.lrb.co.uk/v40/n11/andrew-ohagan/the-tower

Parot, Françoise and Marc Richelle, eds. *Psychologues de langue française*. Paris: PUF, 1992.

Pitts, Victoria. *In the Flesh*. Basingstoke: Palgrave Macmillan, 2003.

Proust, Marcel. *A l'ombre des jeunes filles en fleurs. A la recherche du temps perdu*, vol 1, ed. Pierre Clarac and André Ferré. Paris: Gallimard, 1954 [1918], 431-990.

Rilke, Rainer Maria. *Neue Gedichte* and *Der Neuen Gedichte anderer Teil*. Frankfurt: Insel, 1974 [1907, 1908].

Ritchie, Ian. 'Fusion of the Faculties: A Study of the Language of the Senses in Hausaland'. In *The Varieties of Sensory Experience,* edited by David Howes. Toronto, Buffalo, London: University of Toronto Press, 1991: 192–202.

Rodaway, Paul. *Sensuous Geographies*. London and New York: Routledge, 1997.

Sacks, Oliver. *The Man who Mistook his Wife for a Hat*. London: Picador, 1986 [1985].

Saint-Exupéry, Antoine de. *Vol de nuit*. Paris: Gallimard, 1931.

Sartre, Jean-Paul. *L'Être et le néant*. Paris: Gallimard, 1943.

Sartre, Jean-Paul. *L'Idiot de la famille: Gustave Flaubert de 1821 à 1857* vol 2. Paris: Gallimard, 1971.

Sartre, Jean-Paul. *Le Mur*, Paris: Gallimard, 1939.

Schilder, Paul. *The Image and Appearance of the Human Body*, New York: International Universities Press, 1978 [1950].

Segal, Naomi. '"L'échange de deux fantaisies et le contact de deux épidermes": skin and desire'. In *Sensual Reading*, edited by Michael Syrotinski and Ian Maclachlan. Lewisburg and London: Associated University Presses, 2001: 17–38.

Segal, Naomi. *The Adulteress's Child: Authorship and Desire in the Nineteenth-century Novel*, Cambridge: Polity, 1992.

Segal, Naomi. *André Gide: Pederasty and Pedagogy*. Oxford: Oxford University Press, 1998.

Segal, Naomi. *Consensuality: Didier Anzieu, Gender and the Sense of Touch*. Amsterdam and New York: Rodopi, 2009.

Serres, Michel. *Les Cinq Sens*. Paris: Grasset, 1985.

Smith, Marquard and Joanne Morra, eds., *The Prosthetic Impulse*. Cambridge MA & London: MIT Press, 2006.

Smith, Marquard. 'The Vulnerable Articulate'. In *The Prosthetic Impulse,* edited by Marquard Smith and Joanne Morra. Cambridge, MA & London: MIT Press, 2006: 43–72.

Sobchack, Vivian. 'A Leg to Stand On'. In *The Prosthetic Impulse,* edited by Marquard Smith and Joanne Morra. Cambridge, MA & London: MIT Press, 2006: 17–41.

Sobchak, Vivian. *Carnal Thoughts*. Berkeley, Los Angeles & London: University of California Press, 2004.

Stelarc, 'Zombies, Cyborgs and Chimeras'. Filmed [August 2014]. YouTube video, 57:09. Posted [August 2014]. https://www.youtube.com/watch?v=TqtiM1hK6lU

Stenslie, Stahl. 'Vernetzung des Fleisches'. *Die Zukunft des Körpers I, Bd.* 132 (1995): 178–187.

Tyler, Imogen. 'Skin-Tight: Celebrity, Pregnancy and Subjectivity'. In *Thinking Through the Skin*, edited by Sara Ahmed and Jackie Stacey. London and New York: Routledge, 2001: 69–83.

Van Rysselberghe, Maria. *Les Cahiers de la Petite Dame, Cahiers André Gide* vol 5. Paris: Gallimard, 1974.

Virilio, Paul. *Open Sky*. Translated by Julie Rose. London & New York: Verso, 1997.

Winnicott, D. W. 'The Theory of the Parent-Infant Relationship'. In D. W. Winnicott, *The Maturational Processes and the Facilitating Environment*, London: Karnac, 1962 [1960], 37–55.

Wober, Mallory. 'The Sensotype Hypothesis' In *The Varieties of Sensory Experience*, edited by David Howes. Toronto, Buffalo, London: University of Toronto Press, 1991: 31–42.

Yeats, William Butler. *W. B. Yeats: The Poems*, ed. Daniel Albright, London: Dent, 1990.

Zylinska, Joanna, ed. *The Cyborg Experiments*, London & New York: Continuum, 2002.

A Touching 'Contract'

Jan Hogan

On an island surrounded by the Southern Ocean, an arduous ascending trail carves a pathway between a river and a mountain range. This trail, which I will call the 'Track', is a border zone between urban developments and the wilderness the island is known for. As the human population increases, the Track is becoming more susceptible to damage, becoming gradually wider, with vegetation being pushed back and the dense basalt rock face becoming exposed. The Track follows a creek bed before mounting towards the summit. I stop at a waterhole, unpack my equipment and set up to spend the afternoon drawing. As usual, I have sketchbook, pencils, water, fruit, hat, jumper, jacket and boots but this time I have also carried a large heavyweight roll of imported French paper, 18 metres long and over a metre wide.

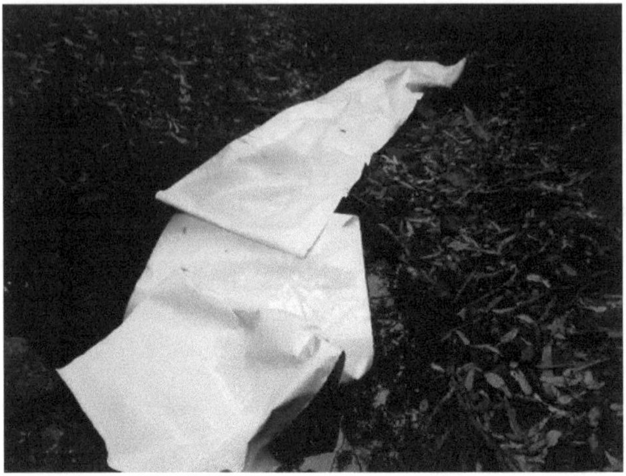

I soak the roll of paper in the waterhole, which is deeper than I thought. The boots, socks and tights come off as I enter the freezing water to gently unravel the paper down the creek bed ensuring the water soaks into every fibre of the paper. With difficulty, as my feet, blue with cold, are stabbed by the rocks and branches in the creek bed, I drag the paper up onto a section of the Track. Here, the ground is softer and a canopy of trees provides shelter from the elements. The paper settles along the indentations and curvature of the Track wending its way around a bend and beyond sight. It matches exactly the width of the Track and to save my feet I walk back along the paper. The soaked fibrous surface reveals the contours of what lies beneath, like the membrane of skin over our bodies, the hard, bony skeleton of the earth presses and stretches the surface. This membrane inhales the touch of everything it comes into contact with, retaining traces of a memory of an encounter across space, time, matter: a 'contract.'

Michel Serres suggests we engage with the Earth through its language of 'forces, bonds, and interactions', entering us into a natural contract binding 'each one of the partners' in 'symbiosis' to a commitment of 'life to the other under penalty of death.'[1] The 'contract' I engage with on the Track folds the parties into the matter of paper, into a legible form, and into an ethical entanglement. The exchange of matter between things becomes tangible in this expanded form of drawing, exploring what Stacy Alaimo in her theory of 'trans-corporeality' calls 'the interconnections, interchanges, and transits between human bodies and nonhuman natures.'[2]

Vicky Kirby in her quest for a radical reconceptualisation of nature asks, 'What do we forfeit if we concede that Nature reads and writes, calculates and copulates with itself in the most perverse, creative, and also destructive ways?' What if it is political through and through, and this very discussion … is a manifestation of natural intent?'[3] Extending Kirby's thinking I propose that processes of art can take on this language of the land, becoming an intermediary, paying attention and revisiting sites to renegotiate the shifting terrain that this more-than-human world constantly engages in, never stable, always changing.

---

1 Michel Serres and Felicia McCarren. 'The Natural Contract', *Critical Inquiry* 19, no.1 (1992): 1–21.

2 Stacy Alaimo. *Bodily Natures: Science, Environment, and the Material Self* (Bloomington: Indiana University Press, 2010), 2.

3 Vicky Kirby. *Quantum Anthropologies: Life at Large* (Durham: Duke University Press, 2011), 86.

This large roll of paper is a witness to the exchanges that occur on the Track, shifting the prevalence of law's discourse where a contract is considered an 'arms-length' transaction between two parties, to a haptic natureculture continuum where the laws of nature are acknowledged and entwined in humanity's legal theories. In contract theory, a 'fundamental feature of law's self-understanding is that it presumes a close link between law and morality. More specifically, laws are understood, from the inside, as providing morally good or justified reasons to do what the law requires.'[4] Opening out the ground of a contract to include the haptic exchange that occurs in place, encourages an ethical exchange, entwining nature's laws into concepts of morality and ethical engagement. If law's reach extends into the atmosphere, as Andreas Philippopoulos-Mihalopoulos contends, then a natural contract could find ways to engage with what the world is telling us.[5] Immersing the paper on the Track allows for process to engage the world of materials in a zone where flows and counterflows occur, inhabiting paper, a form that can be interpreted and used by all parties concerned.

The Western landscape tradition separates the viewer from the natural environment. W.J.T. Mitchell eloquently states, 'the concept of landscape that dominates the discourse of Western art history is one that is resolutely focused on visual and pictorial representation, the scenic, picturesque, and superficial face presented by natural

[4] Stephen A. Smith. *Contract Theory* (Oxford Scholarship Online, 2012), 15.

[5] Andreas Philippopoulos-Mihalopoulos. *Spatial Justice: Body, Lawscape, Atmosphere* (London: Routledge, 2014).

terrain. Landscape is something to be seen, not touched.'[6] As Mitchell expands in his treatise *Landscape and Power*, the development of the representation of the landscape has a dark side that is 'not merely mythic, not merely a feature of the regressive, instinctual drives associated with nonhuman "nature" but a moral, ideological, and political darkness'.[7] He traces the rise and development of landscape paintings with the rise of capitalism and the drive of imperialism where the violence perpetrated in the land is cleansed with a better 'view'. 'Landscape', Mitchell writes, 'is a medium not only for expressing value but also for expressing meaning, ... most radically between the Human and the nonhuman.'[8]

I spend over a year revisiting the Track each week with the roll of paper. After walking along the paper in my bare feet, I decide to limit the materials and processes used. The sense of touch becomes the dominant mode of engagement. Due to the size of the paper I cannot hold it in my gaze or control the flow of materials. More importantly, though, touch requires a more intimate encounter. Being required to walk, crawl and tiptoe on the horizontal surface shifts my perception from the dominating discourse of landscape art, where the viewer is separated from the land. Working on the horizontal employs peripheral vision in the development of the contract. Peripheral vision assists our sensual body

[6] William J. T. Mitchell. 'Holy Landscape: Israel, Palestine, and the American Wilderness', *Critical Inquiry*, 26, no.2 (2000): 197.

[7] William J. T. Mitchell. *Landscape and Power* (Chicago: University of Chicago Press, 2002), 6.

[8] Ibid., 15.

as it negotiates its way through the landscape. It acts to shift the language from landscape's traditional mode of perspectival representation, which makes 'the eye the centre point of the perceptual world' and 'which not only describes but also conditions perception.'[9] The horizontal world of process immerses me in another understanding of the land, making stronger connections with the more-than-human world.

As I negotiate the paper on the ground, I learn to read the shifts in tone, the varied marks from insects and plants, rocks and branches. I become woven into the myriad of networks in this Track, touching and being touched by the more-than-human world as I slow down and become aware of my surroundings. Physicist Karen Barad reminds us that 'so much happens in a touch: an infinity of others – other beings, other spaces, other times – are aroused.'[10] I am careful of my tread as I recognise the smaller creatures scuttling across, under and through the paper. The minute scale of their touch gains momentum over time, as matter is taken away and brought into the paper, microbes and worms beginning the composting process that the forest floor loves.

The sense of touch 'arouses' an intimate, more personal knowledge of the world, engaging us, if we only pause long enough, in an ethical engagement as it shifts from landscape's dominating view. Each touch we make has an impact. The 'contract' picks up the traces of each touch.

---

[9] Juhani Pallasmaa. *The Eyes of the Skin: Architecture and the Senses* (Hoboken: John Wiley & Sons, 2005), 16.

[10] Karen Barad. 'On Touching – The Inhuman That Therefore I Am.' *Differences: A Journal of Feminist Cultural Studies* 23, no.3 (2012): 206.

The paper stretches out, leaving its own touch upon the earth while gaining traces of space and place, the caress of small creatures and the detritus of the bush floor. The way the matter accrues in the paper is from the multiple laws within the atmosphere. The gravitational pull to horizontality, to the lowest point in reach. Liquid's cohesive stickiness forms rivulets in the flow across the surface, gradually transforming back into the atmosphere, leaving residue of matter in patches caused by the hollows in the ground below.

The 'contract' enters and participates in Merleau-Ponty's 'flesh of the world'[11] to mediate in the multiple differences on the site. According to Merleau-Ponty the sense of touch involves a reciprocal arrangement. He describes touch as the double sensation: the hand embodies both the agency of touching and the receptivity of being touched.[12] The paper reveals so sensitively that to touch the earth, the earth touches back. Merleau-Ponty models his theory of the two-sidedness of touch on the Mobius strip, where vision and the invisible form together an atmosphere which guarantees their connection.[13] He contemplates where touch occurs: does the hand sense on its outer surface or from within, from the internal body pressing out? My contract engages in this two-sided, 'Mobius strip' structure of tactile engagement. Constantly rolled and unrolled, my paper has no inside or outside, switching

---

[11] Maurice Merleau-Ponty. *Phenomenology of Perception*, trans. Colin Smith (London: Routledge, 2002), 106–107.

[12] Ibid.

[13] Steven Connor. *The Book of Skin* (London: Reaktion Books, 2004), 275.

between roles on different occasions, one time cast into moist shadows, traversed by light-avoiding critters, and at other times being caressed by the breeze sliding down the mountain's edge. The sense of touch is dispersed in this intermediary form; it is multilayered, being internal and external, and everywhere all at once.

The sense of touch is located in the membrane of our skin but is most sensitive on the extremities of our body; it is our borderland where the world is continuously negotiated. From our fingers stretched out in curiosity, to our toes as they negotiate our passage across the earth, touch is the sense that reveals the way that borderlands and peripheries become the heart of negotiation; a negotiation where the inscribed and the inscriber are in a reciprocal relationship. Elizabeth Harvey comments that 'recent biological research has focused increasingly on the membrane as the cell's command center … the cell membrane functions much as skin does: both are sensory envelopes, boundaries of communication or exchange.'[14] In the 'contract,' the surface of the land, of the paper, of the skin, acts like a cell membrane, allowing communication to occur.

Touch is also a place-based phenomenon. Place is where touch starts, it comes out of place, interacts with place, where else could we place it? For us to understand ourselves as being in existence we need to be 'placed' in the world, our boundaries located in a specific locale, otherwise we would be 'nowhere', in a void. 'A thing is

[14] Elizabeth D. Harvey. 'The Portal of Touch', *American Historical Review* 116, no. 2 (2011): 388–389.

not merely *in* a place,' Edward Casey explains, 'but *a thing constitutes its (own) place*.'[15] Casey emphasises that 'place serves as the condition of all living things.'[16] In order to be in existence, to engage with matter sensually, we need to be in place.

What then, does place bring to existence? Val Plumwood suggests that by 'Looking at the land in ecological and geological, as well as human-cultural terms, we must surely see it as the product of multiple, mixed agencies. For any given piece of the earth's surface, we can, indeed must, tell a story of landforms created by motions of the earth, by volcanoes, tsunamis, earthquakes, meteorites, geological depositions, and weatherings, for example.'[17] Engaging with the Track, the localised events of the land become embedded in the contract, binding me into mutual obligation as the intricacies of place are revealed.

Paul Carter in *Ground Truthing* argues for the role of places and smaller regions in revealing the complexities of a world in motion. In his investigation of the Mallee region in Australia, Carter searches for 'the creative principles that bring regions into being', arguing that these smaller places are microcosms of the world, revealing the world in turmoil.[18] As I settle into this small microcosm of the environment, the generative, creative power

---

[15] Edward Casey. *Getting Back into Place* (Bloomington and Minneapolis: Indiana University Press, 1993), 16.

[16] Ibid.,15.

[17] Val Plumwood. 'The Concept of a Cultural Landscape: Nature, Culture and Agency in the Land', *Ethics & The Environment* 11, no. 2 (2006): 125.

[18] Paul Carter. *Ground Truthing: Explorations in a Creative Region* (Crawley: UWA Publishing, 2010), 2.

of the place becomes animated and seeps out into the imagination that sustains places. Carter points out that the 'ground is not passive, it is the generative matrix of an understanding that exists solely at that spot – situated, timely and often rubbed out.'[19] The 'contract' recognises the ground as a palimpsest, that touching can both erase and uncover the more-than-human world. The Track has an interweaving narrative of marks, the minutiae of ants and insects interlace with small mammals and birds that scurry over the broader path caused by the human body. As Carter points out, this is a creative region, often overlooked or walked through quickly, but essential for the co-existence of the human with the nonhuman.

The site of the 'contract', this Track in place, bears the name of Truganini, contentiously labelled Tasmania's 'last full blood Aboriginal',[20] revealing the entanglement of Australia's colonial past with the matter of nature. The landscape is haunted by the past lives of the land, the once-was sea-bed encrusted and forced to the surface, the impressions of joggers and dog walkers entwined with the creek's original passage, the weaving of multiple footsteps following Aboriginal passages across mountains.

Truganini's spectre haunts this path. The Track is Mouheneener land and Truganini was a Nuennone woman from Bruny Island situated not far away in the Derwent River's broadening estuary. Though forced to move to areas around Australia as she negotiated to save

19 Ibid., 4.

20 Lyndall Ryan. *The Aboriginal Tasmanians* (St. Leonards: Allen & Unwin 1996), 75.

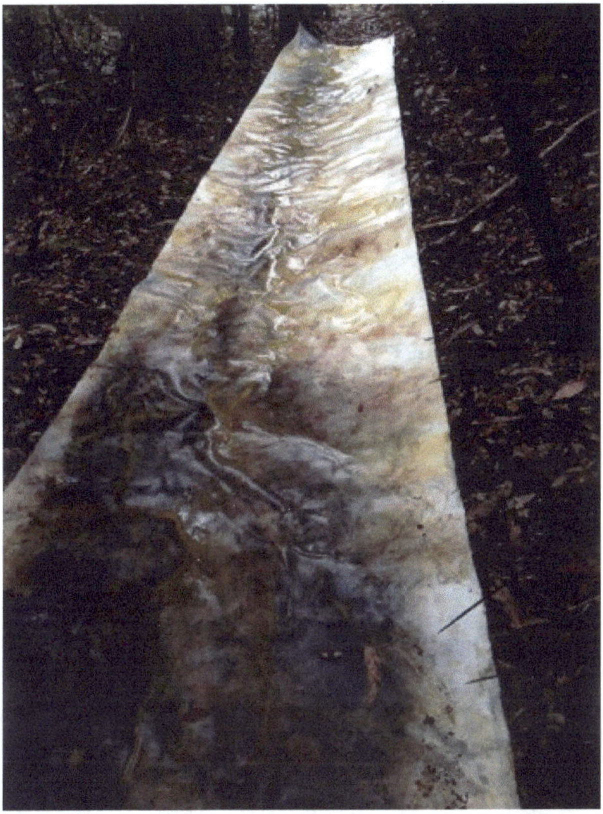

Aboriginal people from genocide, it is hard to fathom a reason for her to walk on this particular track. But then there are trails in the Victorian bush on the mainland of Australia that have felt her feet traipsing the terrain in her brief stint as a bushranger. Her life is an entanglement of the possible and impossible. By 1829 when settlement extended to her country 'her mother had been killed by sailors, her uncle shot by a soldier, her sister abducted by sealers, and Paraweena, a young man who was to have been her husband, murdered by timber-getters.'[21]

Tasmanian Aboriginal academic Greg Lehman mourns 'the fact that Truganini is still held as a symbol of 'rape, murder, invasion', when she should be so much more. 'An artist-maker of maireener necklaces and baskets, a diplomat seeking treaties to end Tasmania's Black War, a guerilla fighter seeking justice denied.'[22] The naming of this Track as the *Truganini Track* aims at acknowledging injustices of the past, but its strange location, away from her country on Bruny Island, continues the disturbance. The ongoing problems of colonisation result in the wishes of Tasmanian Aboriginal people not being heard. Truganini holds particular significance for Tasmanian Aboriginal people who 'spent decades scouring the collections of the world to obtain the return of ill-gotten artifacts and grave-robbed remains', as Lehman observes, and 'fought tirelessly for the release of her bones from the basement of the Tasmanian Museum and Art Gallery, and who sought peace for this woman as her ashes were scattered in the waters of her mother's country.'[23]

Each time I revisit the Track, I soak the paper in the small waterhole surrounded by large dolerite rocks that have been manoeuvred into the creek as stepping-stones. I attempt to wet the paper without having to enter the cold creek water but I am forced to take my boots off each

---

[21] Ibid.
[22] Greg Lehman. 'Fearing Truganini', *Artlink* 31, no.2 (2011): 52.
[23] Ibid.

time in my fear of tearing the paper. Sometimes the minute residents of the creek have begun to inhabit the dark recesses of the paper before I pull it out of the waterhole. The small pearly white inhabitants are rudely exposed to the light and quickly scuttle back into the water or below the paper's surface, hiding in its shadows.

In the early stages of negotiations, the expanse of white paper is in high contrast when placed in the environment – an alert to both humans and nonhumans of an intrusion. My use of paper is instinctual to my training as an artist, but where do all the other responses come from? Why this place, at this time, in these conditions? Brian Massumi in his examination of animal instinct states that the conditions of adaptation and behaviour induce the 'performance of an "improvisation"'.[24] In reflecting on my decisions in engaging in this 'contract' I realise that I am entering into improvisations within the patterns of my cultural tendencies, but also that these actions 'jump start' an active dialogue. My instinct to wet the paper in the waterhole initially seemed informed by a desire to fully immerse it in the environmental conditions, but it also allows for a reply from the environment. The water softens the fibres and allows matter to begin its improvised reply. An opportunity arises and modifications begin between the seemingly disparate cultural and natural tendencies of the parties concerned.

---

[24] Brian Massumi. 'The Supernormal Animal', in *The Nonhuman Turn*, ed. Richard Grusin (Minneapolis: University of Minnesota Press, 2015).

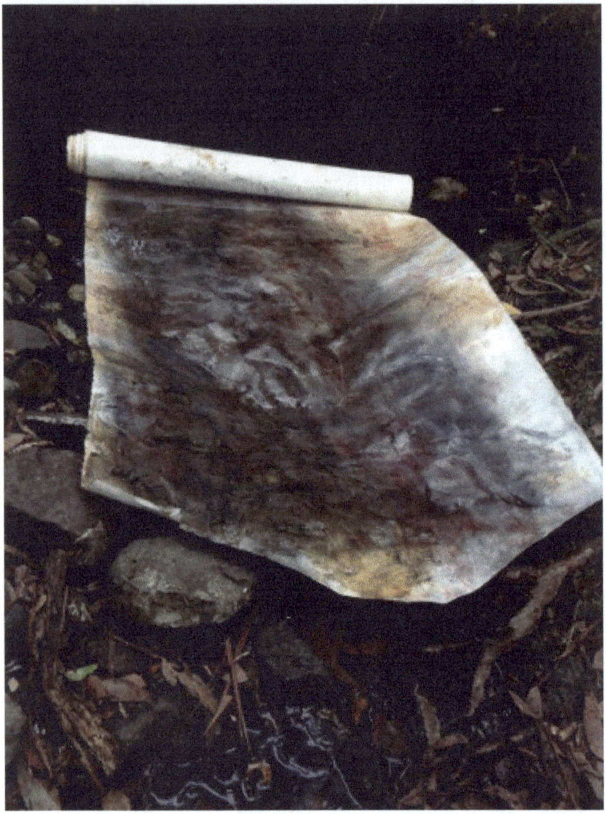

I leave the paper on the Track and continue to investigate around the site. I pick up some ochres found tumbled from a rock face onto the path. The earth gives up a beautiful array of colours, from whites and greys to yellows and reds. I treasure these gifts and take them home to grind and smooth into a paste to make a softer, more tactile, more malleable ochre that I can rub with my own fingers. I collect leaves and barks also found scattered around where I feel the removal will have least impact on the resident life forms and the building up of detritus and decaying matter required for renewal. I boil these into a eucalyptus-infused ink that I leave in the soup tureen to continue brewing in the backyard.

My behaviour is an improvisation of the moment. Why do I decide to keep to natural materials? I am worried that if I over think or plan too much I will lose the moment, I will analyse and block the fluid collaboration and begin to make decisions based on aesthetics or purely social and cultural forces. I return again with the ink generated from the site's refuse. I re-soak the paper in the waterhole and unroll it down the Track. The flow of the ink and its reception on the paper are influenced by the environment; the shadows formed by the angle of the sun at that moment of time and season of the year, the humidity, wind velocity and the pressures of the ground beneath the paper all have their input. I pour the ink from jars I have carefully carried along the path. The ink follows the laws of gravity, tenderly finding the lowest points to trickle their way across the fibres. The paper continues its transformation.

Chance, intention and intuition make the first marks and I was mesmerised by how quickly the paper melded into the environment. It revealed the contours of the land beneath, with sharp edges of rocks and winding roots being exposed by the rivulets of ink. The shadows, having already moved with the rotation of the earth, emphasised the temporality of the moment. The canopy of trees, the narrowness of the path and the warmth of the sun formed a eucalyptus-infused cocoon that acknowledged the intention of the moment.

My skin acts as a sensitive border to shadows that alert me to change in the weather, or more importantly to the presence of something else. My behaviour changes in this environment. I enter into the dynamics of the earth. An itch, a slight irritant on my leg, alerts me to the onslaught of leeches that made their way across the paper's surface in response to the lovely, insanely attractive warmth of my flesh. I have learned to get leeches to drop off through the use of whiteboard markers that make them release without damage to my skin or to the leech. Do the drops of my blood and the creatures 'unclotting' saliva from this improvisation become part of the contract? I'd like to think there was some positive from this interaction, but the encounter also highlights the scales of time: the leech is a fleeting life in human terms, and one human life is also fleeting in the life of a mountain.

In 'The Supernormal Animal', Brian Massumi reflects on the nature of instinct and the inspiring achievements of the natural world. 'The complex weave of the orb spider's web' and the 'productive beauty of the hive' highlight the accomplishments of instinct, but Massumi goes on to question its reputation to always respond appropriately. He states that 'the same drive that so naturally leads it through to its normative accomplishments seems to push it, just as naturally, to overshoot its target.'[25] This 'impulse

[25] Ibid., 480.

to excess', he argues, suggests a different type of aesthetics beyond 'the beauty of utility.'[26]

Massumi's writing builds on Deleuze and Guattari's philosophy linking the theory of the animal to the theory of art. He writes, 'Deleuze and Guattari replace adaptive evolution under pressure of selection with the concept of becoming as the pilot concept for the theory of the animal. Becoming is taken in the strongest sense, of emergence. "Can this becoming, this emergence, be called Art?"'. Massumi extrapolates on the possibilities of this thought: 'Called "art," the formative movement of animal life is no longer analyzable exclusively in terms of adaptation and selection. Another name is called for: expression. In what way do the animal and the human, each in its own right, as well as one in relation to the other, participate in this expressive becoming? Together in what natural "sympathy"?'[27]

Massumi highlights the instinctive qualities of the human, placing us back in the field of nature. He outlines the 'creative life of instinct', quoting the science philosopher Raymond Ruyer that it is 'of the nature of instinctive activity to produce an 'aesthetic yield.'[28] The aesthetic excess that becomes art, placed in the cultural domain, is due to our instinctive improvisations, our distinctly animal instincts. The urge of the supernormal animal to

---

[26] Ibid.
[27] Ibid., 489.
[28] Ibid.

excess, suggests that our mutual improvisations assist in sympathetic 'becomings'.[29]

To consider the paper as a contract is an instinctive reaction on my behalf, as is the site, the times of engagement and the materials used. Does the site draw me into this location? Is it a natural meeting place for many elements of the natureculture continuum, a patch of ground that allows for interaction? It is protected from wind and sun, has flowing water, soft earth and rocks that encourage habitation by multiple species. This instinctual response allows me to think past my 'authorship' of the work, allowing agency to be shared with the other inhabitants of the site, animate and inanimate.

Deleuze and Guattari explain that the 'painter and musician do not imitate the animal, they become animal at the same time as the animal becomes what they willed, at the deepest level of their concord with Nature.'[30] In the 'contract' I engage in interspecies intermingling, improvisations with matter and across matter, to become intimate with the 'flesh of the world'. Adopting Deleuze and Guattari's thesis that 'becoming is always double',[31] the contract binds me to this place as this place enters my pores and becomes part of me. By attending to touch, the connection between the human and nonhuman world conjures a responsibility to matter.

[29] Ibid., 664.

[30] Giles Deleuze and Felix Guattari. *A Thousand Plateaus*, trans. Brian Massumi (London: Bloomsbury, 2014), 355.

[31] Ibid.

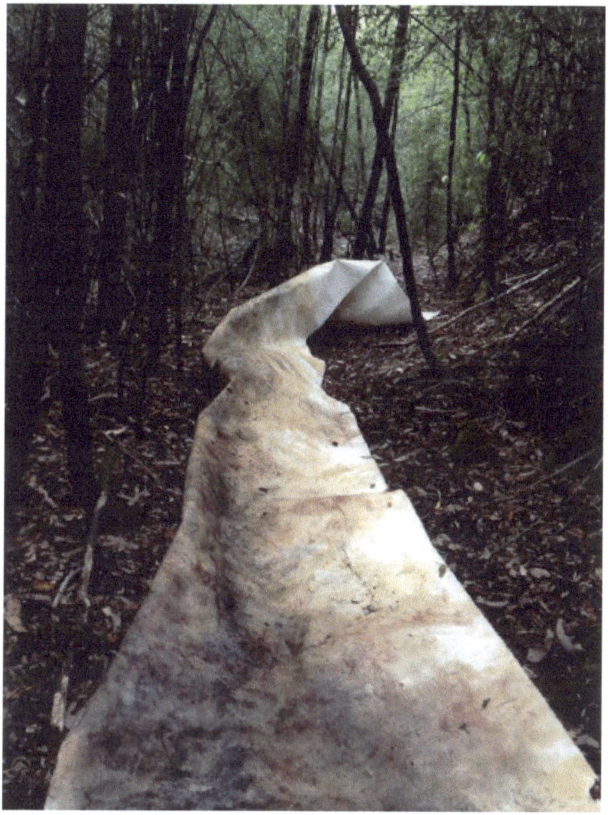

On the horizontal surface, where matter can interplay on the same level, with the weather and the lay of the land influencing the marks, the continuing negotiations become part of the phenomena of the world, allowing the differences across our natures to meet for a moment in 'sympathy'. Jane Bennett argues that 'materiality is a rubric that tends to horizontalize the relations between humans, biota and abiota'.[32] The multiple traces hold a memory of the meeting across differences. And while all parties are never present at the same moment, the intention is to enter into what Barad terms 'the *spacetimemattering* of the universe.'[33] The 'contract' under the weight of its sensual engagement with more-than-human matter absorbs and holds together events from the past at the moment of the present viewing, and through the repetition of phenomena at this same location over time I gain an imprint of 'memory', so that 'the pattern of sedimented enfoldings of iterative intra-activity … written into the fabric of the world'[34] will be materially present as a contractual agreement.

Each visit I become more intimate with both the paper and the site. I get down on my hands and knees and caress the paper with combinations of ochres and the dirt of the Track. There is no longer a distinction apparent as the paper lies on the ground. There appears a palpation, a lifting of the surface as if the earth's crust could be peeled back. On the ground I gently massage the paper, sometimes lifting it to see the textures my fingers have encountered. I come across a rock bed containing thousands of shell fossils, pitting the surface like a discarded snakeskin embossed in the earth.

---

[32] Jane Bennett. *Vibrant Matter: A Political Ecology of Things* (Durham: Duke University Press, 2010),112.

[33] Barad. 'On Touching', 216.

[34] Karen Barad. 'Quantum Entanglements and Hauntological Relations of Inheritance: Dis/continuities, SpaceTime Enfoldings, and Justice-to-Come', *Derrida Today* 3, no.2 (2010): 261.

Edward Casey claims that the 'sensuous surface' of wild places engages with our sensory systems. The texture 'embodies the peculiar tangibility, or "feel"'[35] of a place. What texture offers in particular, is a 'place's distinctive configuration, its physiognomy.'[36] And in wild places such as bush tracks, or passages of land away from the manicured garden and tended suburban plots, Casey states their sensuous surface 'can be construed as an exemplary instance of the flesh of the world.'[37]

Tears are starting to occur in the paper, and the porous seepage through the paper's matter is becoming apparent. The duality of front and back, light and dark, is broken down as the repeated dousing in water leaches out the paper's manufactured starches, replacing them with particles of dust, eucalyptus, animal droppings, plant inks and rock ochres. The paper shifts in texture and starts to resemble an animal's hide or a cloth made from hand-beaten plants, like the Tapa cloths of the Pacific Islands, more than a traditional Western art paper.

The contractual paper develops its own patterns; every part of its surface has built new relationships but it still maintains its laws, it still retains the paperyness of paper: it bends, it folds, it absorbs. It reveals, though, that it is not neutral: it is matter that sits alongside other matter and it can hold many differences within its borders. The ground and the meaning are inseparable in the expression of drawing.

---

[35] Casey. '*Getting Back into Place*', 210.

[36] Ibid.

[37] Ibid.

My fingers press and release against the surface, creating nuances in tone and texture as I enter into the contract. Matter and stories are folded into its creases, seeking to touch and be touched. The work develops with all my senses as I feel the land beneath my hands and knees and feet. I feel softer areas where clay has collected between rock beds and where animals have made networks of pathways in the undergrowth. The memory of the rock's creation and the development of this particular environment become integral to the mark-making. I begin to see where plants grow according to their desire for sun or shade. Sometimes the stench of decaying matter forces me to leave the site but still imprints itself on my memory of the place and in the memory of the paper.

The 'contract' on Truganini Track emphasises the role of matter in having its say. The material of manufactured paper that I introduced as cultural, combined fluently in conversation with the 'natural' elements. Matter has agency in these negotiations. Barad comments that matter 'continually opens itself up to a variety of possible and impossible reconfigurings … nature is not mute, and culture the articulate one. Nature writes, scribbles, experiments, calculates, thinks, breathes, and laughs.'[38] This is becoming apparent through the ongoing negotiations. I begin to see myself more as an element, where I even begin to question how the intention of the contract was formed. Am I the instigator or just a cell floating by in one small exchange of data?

---

[38] Barad. 'On Touching', 268.

The paper is not a neutral 'ground', to take meaning into, to become representative of a particular place and time, to be viewed and possessed as culture, it is a part of the matter of the world. It creases, ages and disintegrates back into the earth. For a small moment in time it is a milieu, an environment, a folding and unfolding between figure and ground. A line on the land that is itself inscribed with lines by the nonhuman, a place for learning and philosophising. Susan Merrill Squier, in *Liminal Lives: Imagining the Human at the Frontiers of Biomedicine*, states that 'material conditions shape and reshape what we can put into words'.[39] I would argue that it structures what we can even think; that the tactile immersion of art allows humans to recognise and imagine themselves within and continuously become matter within nature.

The Track becomes a site of reading nature, moist, undulating, complex and shifting; with changes of weather, time of day, or season, the ground feels different and reveals different traces and patterns. I gain a heightened awareness of the forces in our environment, of the past leaking into the future, of particles intermingling. In the tactile time-based immersion on the site both the paper and I began to change as Deleuze and Guattari predict. The initial state of the paper as a 'cultural' form became more in tune with the natural matter that it was composed of, and I become aware of the matter that I am made up of. Quantum experiments confront us with evidence that finds 'initial conditions' within 'final conditions' and signs of what comes second in what

---

[39] quoted in Alaimo. *Bodily Natures*, 8.

must logically come first. Consistent with this spacetime condensation, the difference between concepts (ideality) and material reality (physical objects) seems to collapse, or at least to go awry in some way that no longer makes sense.'[40] The sequence of events that was put in place to make the contract becomes difficult to untangle. When placed on the Track, the differences become less apparent, the contract becomes camouflaged and suggests that this is its true resting place; the land where all matter will compost and renew itself in vital exchanges.

Taking the contract back to my home to repair some damage, I pull the paper onto my lap to mend a tear. As I work with the drawing draped across the room and over myself I am astounded at the tenderness for the materials and the traces of the site embedded in the paper. Rhythms of daily life, of care, the act of repairing in a domestic setting, weave the story of the contract into my everyday life. The processes of art making, in a time and place-based haptic encounter, shift the knowledge of the historical past into a physical, material and empathetic encounter. The land shifts from being a background, the ground where history and events have occurred, to an elemental and agential force in the events. This paper becomes flesh, it has been stretched out, an epidermal layer sensitive to each step, each nibble, each rock and stick stabbing into its underbelly. What happens when we imagine the land as this biological flesh, capable of haptic sensibilities? As Vicky Kirby probes; 'If it is in the nature of biology to be cultural – and clearly, what

[40] Kirby. *Quantum Anthropologies*, 96.

we mean by 'cultural' is intelligent, capable of interpreting, analyzing, reflecting and creatively reinventing and memorializing – then what is this need to exclude such processes of interrogation from the ontology of life? The difference between ideality and matter, models and what they purportedly represent, or signs of life and life itself, is certainly difficult to separate here'.[41]

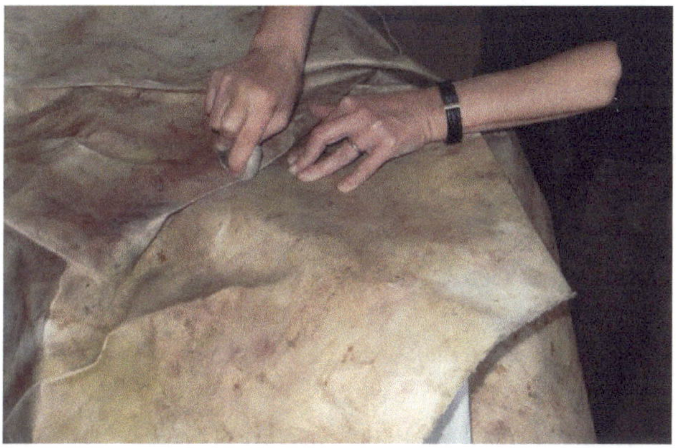

By some strange instinct I decide to iron the paper. Perhaps to preserve the contract a bit longer, to define sections and clauses or to bring back the nature of paper, its ability to bend and fold, to erase marks only for them to leave a ghostly presence? But I suspect it is my maternal instinct, my rhythm of behaviour when returning from camping: I lay all the equipment out, wash, dry, iron and fold it for future use. Through this touching, washing, caressing, erasing and dusting of the paper I become

[41] Ibid., 75.

intimately entangled with its terrain. I am no longer a separate entity that visits 'place', I become ethically engaged, much as Barad observes 'entanglements are … irreducible relations of responsibility'.[42] Through our contractual obligations the Track and I have become entangled in what I can only term 'empathy'. Barad remarks:

> How truly sublime the notion that it is the inhuman—that which most commonly marks humanity's inhumanity as a lack of compassion—that may be the very condition of possibility of feeling the suffering of the other, of literally being in touch with the other, of feeling the exchange of e-motion in the binding obligations of entanglements.[43]

These traces make environmental justice very close. There is a continuous interface and exchange through the corporeality of our body and other bodies and atmospheres. The paper no longer becomes a surface or a 'ground' but material matting, a part of the earth. It is activated and determines meaning through this interface in the same way that our body determines meaning and knowledge of the world through touch.

The contract grounds memory and makes it matter. It reveals the forces that press the body to the earth, reminds us of our future fate and the past that informs our present. As a membrane that records the imprint and traces of touch, Art begins to immerse the viewer in the world. As previously mentioned, the stimulus of the paper is an 'irritant' to the flesh of the world, it 'provokes' and 'stirs'

---

[42] Karen Barad. 'Nature's Queer Performativity', *Qui Parle* 19, no.2 (2011): 149.

[43] Barad. 'On Touching', 219.

responses from the nonhuman world, creating an 'aesthetic excess'. The contract if left in place would follow this to its natural conclusion, breaking down into matter, becoming one with place. Is this then culture's problem, the archiving of all documents? The fear of the earth's pull back into its flesh, for us to be the internal matter assisting in the pull to the dark, rather than the surface irritant? The full cycle is what a natural contract reveals and which we attempt to break, as I have, by separating it from the land's forces and rhythms, into concrete rooms. I have recognised more fully that we are compost, but this composting, this inter-intra species networking is healthy and rich. We need to enter into negotiations, in recognition of our part in the cycle of the world. As Haraway contends, 'Who and whatever we are, we need to make-with—become-with, compose-with—the earth-bound'.[44]

Michel Serres in the 'Natural Contract', which provoked this investigation, asked:

> 'What language do the things of the world speak; how can we come to some understanding with them, make a contract? After all, the old social contract itself remained unstated, unwritten; no one has ever read the original, no one has even read a copy. We do not know the language the world speaks, or rather we only know its various animist, religious or mathematical versions. When physics was invented, the philosophers said that nature was hidden in the code of numbers or algebraic word code came from law.'[45]

[44] Donna Haraway. 'Anthropocene, Capitalocene, Plantationocene, Chthulucene: Making Kin', *Environmental Humanities* 6 (2015): 161.

[45] Serres. 'Natural Contract', 12.

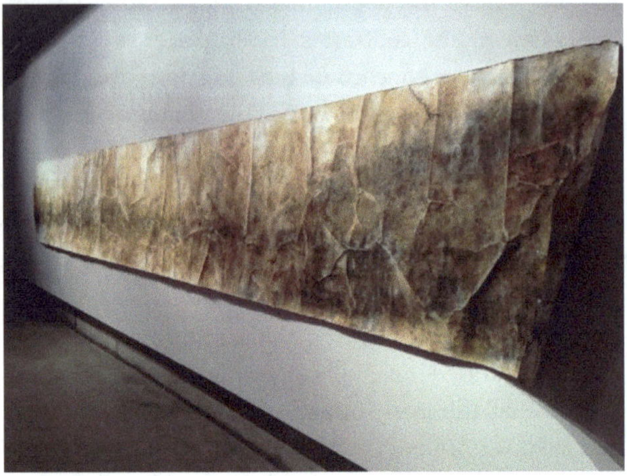

Jan Hogan, *Memory: Truganini Track, Mt Nelson,* Eucalyptus ink, ochre, charcoal, pencil, washed & ironed Rives BFK, 107 x 790 cm, 2014

Perhaps this natural rhythm of composting is why we do not know the language of the world, because we spend our time trying to be apart from it. This natural conclusion seems to be what we most fear but what our contract with nature is really about. We will return to the earth and become active matter again. Deleuze and Guattari reflect that 'the cosmic force was already present in the material, the great refrain in the little refrains, the great maneuver in the little maneuver. Except we can never be sure we will be strong enough, for we have no system, only lines and movements'.[46] My line of enquiry has for a short time followed these movements. The contract initially followed the laws of resemblance, it began to camouflage

[46] Deleuze and Guattari. '*A Thousand Plateaus*', 408.

itself within the environment but it became more than resemblance through tactile immersion, its direct touch with the earth becoming of the earth, it is the flesh of the world and can so easily return without damage, but with perhaps a soft powdery activity on the Track. A possibility of what happens when a contract is honoured. A passage to another future.

References

Alaimo, Stacy. *Bodily Natures: Science, Environment, and the Material Self.* Bloomington, IN: Indiana University Press, 2010.

Barad, Karan. 'Quantum Entanglements and Hauntological Relations of Inheritance: Dis/continuities, SpaceTime Enfoldings, and Justice-to-Come'. *Derrida Today* 3, no. 2 (2010): 240–268.

Barad, Karan. 'Nature's Queer Performativity'. *Qui Parle* 19, no.2 (2011): 121–158.

Barad, Karan. 'On Touching — The Inhuman That Therefore I Am'. *Differences: A Journal of Feminist Cultural Studies* 23, no. 3 (2012): 206–223.

Bennett, Jane. *Vibrant Matter: A Political Ecology of Things.* Durham, NC: Duke University Press, 2010.

Carter, Paul. *Ground Truthing: Explorations in a Creative Region.* Crawley, WA: UWA Publishing, 2010.

Casey, Edward. *Getting Back into Place.* Bloomington, IN: Indiana University Press, 1993.

Connor, Steven. *The Book of Skin.* London: Reaktion Books, 2004.

Deleuze, Gilles and Felix Guattari. *A Thousand Plateaus.* Translated by Brian Massumi. London: Bloomsbury, 2014.

Haraway, Donna. 'Anthropocene, Capitalocene, Plantationocene, Chthulucene: Making Kin'. *Environmental Humanities* 6 (2015): 159–165.

Harvey, Elizabeth D. 'The Portal of Touch'. *American Historical Review* 116, no. 2 (2011): 385–400.

Kirby, Vicky. *Quantum Anthropologies: Life at Large*. Durham, NC: Duke University Press Books, 2011.

Lehman, Greg. 'Fearing Truganini'. *Artlink* 31, no. 2 (2011): 50–53.

Massumi, Brian. 'The Supernormal Animal'. In *The Nonhuman Turn*, edited by Richard Grusin, Minneapolis, MN: University of Minnesota Press, 2015.

Merleau-Ponty, Maurice. *Phenomenology of Perception*. Translated by Colin Smith. London: Routledge, 2002.

Mitchell, William J. T. 'Holy Landscape: Israel, Palestine, and the American Wilderness'. *Critical Inquiry* 26, no.2 (2000): 193-223.

Mitchell, William J. T. *Landscape and Power*. Chicago, IL: University of Chicago Press, 2002.

Pallasmaa, Juhani. *The Eyes of the Skin: Architecture and the Senses*. Hoboken, NJ: John Wiley & Sons, 2005.

Philippopoulos-Mihalopoulos, Andreas. *Spatial Justice: Body, Lawscape, Atmosphere*. London: Routledge, 2014.

Plumwood, Val. 'The Concept of a Cultural Landscape: Nature, Culture and Agency in the Land'. *Ethics & The Environment* 11, no. 2 (2006): 115–150.

Ryan, Lyndall. *The Aboriginal Tasmanians*. St. Leonards, NSW: Allen & Unwin, 1996.

Serres, Michel and Felicia McCarren. 'The Natural Contract'. *Critical Inquiry* 19, no.1 (1992): 1–21.

Smith, Stephen A. *Contract Theory*. Oxford Scholarship Online, 2012. DOI: https://doi.org/10.1093/acprof:oso/9780198765615.001.0001

Squier, Susan Merrill. *Liminal Lives: Imagining the Human at the Frontiers of Biomedicine*. Durham, NC: Duke University Press, 2004.

Depression, Shock and Stimulation: Regimes of Touch in the Field of Psychiatry

Moritz von Stetten

No other therapies of mental illnesses have been confronted so harshly and strongly with criticism as brain surgery and brain stimulation. Terms like electroshock, psychosurgery and lobotomy are firmly anchored as traumatic experiences in the collective memory of historic delusions in psychiatric care.

Nevertheless, therapy and research in the field of brain stimulation have not been abandoned. Quite on the contrary, psychiatric research on brain stimulation for treating depression is widespread and growing. Apart from the development of antidepressants, forms of brain stimulation and brain surgery are the most important innovations of biological psychiatry in the twentieth century.

Electroconvulsive therapy (ECT) has been experiencing a renaissance since its decline in the 1960s and 1970s.[1] Some forms of brain stimulation – especially transcranial magnetic stimulation (TMS) and deep brain stimulation (DBS) – have been developed only since the 1980s. There is no comparable history of stigmatisation for these new technological developments.

In the following, I will discuss the *regimes of touch* underlying practices of therapeutic help in the context of biological and neurological psychiatry.[2] In order to illustrate the regime of touch underlying biological psychiatry, I will deal with the example of brain stimulation in the case of major depression. A regime is defined as a social order of norms, experiences and affects structuring the net in which human beings and their bodies are embedded. It cannot be reduced to mere semantics, discourses, institutions or other emergent social structures. It directly affects the bodily self, its sensitiveness, its vulnerability.

In what follows, I show that biological psychiatry presupposes an inadequate and insufficient regime of touch. As an alternative, I suggest a regime of touch informed by the tradition of body-oriented phenomenology. Body phenomenological approaches focus on the 'sense of

---

1 Timothy W. Kneeland and Carol A. Warren. *Pushbutton Psychiatry: A Cultural History of Electroshock in America* (Westport: Praeger Publishers, 2002), 85–102.

2 Biological psychiatry is one of the most important fields of modern psychiatry. Psychiatric thinking also entails traditions like social psychiatry and anti-psychiatry. Since the 1980s, biological psychiatry has increasingly become the most dominant discourse in psychiatric research.

atmosphere' ('Gespür für Atmosphärisches') as a central dimension of psychiatric and psychotherapeutic help.[3] Here, the structures, continuities and disruptions of touch can never easily be decoded, they never become emergent structures of unambiguous orientation. Practices of therapeutic help are exchanged and negotiated within the contingent situation between those who seek, and those who offer help. Any therapeutic success in the field of mental illness and suffering relies on practices of touching and being touched.

The text is divided into four sections. The first section elaborates on the theoretical concept of regime and its relation to the question of touch in the tradition of body phenomenology following Helmuth Plessner. In the second section, I briefly reconstruct the decline and renaissance of brain stimulation in the modern history of psychiatry. I then discuss some ethical issues raised by modern psychiatry in order to deepen the contextual understanding of psychiatric research on brain stimulation. I conclude in the fourth section by pointing at the role of body phenomenology as a mediator between psychiatric research on the one side and the phenomenon of depression on the other.

1. Body Phenomenology and Regimes of Touch

The suggested understanding of regime follows a theoretical position mediating between phenomenological and

[3] Hubertus Tellenbach. *Geschmack und Atmosphäre. Medien menschlichen Elementarkontaktes* (Salzburg: Otto Müller Verlag, 1968), 49.

poststructuralist, between subject-oriented and structuralist perspectives. It is informed by a body phenomenological tradition from Helmuth Plessner and Maurice Merleau-Ponty to Gesa Lindemann and Thomas Fuchs, replacing the concept of the subject by concepts of 'corporeity' and of the 'Leib' ('living body').[4] Here, the body is always both: a subjective form of lived experience, and an objective form of material being. The living body can neither be reduced to an apperception (Husserl), nor to a material entity separated from any understanding of the conscious self. Plessner suggests another interpretation of the 'Leib', described in the following formula: 'this strange relation of indirect directness, of mediated immediacy between organism and world'.[5] The 'Leib', the living body, is a relational phenomenon that cannot be reduced to an illusion of human consciousness or to a material form. Plessner considers the living body as a relational operation embedded in the ecology of organism and its environment. He states: 'Only indirectness creates directness, only separation allows touch.'[6] Thus, the concepts

---

[4] Helmuth Plessner. *Die Stufen des Organischen und der Mensch: Einleitung in die philosophische Anthropologie* (Berlin: de Gruyter, 1975); Thomas Fuchs. *Leib – Raum – Person: Entwurf einer phänomenologischen Anthropologie* (Stuttgart: Klett-Cotta, 2000); Gesa Lindemann. 'Leiblichkeit und Körper', in *Handbuch Körpersoziologie. Band 1: Grundbegriffe und theoretische Perspektiven*, eds. Gugutzer, Klein and Meuser (Wiesbaden: Springer VS, 2017); Thomas Fuchs. *Ecology of the Brain. The Phenomenology and Biology of the Embodied Mind* (Oxford: Oxford University Press, 2017); Maurice Merleau-Ponty. *Phenomenology of Perception* (New York: Routledge, 2012).

[5] Plessner. *Die Stufen des Organischen und der Mensch*, 260, own translation.

[6] Ibid., 332, own translation.

of 'Leib' and eccentric positionality also entail a certain understanding of touching and being touched.

This understanding of touch is based on the principle of 'mediated immediacy' ('vermittelte Unmittelbarkeit') also formulated by Plessner.[7] The principle requires that any form of touch – as well as any other form of human experience – must be understood from two sides: as an inner experience and as a material body. The principle of 'mediated immediacy' is here used as a theoretical and methodological instruction that allows us to identify the artificial nature of bodily experience. Even if bodily experiences are always unique and irreducible, they are embedded and folded into material, social and cultural systems; even if they are highly symbolic and representative, they also remain the situational experience of living beings.

The mediated immediacy of touch does not only presuppose mediated encounters between humans and other bodies – things, technological objects, plants, animals, other human beings. It also implies a concept of the human being as a living body different from other bodies. Plessner differentiates human existence from other living beings by assigning human nature a specific form of 'positionality'. The human body presupposes the mediated and relational nature of the human body *to itself*. Plessner calls this the 'eccentric positionality' of human existence.[8] Human beings are bound by their own bodies but they are also detached from them. The 'Leib' is the centre, the absolute inner core that enables its paradox

[7] Ibid., 321–341.
[8] Ibid., 288–346.

and conflicting positionality. The 'Leib' is the material *and* symbolic operation combining self-reflection and inner experience. The radical relational nature of the 'Leib' forbids any subjective understanding of human experience. At the same time, it considers eccentric positionality as the specific form of living existence that reflects itself *as* subjective. Here, one should not make the mistake of categorising the operation of reflection as the rational act of a conscious subject. Reflection is an operation of living beings embedded in the artificial nature of the relational body. There is no singular, detached and isolated subject. There are living bodies reflecting on the relations in which they are situated and in which they situate themselves.

Here we also find one crucial difference to recent literature on affect theory.[9] Poststructuralist and ontological accounts following Spinoza, Deleuze and Massumi argue in favour of a symmetric anthropology including nonhuman bodies.[10] This sometimes leads to the idea of a symmetrical relation between various bodies – humans, animals, plants, technological objects, etc. If we are to follow Plessner's anthropology, however, we must reject any form of radical symmetry while avoiding a relapse into anthropocentric accounts. Body phenomenology underlines the specific features of human existence without supporting any ethics of human dominance. Eccentric

---

[9] Patricia Ticineto Clough and Jean Halley, ed. *The Affective Turn: Theorizing the Social* (Durham: Duke University Press, 2007); Melissa Gregg and Gregory J. Seigworth, ed. *The Affect Theory Reader* (Durham: Duke University Press, 2010).

[10] Robert Seyfert, 'Beyond Personal Feelings and Collective Emotions: Toward a Theory of Social Affect', *Theory, Culture & Society* 29, 6 (2012).

positionality is not a concept of human hegemony. It is rather a methodological tool that further investigates the tragedy of human existence.

This leads to an analytical concept widening the perspective on the phenomenon of touch. We can now further investigate the operation of touch itself. The operation of touch is based on two central theoretical assumptions.[11] Both of these assumptions aim at a more coherent, broader definition of touch.

First, skin contact is understood as only one possible form of touch. The intimidating power of gazing, the violence of spoken words and the atmospheric materiality of interior spaces are dimensions of touching without any actual skin contact. Here, the regime of touch refers to inner bodily experiences like being affected and moved, protected and loved, embarrassed and assaulted. Thus, touch is not restricted to a form of sensual or synaesthetic experience. Touch appears as a state of bodily immanence embedded in the immaterial and material ecology of human existence.

Second, reflection and tact on the one side, and touch and affection on the other side, do not face each other as mutually exclusive oppositions. There is no clear-cut definition of touch as a sensation of direct, immediate and vulnerable, even physical contact. This definition of touch appears as a mystification of never-occurring direct

---

[11] Here I follow the remarks of Christian Fritz-Hoffman, who has brought forward some theoretical and methodological suggestions to reconcile phenomenological and poststructuralist traditions of thinking about touch. See Christian Fritz-Hoffmann, 'Grundzüge eines erweiterten Berührungsbegriffs. Zur Materialität des Hautkontakts und darüber hinaus', *Soziale Welt* 68, nos.2–3 (2017).

affection. Instead, touch is a mediated social operation as any other sensual experience. This entails that any understanding of touch as a more *direct* or *immediate* form of sensual experience than seeing, smelling or hearing is strongly rejected. Touching is not to be equated with naturally given feelings, emotions and moods, but it also isn't an exclusion of event-based moments of contingent and spontaneous affection. At the same time, touching and being touched *can* imply great intensity. Intensity is a feature of the paradoxical nature of touch. But there is no hierarchy of intensity with regard to different forms of sensual experience. The reason is rather simple: touching and being touched is not one sensual experience among others. Following the ideas of body phenomenology, we can consider touch as an operation embedded in all of the senses.

Any experience of human existence must be understood as a relational form embedded in a variety of environments. Here, Plessner's idea of mediated immediacy is understood, among other things, as a sociological thought.[12] In this sense, any form of direct touch is always mediated by social norms and symbolic structures, as well as the material and technological environments involved. Human beings and their bodies are characterised by their expressive and immanent position within the social world and its ecologies.

---

[12] Gesa Lindemann has comprehensively contributed to this interpretation of Plessner's work. See Gesa Lindemann, *Weltzugänge: die mehrdimensionale Ordnung des Sozialen* (Weilerswist: Velbrück Wissenschaft, 2014); Gesa Lindemann, 'The Body of Gender Difference', *European Journal of Women's Studies* 3, no. 4 (1996).

Following this sociological understanding of Plessner's anthropology, any form of touch is a twofold phenomenon. On the one side, touch is understood as a form of bodily experience. On the other side, touch relies upon norms, constraints, and conventions of social orders and cultural traditions. This also means that the social, cultural and symbolic embeddedness of affection and touch does not entail any ontological basis or moral need for anticipation, discipline or control. It only points at the inevitability of *ecological embeddedness and relationality.* There is no institutional, normative or social instruction resulting from this understanding of touch. Nevertheless, the socially contingent nature of touch has to be taken into account.

Now, this understanding of touch must be understood as an alternative to the widespread conception of biological and neurological reductionism in the field of psychiatry. However, it does not simply oppose the field of psychiatry. It rather uncovers the contradicting and inadequate assumptions of biological psychiatry; it reacts to the insufficient and inadequate concepts of neurological reductionism.

Neurobiological psychiatric research is based on the hypothesis that the clinical diagnosis of mental illness is *primarily* caused by brain dysfunctions. Therefore, the history of psychiatry is inseparably linked with the rise of biological and neurological reductionism. From a body phenomenological perspective, the human brain is not an isolated control centre of one's behaviour, personality and feelings.[13] Rather, it is embedded in the environ-

[13] Fuchs. *Ecology of the Brain. The Phenomenology and Biology of the Embodied Mind.*

ment of the human body (here as the 'Leib') as a relational operation. I will now look at the medical procedure of brain stimulation in order to illustrate the theoretical differences between body phenomenological and neurobiological approaches. This enables a closer look at the regime of touch underlying the practices of biological psychiatry.

2. Decline and Renaissance: Psychiatry and Brain Stimulation

Let me now elaborate on the historical rise of brain stimulation in order to provide the context of the empirical examples I am referring to. The history of brain stimulation is a history of gaining experience about the mystery of mental illness. Since the eighteenth century modern psychiatry has dreamt of the discovery of biological grounds for schizophrenia, melancholia or depression. Protagonists like Philippe Pinel, Jean Esquirol and William Cullen were trying to locate the causes of mental illness inside the body, as a disorder of the nervous system and the brain. To this day, modern psychiatry relies upon the premise of being able to find the biological or neurological reasons for mental suffering. However, the use of electricity in medical care has a much longer tradition than electric brain stimulation. Since the sixteenth century, amber stones and different fish (catfish, eel, ray) have served as sources of electric medical treatment.[14] In the nineteenth century, 'electrotherapeutics' became a key

[14] Kneeland and Warren. *Pushbutton Psychiatry*, vii-ix.

concept of medical terminology – and a common practice beyond the medical realm. Kneeland and Warren note: 'There were machines in public spaces that would, for a penny or nickel, provide a charge of electricity to cure nervous ailments or rheumatism. Congress had a cellar room in the Capitol filled with electrical medical apparatus in the 1880s […].'[15] The end of the nineteenth century also marks the first ever experiments of electric *brain* stimulation – with the first one probably taking place in 1874.[16]

Modern psychiatry continued the search for the biological causes of symptoms of depression in the beginning of the twentieth century. The invention of electroshock therapy in the 1930s can be considered the breakthrough of brain stimulation. For the first time, modern psychiatry was able to refer to a concrete treatment bridging the gap between medical speculations and individual cases.[17] Electroshock therapy – or Electroconvulsive therapy (ECT) – fulfilled two purposes. First, it somehow worked for some patients. Second, it satisfied the needs of psychiatric research and its medical industry. Even if the mechanism of ECT was poorly understood – and still is today[18] – it served as an experimental basis for the treatment of

---

[15] Ibid., xix.

[16] James P. Morgan. 'The First Reported Case of Electrical Stimulation of the Human Brain', *Journal of the History of Medicine and Allied Sciences* 37, no. 1 (1982).

[17] Alain Ehrenberg. *The Weariness of the Self: Diagnosing the History of Depression in the Contemporary Age* (Montreal: McGill-Queen's University Press, 2010), 45–69.

[18] Tom G. Bolwig. 'How Does Electroconvulsive Therapy Work? Theories on its Mechanism', *The Canadian Journal of Psychiatry* 56, no. 1 (2011).

depression. Alain Ehrenberg has shown how the invention of ECT led to the requirement of a clinical understanding of melancholia.[19] This is how the diagnosis of depression has become much more relevant to the medical discourse than ever before. In fact, the invention of ECT is the beginning of the diagnosis of depression as a mass phenomenon.

Today, the technology and the diagnosis of depression go hand in hand. ECT and other forms of brain stimulation are meant to prove the (neuro)biological grounds of depression; and psychiatrists can emancipate depression from the rather unpopular and 'old-fashioned' concept of melancholia. As Susan Sontag put it in the 1970s: 'Depression is melancholy minus its charms—the animation, the fits.'[20] That is exactly what biological, modern psychiatry needed: a more clinical, undecorated definition.

Recent studies on the history of psychiatric brain stimulation and shock therapy remember – some painfully – the strong public impact of the powerful images shown in *One Flew over the Cuckoo's Nest* from 1975.[21] The movie showed electroshock therapy as one element within a 'mechanized, machine-centered, emotionless world'.[22] It also visually exemplified electroshock as an effective regime of touch at the service of political and social control, with the power of reducing human beings to

---

[19] Ehrenberg. *The Weariness of the Self*, 45–69.

[20] Susan Sontag. *Illness as Metaphor* (New York: Farrar, Straus and Giroux, 1977), 50.

[21] David Healy and Edward Shorter. *Shock Therapy: A History of Electroconvulsive Treatment in Mental Illness* (Piscataway: Rutgers University Press, 2007), 9, 213–214.

[22] Kneeland and Warren. *Pushbutton Psychiatry*, 64.

helpless bodies, to submissive elements of society. However, the slow decline of ECT and other forms of brain stimulation and surgery had already started in the 1950s. Many patients unknowingly became part of dangerous experiments of psychiatrists, and many of them suffered long-term damage. Especially the so-called lobotomy (or leucotomy) stands as evidence for the brutality and ruthlessness of modern psychiatry. António Egas Moniz received the Nobel Prize for his neurosurgical innovations in the field of lobotomy in 1949. Only fifteen years later, however, the bad reputation of the treatment led to its disappearance.

Several reasons have paved the way for the rebirth of non-invasive as well as invasive forms of brain stimulation since the 1980s. The situation of psychiatry in the twenty-first century is highly influenced by these developments. First, the disappointment in pharmaceutical products like antidepressants has reached the heart of the medical industry. It became clear that the industry would have to seek for alternative research fields that promise better efficacy and reduced side-effects. Second, new technologies of neuroimaging have led to an explosion of research on the function of different brain areas in order to correlate their activities with different forms of mental illness and suffering. In this way the digital revolution of neuroimaging has extensively contributed to the renaissance of brain stimulation. Research on TMS and DBS are the results of this process. Third, the publication of the third (1980) and fourth catalogue (1994) of the *Diagnostic and Statistical Manual* (DSM) developed by the American Psychiatric Association (APA) put an even larger emphasis on the somatic, genetic and biological symptoms of mental disorders. Thus, the DSM manuals provided a narrative and justification in order to call for more research on neuroimaging and brain stimulation to tackle those symptoms in a more efficient way. The DSM and its 'checklist of symptoms' reflected and rigidified the 'tone of medical authority' in psychiatric diagnosis and treatment.[23] Fourth, the conditions of performing ECT have comprehensively improved. New anaesthetics, muscle relaxants and refinements in electrode placement enable psychiatrists and surgeons to increase effectiveness and minimise side-effects. Furthermore, the effectiveness of generalised seizures for therapeutic purposes has never been completely negated or refuted. Now, psychiatry could connect older achievements with technological innovations.

The efficacy of brain stimulation in the treatment of movement disorders like Parkinson's, tremor and dystonia since the 1990s has encouraged psychiatric research to tackle mental illnesses with identical methods. Here, hopes were raised that the precise stimulation of different areas of the brain can relieve individuals from the heavy burden of long-term depression.

Nevertheless, the causes of many forms of mental illness remain an open question to psychiatric and neuroscientific research to the present day. In recent research literature we find descriptions like the following about ECT: 'Any formulation of the mechanism of ECT will

[23] Ann Cvetkovich. *Depression. A Public Feeling* (Durham: Duke University Press, 2012), 99.

encounter numerous difficulties. ECT is effective in various illnesses such as depression, mania, schizophrenia, and catatonia, but it remains an unresolved issue whether ECT exerts differential effects, or whether these obviously different disorders have common pathophysiological bases.'[24] We might add here: it also remains unclear whether there is a pathophysiological base for all of those mental disorders *at all*. This applies in particular to the diagnosis of severe depression. With regard to research on deep brain stimulation, it is not even clear which area of the brain can be considered as an effective and reliable target of stimulation to treat severe depression.[25] During informal discussions, psychiatrists tend to judge prospective research on brain stimulation in the case of major depression with great caution or scepticism. This leaves the impression of neurobiological psychiatry building its theories on false concepts of stimulation, shock and therapy. In other words: touch. I will come back to the understanding of touch and the body underlying neurobiological psychiatry. But before that, I will discuss some ethical issues discussed in recent psychiatric literature dealing with brain stimulation.

3. The Ethics of Brain Stimulation

A regime is a bundle of norms, experiences and affects embedded in discourses and their practical operations. It

---

[24] Bolwig. 'How Does Electroconvulsive Therapy Work?', 14.

[25] Sibylle Delaloye and Paul E. Holtzheimer. 'Deep Brain Stimulation in the Treatment of Depression', *Dialogues in Clinical Neuroscience* 16, no. 1 (2014).

entails normative and ethical issues concerning a heterogeneous field of social phenomena. I will not investigate any further ethical dimensions underlying the treatment of severe depression in the context of psychiatric brain stimulation. Instead, I will briefly summarise the criticism raised against brain stimulation in the twentieth century, and show how psychiatry has reacted to this criticism with regard to the diagnosis of major depression. Since the 1980s, the field of neurobiological psychiatry has been highly engaged with questions of medical ethics in order to position itself in the public debate about psychiatric care. I will discuss the problems of free will and personal identity as two key debates in this context.

Today, brain stimulation still carries the stigma of behavioural control and suppression, of capitalist ruthlessness and modern torture. Various issues can be mentioned here. First, we have already seen that psychiatry has widely contributed to this image of megalomania. Prominent psychiatrists like Ugo Cerletti, António Egas Moniz, Walter Freeman and others have violated patient rights in order to develop their ideas in hidden experimental studies. Second, modern psychiatry did not only produce violent hierarchies of all sorts, it also implied a persistent gender bias from its very beginning.[26] In 1994, New York psychologist and ECT specialist Harold Sackheim threw a party in honour of ECT icon Max Fink to celebrate the founding of the journal *Convulsive Therapy*. The picture of the most prominent guests shows eleven

---

[26] Kneeland and Warren. *Pushbutton Psychiatry*, 21–40, 69–75.

men.[27] Third, forms of brain stimulation evoke pictures of political manipulation, state control and modern torture. The 'Birth of Electroshock' in 1938 already supports this impression. Ugo Cerletti, Lucio Bini and other psychiatrists and neurosurgeons developed ECT with the support of Italian fascism: 'The research, funded by and conducted during the Italian fascist movement, formed part of broader efforts of a variety of experts in medicine and social science to assume the role of social managers and engineers.'[28] Later on, many key figures of ECT further developed the treatment in the United States. But the relation of ECT to greater ideas of political control remains. Naomi Klein has shown how electroshock therapy has been used by governments as part of a greater strategy of neoliberal oppression, brain-washing and ideological struggle.[29] Here, electroshock therapy enables societal authorities to break the will and spirit of individuals just as social catastrophes open the way for neoliberal policy reforms.

Recent psychiatric research on brain stimulation in the case of severe depression is very aware of this history of stigmatisation and critique. It has tried to bring forward an active response to these challenges. During the last twenty years, neuropsychiatric publications have dealt with several dimensions of ethical concerns with forms of brain stimulation in the case of depression. This applies in

---

[27] Healy and Shorter. *Shock Therapy*, 239.

[28] Kneeland and Warren. *Pushbutton Psychiatry*, 48.

[29] Naomi Klein. *The Shock Doctrine: The Rise of Disaster Capitalism* (London: Penguin Group, 2007).

particular to the debate about deep brain stimulation.[30] I pick out two prominent examples to illustrate some contents of this debate: the problem of autonomy and free will, and the problem of personality and identity.

First, adherents of new technologies in brain stimulation have discussed the question of *autonomy* and *free will*. The philosophical debate about autonomous decision-making and freedom of consent has been adapted to defend treatments like DBS in interdisciplinary and public debates.[31] The general argument is the following: even if people suffer from severe depression, they cannot be deprived of the ability to speak up for themselves and they should not be deprived of the right to refuse treatments – including brain stimulation. The possibility of using brain stimulation technology in order to prevent convicted offenders from committing further crimes is considered a very rare exception to this general principle, restricted to the realm of forensic psychiatry.

[30] Frederic Gilbert. 'Self-Estrangement and Deep Brain Stimulation: Ethical Issues Related to Forced Explanation', *Neuroethics* 8, no. 2 (2015); W Glannon. 'Stimulating Brains, Altering Minds', *Journal of Medical Ethics* 35, no. 5 (2009); Matthis Synofzik and Thomas E. Schlaepfer. 'Stimulating Personality: Ethical Criteria for Deep Brain Stimulation in Psychiatric Patients and for Enhancement Purposes', *Biotechnology Journal* 3, no. 12 (2008); Christian Katzenmeier, Björn Schmitz-Luhn and Christiane Woopen. 'Law and Ethics of Deep Brain Stimulation', *International Journal of Law and Psychiatry* 35 (2012).

[31] Joseph J. Fins, Thomas E. Schlaepfer and Matthis Synofzik. 'How Happy Is Too Happy? Euphoria, Neuroethics, and Deep Brain Stimulation of the Nucleus Accumbens', *AJOB Neuroscience* 3, no. 1 (2012); Timo Beeker, *Tiefe Hirnstimulation als Ultima Ratio? Eine medizinethische Untersuchung am Beispiel der therapieresistenten Depression* (Münster: Mentis, 2014).

In order to maintain and guarantee the use of such an exception, psychiatry has focused on two objective standards. The criterion of *treatment resistancy* enables the preselection of patients by only choosing individuals with an 'adequate' history of failed treatments. In the case of brain stimulation, this usually includes up to four unsuccessful attempts of medication. However, only one third of depressive patients are actually classified as 'treatment-resistant'.[32] The second standard is the concept of *informed consent*.[33] In the case of brain stimulation for severe depression this is characterised by three criteria. All relevant information has to be disclosed to the patients. The patients need to demonstrate competence to understand the information. And finally, the decision based on this medical information has to be taken voluntarily and free from manipulative influence. The criterion of informed consent lacks clarity, however, particularly with regard to the nature of treatments with brain stimulation. The history of treating depression with brain stimulation – as well as medication – is a history of highly experimental studies with no reliable biological basis. The ontological situation of brain stimulation always remains a non-hierarchical situation of interacting amateurs. Both – experts and patients – gain their knowledge by being involved within a dynamic situation of mutual touch and

[32] Timo Beeker, Volker Coenen and Thomas Schlaepfer. 'Autonomy in Depressive Patients Undergoing DBS-Treatment: Informed Consent, Freedom of Will and DBS' Potential to Restore It', *Frontiers in Integrative Neuroscience* 11, no. 11 (2017): 2.

[33] Ibid., 3; Katzenmeier, Schmitz-Luhn and Woopen, 'Law and Ethics', 133–136.

experience. 'Therapeutic misconception' is not a form of self-deception on the patients' side; it is rather a possible risk of any form of brain stimulation with severe depression. However, the legal, moral and medical hierarchical position of psychiatrists often hides this fundamental uncertainty. Furthermore, the use of external assessments – psychiatrists assessing the patients' autonomy – is very common and widespread. This procedure also affects the inner wishes and hopes of suffering patients, who may experience major disappointment if those desires remain unfulfilled.

This brings us to the second example of ethical issues concerning brain stimulation with major depression. Even if autonomy is considered an attainable goal, the problem of manipulation with regard to one's *personal identity* remains. Brain stimulation still implies the stigma of behavioural control in terms of changing one's personality. This is the psychiatric rationale in response to this critique: even if brain stimulation changes the individual's personality and identity, there is no reason to consider this as exceptional and unusual.[34] Quite the contrary, the development and change of personality and identity is considered a natural process of becoming one's self throughout different stages in one's life. Additionally, patients suffering from severe depression usually *wish* to change their lives and personalities in order to have a fresh start. Since the 1950s neurologists and psychiatrists have been speculating about the existence of some kind of 'pleasure centre', usually identified with the nucleus

---

[34] Gilbert. 'Self-Estrangement'; Beeker, 'Tiefe Hirnstimulation'.

accumbens. Simply by increasing the voltage amount for DBS patients suffering from depression, it is now possible to change the mood of some patients from 'anxious' to 'relaxed' and 'too euphoric'.[35] In this context, the standard of 'self-estrangement' is suggested as one possible red line to distinguish unwanted side-effects from the 'normal feeling of self'.[36] The neuro-ethical philosopher Frederic Gilbert elaborates: 'In that respect, postoperative self-estrangement may enhance or restore one's control over one's life or illness. However, in some cases, DBS radical modifications of the self may lead to a loss of control or experiencing feelings of powerlessness.'[37] This also implies suicidality.

All these philosophical reflections consist of non-binding speculations and blurred ethical lines. They seek to reconcile the very basic principles of modern biological psychiatry with public and ethical criticism. At the same time, they continue a tradition of neurological reductionism. They limit the human body to its material form and brain functions.

4. Brain Stimulation and its Regime of Touch

In this last section, the regime of touch underlying recent psychiatric research about brain stimulation is contrasted with the understanding of touch developed in the beginning of this chapter. I argue that neurological reductionism

---

[35] Fins, Schlaepfer and Synofzik, 'Too Happy?'.

[36] Gilbert. 'Self-Estrangement', 109.

[37] Ibid.

has to be confronted with a different perspective on the human body and its regime of touch.

Until today, psychiatric research has not found any definitive pathophysiological base of depression. Despite the great efforts since the renaissance of ECT, it is very unlikely that effective forms of brain stimulation will be found in order to provide a long-lasting treatment for severe depression. All concerned patients depend on pharmacological and social support to cope with everyday life. And there is strong evidence that depression must be considered an 'intercorporeal', social phenomenon.[38] However, neurological regimes of touch in psychiatry still exclude any form of social and cultural embeddedness from possible therapeutic approaches. Rather, the neurological status of the human body is considered the source of depression. Consequently, the regime of brain stimulation tends to neglect the radical individual contingency of effects and outcomes in order to reinforce these underlying basic principles.

The concept of stimulation evokes the image of causal effects between the brain stimulus and a person's life and health. Thus, it implies powerful hopes for patients suffering from depression. This opens up doors for great hopes and even greater risks and dangers. On the one side, it contains the promise of healing the person as a whole while avoiding any further moments of painful inner and social touch. Patients are presented with seemingly miraculous healing powers. On the other side, an abyss of even greater

---

[38] Thomas Fuchs. 'Depression, Intercorporeality and Interaffectivity', *Journal of Consciousness Studies* 20, nos. 7–8 (2013).

detachment and vulnerability appears, situated between the suspicion of possible manipulations and profound disappointments.[39] If the miracle fails to occur, the consequences are unforeseeable. Shock and stimulation equally create hopes and dangers. Affects may be a source of criticism but they are also the source of emptiness and horror.[40] Post-traumatic stress disorder is one of the greatest blind spots in this context.

From a body phenomenological perspective, this understanding of the human body and of touch is disconnected from any concept of human existence and the 'Leib'. This leads to a different description of the self and of depression. Severe depression is the most extreme case of self-destructive, inwardly turned intensity. It appears as a threat to any assurance of one's self, one's identity as the necessary *centre*, *perspective* and *presence* of self-becoming *within* the inevitable, ontological fundament of ecological existence. Any 'biological dysfunction' must be understood as 'the meaningful expression of a disorder of intercorporeality and interaffectivity on the psychosocial level'.[41] Individuals suffering from depression are thrown back on themselves, to their own flesh and body, to their very own individualised vulnerability.

This also entails a different perspective on the ethical issues discussed in this text. First, autonomy and free

---

39 One setback is mapped out long before the treatment has even begun. The vast majority of patients of brain stimulation rely on antidepressants to receive brain stimulation, and depend on antidepressants long after the treatment.

40 Clough and Halley, eds., *The Affective Turn*.

41 Fuchs. '*Depression, Intercorporeality and Interaffectivity*', 234.

will are not understood as characteristics of an isolated subject taking conscious decisions. They are embedded in intercorporeal relations. Second, personality and identity are not considered features of individual subjects. The relational character of bodily existence can only manifest itself in relational operations of becoming, not of being. So, body phenomenology agrees with neuropsychiatry in saying that a person's identity is a process of becoming, not a state of being. However, it disagrees with neuropsychiatry in not reducing the regime of touch to the practice of brain stimulation itself. Becoming is a relational category of the 'Leib', not an isolated biological, neurological or individual narrative.

Like any medical treatment of mental illness discussed as an isolated practice, the procedure of brain stimulation tends to some form of self-fulfilling prophecy. In theory, it reduces depression to a form of brain dysfunction and it only refers to factors confirming this view. It follows a logic of reset and reload, erasing bad signals and trying to build up new ones. The genealogy and ecological dynamics of depression and the ongoing treatment are left out – or they are dismissed as dimensions of failed attempts of previous treatments. The normative force of treatment resistancy, for example, severs all links of brain stimulation to an individual's history of failed attachment and desperate isolation. It generates a realm of a very abstract double bind effect by fuelling hopes and expectations without ever leaving the grounds of radical experimentation and unconcerned non-responsibility at any time.

If the requirement of ecologically embedded depression is taken seriously, this normative effect cannot be dissolved by only pointing at conceptual transformations manifest in philosophical coherence. It can only be tackled by reflecting the painful and contradictory processes of touching and being touched within any 'shared space of attunement' pervaded by depression.[42] Body phenomenology provides a coherent concept of the living body in order to leave room for a relational and social understanding of human existence that does not fall back into subjective, individualist, dualistic or highly normative accounts.

Helmuth Plessner's *Die Stufen des Organischen* (1928) was meant to address the conflicts between the natural sciences and philosophy, between empirical and non-empirical sciences in the beginning of the twentieth century. Plessner underlines the important mediation of ontological and empirical, of philosophical and biological concepts. In his view, phenomenology bridges the gap between different disciplines, discourses and ways of thinking. Following this thought, body phenomenology should not be misunderstood as a general rejection of psychiatric research and treatment. It rather seeks to reconcile theoretical models with our social reality by emphasising the tragic and eccentric positionality of human existence.

References

Beeker, Timo. *Tiefe Hirnstimulation als Ultima Ratio? Eine medizinethische Untersuchung am Beispiel der therapieresistenten Depression*. Münster: Mentis, 2014.

[42] Ibid., 233.

Beeker, Timo, Volker Coenen and Thomas Schlaepfer. 'Autonomy in Depressive Patients Undergoing DBS-Treatment: Informed Consent, Freedom of Will and DBS' Potential to Restore It'. *Frontiers in Integrative Neuroscience* 11, no.11 (2017): 1–11.

Bolwig, Tom G. 'How Does Electroconvulsive Therapy Work? Theories on its Mechanism'. *The Canadian Journal of Psychiatry* 56, no.1 (2011): 13–18.

Cvetkovich, Ann. *Depression. A Public Feeling*. Durham: Duke University Press, 2012.

Delaloye, Sibylle and Paul E. Holtzheimer. 'Deep Brain Stimulation in the Treatment of Depression', *Dialogues in Clinical Neuroscience* 16, no.1 (2014): 83–91.

Ehrenberg, Alain. *The Weariness of the Self. Diagnosing the History of Depression in the Contemporary Age*. Montreal: McGill-Queen's University Press, 2010.

Fins, Joseph J., Thomas E. Schlaepfer and Matthis Synofzik. 'How Happy Is Too Happy? Euphoria, Neuroethics, and Deep Brain Stimulation of the Nucleus Accumbens', *AJOB Neuroscience* 3, no.1 (2012): 30–36.

Fritz-Hoffmann, Christian. 'Grundzüge eines erweiterten Berührungsbegriffs. Zur Materialität des Hautkontakts und darüber hinaus.' *Soziale Welt* 68, nos.2–3 (2017): 199–223.

Fuchs, Thomas. *Leib – Raum – Person: Entwurf einer phänomenologischen Anthropologie*. Stuttgart: Klett-Cotta, 2000.

Fuchs, Thomas. 'Depression, Intercorporeality and Interaffectivity'. *Journal of Consciousness Studies* 20, nos.7–8 (2013): 219–238.

Fuchs, Thomas. *Ecology of the Brain. The Phenomenology and Biology of the Embodied Mind*. Oxford: Oxford University Press, 2017.

Gilbert, Frederic. 'Self-Estrangement and Deep Brain Stimulation: Ethical Issues Related to Forced Explanation', *Neuroethics* 8, no.2 (2015): 107–114.

Glannon, W. 'Stimulating Brains, Altering Minds'. *Journal of Medical Ethics* 35, no.5 (2009): 289–292.

Healy, David and Edward Shorter. *Shock Therapy: A History of Electroconvulsive Treatment in Mental Illness*. New Jersey: Rutgers University Press, 2007.

Katzenmeier, Christian, Björn Schmitz-Luhn and Christiane Woopen. 'Law and Ethics of Deep Brain Stimulation'. *International Journal of Law and Psychiatry* 35, (2012): 130–136.

Klein, Naomi. *The Shock Doctrine: The Rise of Disaster Capitalism*. London: Penguin Group, 2007.

Kneeland, Timothy W. and Carol A. Warren. *Pushbutton Psychiatry: A Cultural History of Electroshock in America*. Westport: Praeger Publishers, 2002.

Lindemann, Gesa. 'The Body of Gender Difference'. *European Journal of Women's Studies* 3, no.4 (1996): 341–361.

Lindemann, Gesa. *Weltzugänge: die mehrdimensionale Ordnung des Sozialen*. Weilerswist: Velbrück Wissenschaft, 2014.

Lindemann, Gesa. In *Handbuch Körpersoziologie. Band 1: Grundbegriffe und theoretische Perspektiven*, edited by Robert Gugutzer, Gabriele Klein and Michael Meuser, 57-66. Wiesbaden: Springer VS, 2017.

Merleau-Ponty, Maurice. *Phenomenology of Perception*. New York: Routledge, 2012.

Morgan, James P. 'The First Reported Case of Electrical Stimulation of the Human Brain'. *Journal of the History of Medicine and Allied Sciences* 37, no.1 (1982): 51–64.

Plessner, Helmuth. *Die Stufen des Organischen und der Mensch: Einleitung in die philosophische Anthropologie*. Berlin: de Gruyter, 1975.

Seyfert, Robert. 'Beyond Personal Feelings and Collective Emotions: Toward a Theory of Social Affect'. *Theory, Culture & Society* 29, no.6 (2012): 27–46.

Sontag, Susan. *Illness as Metaphor*. New York: Farrar, Straus and Giroux, 1977.

Synofzik, Matthis and Thomas E. Schlaepfer. 'Stimulating Personality: Ethical Criteria for Deep Brain Stimulation in Psychiatric Patients and for Enhancement Purposes'. *Biotechnology Journal* 3, no.12 (2008): 1511–1520.

Tellenbach, Hubertus. *Geschmack und Atmosphäre. Medien menschlichen Elementarkontaktes*. Salzburg: Otto Müller Verlag, 1968.

Not at a Distance: On Touch, Synaesthesia and Other Ways of Knowing

Erin Manning

A thousand other things sing to me.

John Lee Clark

Every possible feeling produces a movement, and that movement is a movement of the entire organism, and of each of its parts.

William James

What if mirror-touch synaesthesia, defined as the experience that ensues when the stimulation of one sensory modality (vision) automatically triggers a perception in a second modality (touch), in the absence of any direct stimulation to this second modality, were not only misnamed, but radically misunderstood? It's not just the nomenclature that I am concerned with here – why a synaesthesia that is said to move between touch and vision isn't called vision-touch synaesthesia like its sisters, sound-taste, colour-grapheme, shape-taste – but the very presupposition that grounds an account of sensation that can be parsed so cleanly between sense modalities and between the bodies that are said to be the locations of sense. For even if it were called vision-touch synaesthesia, it would still take for granted a whole set of beliefs about both how we perceive and what is considered worthy of being perceived: despite a rare admission that for some the experience of being touched-without-touch occurs through an object,[1] mirror-touch synaesthesia is predominantly a humanist concept. To be touched by that which we see is, in most of the literature, to be touched by the human. This is the question I want to ask here: what is assumed in the presupposition that to be moved is to be moved by the human? And what is assumed when we take vision as the predominant activator of the experience of being touched by the world? Circling around autistic perception and DeafBlindness, I want to ask how neurotypicality as the normative standard for human experience operates in the presuppositions of sense.

A Thousand Other Things Sing To Me

The dominant neuroscientific literature works with a deficit model of sensation that is neurotypical through and through, most emphatically in its presupposition of a body

1 'It is unclear if MT synaesthesia is specific to viewing a real person, rather than a dummy figure or an object being touched since in their Supplementary material Banissy and Ward discuss some cases of MT synaesthesia also being induced by viewing objects being touched'. Jörg Jewanski, Sean A. Day, and Jamie Ward. 'A Colorful Albino: The First Documented Case of Synaesthesia, by Georg Tobias Ludwig Sachs in 1812.' *Journal of the History of the Neurosciences* 18, no. 3 (2009): 293–303. DOI: https://doi.org/10.1080/09647040802431946

schema which acts as the normative ground on which all divergent experience is mapped. In this literature, mirror-touch synaesthesia is chiefly described, as mentioned above, as depending on one body seeing-feeling the touch of another directly on their skin: you touch yourself and I feel it because I see it. In this account, the experience of feeling the other is, paradoxically, considered a deficit: it weakens the body schema. With the feeling of you directly experienced on my body, I lose a bit of what separated me from you. The coming into relation is considered a loss.

The deficit model of sensation begins with the presupposition that senses are fixed and located, working with a pre-constituted body schema whose 'sense of agency,' it is said, is fractured by the increase in sensation. Bodies lose their integrity in the encounter with the touch of the other. This approach, which situates 'sense of agency' as central to what it means to have a body, placing what I have called the intentionality-agency-volition triad ahead of the *agencement of* experience coming into itself to activate a bodying, emphasises that bodies are above all individual, separate envelopes that are in the world but not of it. Bodies are only properly bodies when they can fully distinguish themselves from the world, the implication being always that bodies are separate entities that have dominance over their sensations, and, by extension, over their movements. The deficit model perceives any deviation from this norm to be a lack.

> In the context of MTS [mirror-touch synaesthesia], one prediction from this would be that if there were agency-processing deficits these would exacerbate more basic disturbances in bodily awareness. We are

> clearly suggesting here that MTS is primarily a 'dis-order' of ownership, which can have consequences for SoAg [sense of agency] and which in turn can further worsen ownership disturbances.[2]

Bodies that sense too much, bodies that feel the touch of the world and are moved by it, are deficient. When we lack the ability to distinguish our world from the world of others we lose something of what makes us, properly speaking, bodies, and, by extension, human.[3]

Feeling the touch of another body or another object on our body is already a misnomer. It makes too strong a distinction between body and world, a distinction that is everywhere at play in the neuroscientific studies of all forms of synaesthesia, but perhaps even more forcefully so in studies of mirror-touch synaesthesia.

> Individuals with mirror-touch synaesthesia (MTS) experience touch on their own bodies when observing another person being touched. Specifically, the images that participants had initially perceived as containing equal quantities of self and other became more likely to be recognised as the self after viewing the other being touched.[4]

---

[2] Maria C. Cioffi, James W. Moore and Michael J. Banissy. 'What Can Mirror-Touch Synaesthesia Tell Us About the Sense of Agency?'. *Frontiers in Human Neuroscience* 8 (2014): 256. DOI: https://doi.org/10.3389/fnhum.2014.00256

[3] In Amelia Baggs's important video *In My Language*, Amelia (formerly Amanda) Baggs demonstrates the degree to which the way she senses and perceives the world excludes her from the category of the human. https://www.youtube.com/watch?v=JnylM1hI2jc

[4] Lare Maister, Michael J. Banissy, and Manos Tsakiris. 'Mirror-Touch Synaesthesia Changes Representations of Self-Identity'. *Neuropsychologia* 51, no. 5 (2013): 802.

Self-identity is the starting point, and it is in the self-identity that the experience of touch is located: 'These results suggest that observing touch on others not only elicits a conscious experience of touch in MTS, but also elicits a change in the mental representation of the self, blurring self-other boundaries'.[5] There is no mention here of the emergent quality of sensation produced in the world. No attempt is made to explore the ways in which the relational milieu activates this singular composition. Nor is there an effort to explore how the touch that is felt might move beyond the limited concept of 'simple location'[6] – no questions are asked about how that touch alters the feel of the space, the quality of sensation beyond the actual location of the touch. There is no account of body as process – of bodying. What is assumed is always that we know what constitutes a body – a body, it must always be remembered, that, in its neurotypicality, stands in for the normative standard of whiteness.

Because there is no account of a processual bodying, there is no way to articulate what is activated in the sensation, only what is lost. When bodies are mapped in advance as abstracted from their environment and parsed according to the normative (white) standard, the only conclusion can be that what diverges is a loss – a loss of

---

[5] Ibid.

[6] In *Science and the Modern World*, Whitehead writes: 'to say that a bit of matter has *simple location* means that, in expressing its spatio-temporal relations, it is adequate to state that it is where it is, in a definite finite region of space, and throughout a definite duration of time, apart from any essential references to the relations of that bit of matter to other regions of space and other durations of time.' (New York: The Free Press, 1925), 58.

the norm. For this is clearly what is at play here, though never addressed as such. In the mirror-touch example, the activation of sense caused by the overlap of sense means individuality (the neurotypical norm) is weakened: in their 'becoming one' the one who senses too much loses the very boundary that made it a body. In study after study, the assumption is that the field of relation[7] activated by the touch of the world *reduces* the body schema, placing not only the body at risk, but the whole edifice of representation the neurotypicality upholds.'[W]hen MTS individuals view touch on others, it not only elicits a shared tactile experience, but actually alters their body representation'.[8] This altering of the body representation is a deficit because the assumed contours of the body are no longer intact. Without the intactness a body no longer properly feels the distinction between body and world, between self and other.

What if the contours of a body were never intact? In this return to an account of touch ten years after publishing *Politics of Touch*,[9] I hope to do four things: 1) demonstrate that the force of reaching-toward, which is how I defined touch in *Politics of Touch*, troubles the model of 'sense of agency' at the heart of accounts of mirror-touch synaesthesia; 2) build on John Lee Clark's account of distantism as it plays out not only in DeafBlind culture but

[7] See 'Toward a Leaky Sense of Self' in Erin Manning, *Always More Than One: Individuation's Dance* (Durham: Duke University Press, 2013) for a more detailed account of the relational body.

[8] Maister, Banissy and Tsakiris. 'Mirror-Touch Synaesthesia', 802.

[9] Erin Manning. *Politics of Touch: Sense, Movement, Sovereignty* (Minneapolis: Minnesota University Press, 2007).

more broadly in the neurotypical worldview; 3) consider the ways in which accounts of mirror-touch synaesthesia as well as synaesthesia more broadly support a deficit model of sensation that is deeply neurotypical; 4) explore how ProTactile, a movement for language-in-the-making and DeafBlind experience, remaps the spacetime of sensation away from the categorical limitations that come with the imposition of sensory regimes that privilege the body-world separation.

> The word on the breeze, and through the floor
>
> *Liz Ball*

'The TV is off, but I can still hear (and feel on my skin) the current of electricity powering all that equipment,' writes Aspiegrrl on her blog 'Autism and Angels'.[10] Hearing what moves infrasensorially through her surroundings, being moved and changed by the field of relation, makes it impossible for Aspiegrrl to hold onto the neurotypical imposition of body-world separation. Already considered at a deficit by her autistic difference, by the standard of neuroscientific work on synaesthesia, she is doubly pathologised, her divergent sensory processing further evidence of her faulty 'sense of agency'. She suffers from a disturbance of sense perception that will, most likely, be considered as a disadvantage in learning environments: she will be taught, if not through the violent practices of ABA (Applied Behaviour Analysis),[11] then through the

---

[10] Autism and Angels, https://aspiegrrl.wordpress.com.

[11] For an important critique of ABA, see Melanie Yergeau, *Authoring Autism: On Rhetoric and Neurological Queerness* (Durham: Duke

ubiquitous behavioural codes that are systemic in our education systems to direct her perception so as to sense less fully, thereby attempting to craft a less porous body. But this will not actually make her sense less. It will simply make more violently apparent that a sensing body in movement is a deficient body. She will learn that in order to pass she will have to background the feel of electricity on her skin. She will have to act as though she is in control of her surroundings. She will pretend that she has agency over what moves her. She will be told in a thousand ways that value resides in subtracting from the welter of experience. She will learn that the standard of neurotypical life is one of sense-poverty. She will be considered properly treated if she can 'pay' attention, attention no longer dancing at the pace of the more-than.

What if we were to turn the sensory model on its head and ask what it is that keeps so many feeling so little?

Synaesthesia is usually defined as an overlapping or cross-mapping of the senses. In the most widely studied cases of synaesthetes – colour-sound and colour-grapheme – great emphasis is placed on mnemonic systems, focusing on the modality of parsing from the more-than synaesthesia is said to facilitate. Synaesthetes are acclaimed for their unusual abilities: autistic Daniel Tammet,[12] for instance,

University Press, 2017). See also Laura Smith Donohoe's 'Regarding Applied Behavioral Analysis Therapy' in https://laurensmithdonohoe.com/2018/08/11/regarding-applied-behavioral-analysis-aba-therapy/ as well as Anthony Easton, whose articles include 'Why do Autism Specialists want to Stamp out Autistic Traits' in https://www.theglobeandmail.com/opinion/why-do-autism-specialists-want-to-stamp-out-autistic-traits/article28441771/

12 http://www.danieltammet.net

is celebrated for being able to visualise pi to a previously unimaginable degree (22,514 digits), while others inspire wonder by being able to retrace their past to a remarkable degree thanks to a colour-grapheme synaesthesia that enables them to see any day of the week as far back as they want to go.[13] These stories – and there are many of them – are fascinating, and the abilities are remarkable, but they only touch synaesthesia at its limit. In addition, they foreground a model of value that is deeply neurotypical: they emphasise not the qualitative complexity of their sensual fields but what can be culled from those relational fields, and thereby quantified. And, insofar as they include autistics such as Daniel Tammet, they replay the well-worn narrative of autistic savantism, reminding us at every turn that while these abilities may be extraordinary, displaying 'high functioning' traits, they do not tend to carry over into other 'lower functioning' realms of autistic experience. In addition, not only does the narrative of savantism cleave autistics by singling out, for value-added, those who have particular gifts that can be studied, it also provides an ideal opportunity to reinforce the narrative of deficiency among those who do not share these mnemonic talents, keeping autistics in their place as deficiently sub-human.

This approach to diversity as divergence from a neurotypical norm is all over the writing on Tammet. Described as a 'high functioning autistic savant,' his sensitivity to the world is bracketed by functioning labels that only serve to

[13] Lix Buxton. 'Experience: I See Words as Colours', *The Guardian*, 19 August 2016, https://www.theguardian.com/lifeandstyle/2016/aug/19/experience-i-see-words-as-colours

reinstall neurotypical norms. For instance, when describing the ways in which he functions outside his mnemonic synaesthetic abilities, he is said to be unimaginative because 'he tends to take things literally'.[14] The claim is as simplistic as it is widespread in the world of autism: to take things literally is to not be able to hear the undertones of communication that veer it toward subtexts, and thereby not really being able to communicate at all. As autistic Melanie Yergeau argues with rhetorical flourish, this kind of claim to non-communication is well known.

> Autistics are multiply bound to non-rhetoricity. In many respects, the idea of an autistic culture is often rendered as the cute or pathological machinations of autistic people who lack insight into the horrors of their arhetorical circuitry. [...] Autistic culture — and its flirtatious bristling against rhetorical norms — is a queering of rhetoric's conditions.[15]

No inquiry is made by the psychologist Simon Baron-Cohen (see fn. 16, p.158) as to how the excess of sense coursing through Tammet's every thought and movement creates a radically different engagement with the world. No effort is made to understand how the queering of expression in his hypersensorial universe shifts the conditions of sense. If there is indeed a tendency in some autistics toward literality, what is it that cannot easily be parsed from communication? What nuance is

---

[14] Ralph Savarese. 'Reading Fiction with Temple Grandin: Yes, people with autism can understand literature', *Salon*, 2 September 2018 https://www.salon.com/2018/09/02/reading-fiction-with-temple-grandin-yes-autistic-people-can-understand-literature/

[15] Melanie Yergeau. *Authoring Autism*, 42.

reverberating in the field of experience that distracts from the process that would facilitate a neurotypical selection we call irony, or sarcasm? Is it that human communication itself stands out less than other activities in the wash of perception, as a result of which some of its layers of sense are easily missed in the dance of attention? Or that those layers of sense that neurotypicals find so central to communication are less interesting, in the moment, than neurotypicals assume they are? Because there is no question, ever, that autistics are incapable of feeling nuance and, where apt (often in reference to neurotypicals), of using sarcasm.

The obsession with emphasising the 'low functioning' tendencies in neurodiversity, even in cases of autistic savantism, serves to maintain the deficit model of sensation with respect to synaesthesia. If we know that Tammet, despite his extraordinary synaesthetic capacities, 'doesn't notice if someone is upset,' it will be easy to argue that the touch of another on his body decreases his capacity to truly be human. If we read that Tammet 'commits frequent faux pas,' is 'asocial' and 'avoids social situations and finds parties confusing,' we are reinforced in our belief that there is no neurodiverse sociality. If what is foregrounded is that he is 'obsessed,' that 'he has strict routines,' what we learn is that no matter how sensitive he is, there is no real latitude in his capacities. And if we read that he 'showed severe tantrums at change of routine as a child,' that he 'showed head-banging in his cot,' and 'sat with fingers in his ears in primary school and with his eyes tight shut,' we become convinced in our assessment that no matter how extraordinary his reciting of pi, he has nothing on us, we neurotypicals. For Tammet is nothing more than an arhetorical unimaginative mind-blind less-than-human incapable of truly being aware (of us), detached, distanced, apart, 'in a world of his own'.[16]

Or, we recognise that all of this is less about Tammet than about the presuppositions that accompany the imposition of the neurotypical norm on all experience. Turning our attention away from the neurotypical norm, we note that with hypersensoriality comes a sensitivity so powerful that it activates the field of relation in ways sometimes impossible to hold. Bodies collapse under the strain. We learn that what the literature calls tantrums are the undoing, in this collapse, of any boundary between self and world, a body succumbing to the pain of having to hold at bay the forces that shape experience. And we learn to recognise the violence in the account, an account that polices the body-world boundary in order to maintain the well-worn habit of enforcing (white) dominance.

The violence is not only in enforcing this separation by demonising those bodies that collapse under the strain of overstimulation, but in openly recognising as valuable only those who can be reflected in the mirror of neurotypicality. Baron-Cohen writes:

> With age, DT [Daniel Tammet] has developed more of an idea of how to behave and how he seems to others, raising the possibility that mindreading skills are not completely absent but are simply delayed. It helped when, at the age of 13, his mother was able to

---

[16] Simon Baron-Cohen et al. 'Savant Memory in a Man with Colour Form-Number Synaesthesia and Asperger Syndrome'. *Journal of Consciousness Studies* 14, nos. 9–10 (2007): 237–51

> give him some feedback and tell him to look at others' eyes and not at his own feet. This suggests that in individuals on the autistic spectrum, for whom such social insight and consciousness of others' minds does not develop naturally at the right point in development, learning to consciously attend to key parts of the environment (faces, eyes, expressions) may help.[17]

The criteria for inclusion into humanity are always neurotypical. That Tammet prefers not to have eye-contact has absolutely no bearing on what he sees or feels. It is Baron-Cohen and all those who adopt neurotypical standards for body schemas, those who insist that eye contact has anything to do with a regard for the other, who are here displaying their narrow-mindedness, if not mind-blindness. As those of us who do not feel pain when looking others in the eye know, there is nothing easier than to pretend presence through eye contact while being altogether elsewhere. Eye contact is a practiced mechanism for allowing the human to feel that we are at the centre of experience, nothing more.

Daniel Tammet functions just fine. He is neither 'high functioning' as a savant nor 'low functioning' in the rest of his life. Functioning labels, as anyone in the movement for neurodiversity will emphasise, say nothing at all except that neurotypicals are obsessed with categories that keep their way of knowing at the forefront.[18] To function, according to these labels, means to deploy movement,

---

[17] Simon Baron-Cohen et al. 'Savant Memory'.

[18] For an excellent piece on functioning labels in autism see https://ollibean.com/problems-functioning-labels/

expression, sensation in ways that 'pass' for neurotypical: to take on a posture that does not announce too forcefully the sensory processing challenges that come with overstimulation; to be able to meet requirements for independence imposed by a belief in individualism before all; to be able to perform competence in ways that do not endanger the body schema of those for whom the template of neurotypicality has become second nature.

Study after study links autism and synaesthesia. Indeed, this view has become so widespread that even Simon Baron-Cohen, who for decades kept his research on autism and synaesthesia separate, recently decided to bridge them:

> I have studied both autism and synaesthesia for over 25 years and I had assumed that one had nothing to do with the other. These findings will re-focus research to examine common factors that drive brain development in these traditionally very separate conditions. An example is the mechanism 'apoptosis,' the natural pruning that occurs in early development, where we are programmed to lose many of our infant neural connections. In both autism and synaesthesia apoptosis may not occur at the same rate, so that these connections are retained beyond infancy.[19]

In this research, rather than asking how 'apoptosis' might challenge his theory of 'mind-blindness' – the condition of not being able to read 'the mind' of another mentioned above in relation to Tammet as 'mindreading' – by demonstrating that the hypersensorial tendency in autism that is likely in part due to 'apoptosis' results in them

[19] http://www.cam.ac.uk/research/news/synaesthesia-is-more-common-in-autism

being *more* in contact with the world and not less, Baron-Cohen takes it upon himself not only to reemphasise the concept of mind-blindness but to counter other studies that suggest that those with mirror-touch synaesthesia may be more attuned to the world than those without. A recent article, entitled 'Mirror-Touch Synaesthesia is Not Associated with Heightened Empathy, and Can Occur with Autism,' he and his co-writers (Robson and Allison) make their position abundantly clear.[20]

When Baron-Cohen speaks of empathy, he is referring to the Empathy Quotient, a measure for empathy he developed with Sally Wheelwright. Empathy, for Baron-Cohen and Wheelwright, Wikipedia explains is 'a combination of the ability to feel an appropriate emotion in response to another's emotion and the ability to understand the other's emotion.'[21] All of this is of course associated with theory of mind, 'the ability to attribute mental states – beliefs, intents, desires, pretending, knowledge etc. – to oneself and others and to understand that others have beliefs, desires, intentions, and perspectives that are different from one's own.'[22]

---

[20] Simon Baron-Cohen et al. 'Mirror-Touch Synaesthesia is Not Associated with Heightened Empathy, and Can Occur with Autism.' PLoS ONE 11(8) (2016): e0160543. DOI: https://doi.org/10.1371/journal.pone.0160543.

[21] https://en.wikipedia.org/wiki/Empathy_quotient. Note also that the Empathy Quotient suggests that connection to humans over animals is a sign of empathy. As with Theory of Mind, Baron-Cohen seems incapable of imagining the force of relation outside a Humanist paradigm. https://psychology-tools.com/empathy-quotient/

[22] https://en.wikipedia.org/wiki/Theory_of_mind. For more on autism and theory of mind, see Melanie Yergeau, *Authoring Autism*. I have also written about it in 'The Ethics of Language in the Making,' in *Always More Than One* and in 'Coming Alive in a World of Texture,' in Erin Manning and Brian Massumi, *Thought in the Act:*

To be empathetic is to be able to parse from the world that which most closely conforms to what we already recognise as having value. It is to carry forward a power relation that acknowledges similarity and responds benevolently to it. I feel you because your feeling corresponds to what I already recognise as feeling. Empathy, the feeling-in of an interiority that recognises itself in the other, thereby creating a measure of the self-same, must be seen not only as a profoundly humanist marker of self-recognition, but as the neurotypical marker par excellence of exclusion of all that cannot be recognised as self. It is this assumption that feeling is internal to the body that allows Baron-Cohen et al to assume that autistics are mind-blind and, by extension, have no empathy. For when Baron-Cohen says that autistics cannot 'understand that others have beliefs, desires, intentions and perspectives that are different from one's own,' what he seems unable to comprehend is that the definition excludes those modes of feeling proper to the neurodiverse. The concept of empathy simply cannot recognise experience expanded from the normative interiority of a neurotypical body-schema. When Baron-Cohen et al write that 'individuals with MT [motor-touch synaesthesia] have a *reduced* aptitude for social situations,'[23] this is always in reference to the 'in-feeling' of empathy. A neurotypical viewpoint cannot recognise neurodiverse

Passages in the Ecology of Experience (Minneapolis: University of Minnesota Press, 2014). For a nuanced account of empathy reading neuroscientific studies in relation to a project of reading with autistics, see also Ralph Savarese, *See It Feelingly: Classic Novels, Autistic Readers and the Schooling of a No-Good English Professor* (Durham: Duke University Press, 2018).

[23] Baron-Cohen et al. 'Mirror-Touch Synaesthesia'.

sociality precisely because it is always feeling-in, led by a model of interiority that presumes that feeling is only what a body contains, not what a body does in the worlding. There is no feeling-with in this account.

Sympathy – what things do when they shape each other – is a threat to neurotypicality precisely because it challenges the centrality of empathy as in-feeling. Turning to the force of a shaping, sympathy extends care toward the world, highlighting the world's own concern for experience unfolding. When Baron-Cohen et al insist that autistics fail to demonstrate empathy, what they are actually insisting is that we retain empathy as the baseline for experience in order to maintain the account of interiority that keeps body and world separate. This of course includes the Karolinska Directed Emotional Faces Test and the presupposition of identification that comes with it. To be empathetic is to be able to parse human expression according to the normative framework of expressivity. Despite the general knowledge that faces can contort to represent states required of them (much like the bestowing of eye-contact to pacify an interlocutor), despite the widely held experience that we can demonstrate interest we don't share by moving our facial muscles in ways that are normatively recognised, face-tests such as the Karolinska Directed Emotional Faces Test remain the marker for adhesion to humanity by way of a model of empathy that will always exclude those who cannot be recognised and embraced as self-same.

Empathy is a white concept. It requires an identificatory frame that can be mapped onto the other. It requires the extraction from experience of all that does not conform to the choreography of human-human interaction. To be empathetic according to these standards is to be capable of cutting out the feltness of the world activating a body beyond its-(white)self. There is no inability-to-feel relation in neurodiverse sociality: indeed, in the sympathetic force of worlding, a folding-in and through the world is at its height. All is felt-with. The problem for neurotypicality is that feeling-with cannot be contained within the limited category of an Empathy Quotient. Leaky, the sympathetic encounter with what things do when they shape each other, takes over. This synaesthetic feeling-with cannot be measured precisely because it cannot be located in a body precontained. It is of the world. Its feeling-with shapes the conditions of experience in the very same gesture that it shapes a body. Neurodiverse sociality might be described as a sensitivity to this shaping, a commitment to how the shaping orients, unmoors, disturbs any idea of a body as self-enclosed. Neurodiverse sociality lives in and through the force of the shaping, a shaping so deeply alive with the world that it continuously activates new fields of resonance at the edging-into-existence of body-worldings. The force of these body-worldings what explodes when a body collapses under the weight of neurotypicality.[24]

Simon Baron-Cohen deserves no more of our time. I turn to his work only because it is prevalent in the field

---

[24] Many autistics have written important pieces on the consequences of the deficit model, among them Melanie Yergeau in her recent book *Authoring Autism* (2018), David J. Savarese, 'Passive Plants'. *The Iowa Review* 47(1) (2017) https://iowareview.org/from-the-issue/volume-47-issue-1-—-spring-2017/passive-plants, and Tito Mukhopadhyay in *The Mind Tree: A Miraculous Child Breaks the Silence of Autism* (New York: Riverhead Books, 2007).

and therefore affects both the literature on autism and on synaesthesia. To address the claims he makes, and then to move away from him, it is necessary to underscore the following: 1) all models of relation that begin with a preconstituted body schema and make human interaction the only marker for empathy are deeply erroneous. These are models of interaction, not relation.[25] 2) empathy is a humanist construct that privileges a human-centred account of importance that is always organised around preexisting norms. These norms are based on neurotypicality, which also means whiteness, male-centredness, gender normativity and able-bodiedness. 3) synasthesia is never going to be a condition that can be adequately studied with an experimental method that begins with a neurotypical body schema. This is the case not only because the quantifications of sense that are the results of such studies are only the tip of the iceberg, but because all sensation occurs in complex overlaps. 4) sensing is not limited to sense-presentation. All sensing is amodal and amodal sensation can only be mapped, if it can be mapped, topologically. To address synaesthesia, new modes of expression will continuously have to be invented. With them will come new modes of knowing. 5) autism tends to express itself not as a lack of feeling as Baron-Cohen argues, but as an overfeeling, as a feeling-with-the-world of such intensity that it is difficult to

[25] For an important account of the difference between interaction and relation, see Brian Massumi, 'The Thinking-Feeling of What Happens.' *Inflexions: A Journal for Research-Creation* 1 (2008) http://inflexions.org/n1_The-Thinking-Feeling-of-What-Happens-by-Brian-Massumi.pdf

parse into the quotient scientists like Baron-Cohen use to measure humanity. I have defined this tendency of supra-sensation or overfeeling as autistic perception, emphasising that it exists on a continuum of neurodiversity but expresses itself most intensely in classical autism. As I have argued elsewhere, this intensity of feeling is relational to the core. It is alive with the more-than. We all stand to learn from a modality of feeling that is so ecstatically more-than human.

What Things Do When They Shape Each Other

> All things living and dead cry out to me
> when I touch them. The dog, gasping for air,
> is drowning in ecstasy, its neck shouting
> Dig in, dig in. Slam me, slam me,
> demands one door while another asks to remain
> open. My wife again asks me
> how did I know just where and how
> to caress her. I can be too eager to listen:
> The scar here on my thumb is a gift
> from a cracked bowl that begged to be broken.
>
> John Lee Clark *Clamor*[26]

John Lee Clark, to my knowledge, has never been tested for synasthesia. How could he be, when the neurotypical assumption around the sensing body automatically discounts a DeafBlind person from mirror-touch synaesthesia, or any other kind. What would there be to measure? Indeed, the neurotypical view of DeafBlindness suggests

26 John Lee Clark. 'Metatactile Knowledge'. https://johnleeclark.tumblr.com/post/130321809778/metatactile-knowledge

that there really is no life to be experienced without the senses of vision and hearing: 'The loss of both sight and hearing constitutes one of the severest disabilities known to human beings. Essentially, it deprives an individual of the two primary senses through which we acquire awareness of and information about the world around us, and it drastically limits effective communication and freedom of movement, which are necessary for full and active participation in society.'[27]

And yet. What about the synaesthesia so clearly felt in these lines? What of the strength of feeling-felt?

> All things living and dead cry out to me
> when I touch them. The dog, gasping for air,
> is drowning in ecstasy, its neck shouting
> Dig in, dig in. Slam me, slam me,
> demands one door while another asks to remain
> open. My wife again asks me
> how did I know just where and how
> to caress her. I can be too eager to listen:
> The scar here on my thumb is a gift
> from a cracked bowl that begged to be broken.

These words of Clark's are reminiscent of autistic Tito Mukhopadhyay's account of the mining tragedy in Raleigh County, West Virginia in 2010. Mukhopadhyay writes:

> It's true that when I think of the situation, there may be empathy. But my empathy would probably be towards the flashlight batteries of those trapped coal miners if there happens to be a selection on my part. Or my empathy would perhaps be toward the trapped air around those coal miners. There would

[27] John Lee Clark. 'Distantism'. https://johnleeclark.tumblr.com.

> be me watching through the eyes of the flashlight cell the utter hopelessness of those unfortunate miners as my last chemicals struggled to glow the faint bulb so that I didn't leave them dying in darkness. As the air around them, I would try to find a way to let myself squeeze every bit of oxygen I have to allow the doomed to breathe, for I am responsible for their doom. And while I found myself trapped, I would smell the burning rice being cooked with neglect in an earthen pot.[28]

For Clark, the touch carries a proximity that is also felt in Mukhopadhyay, though in Mukhopadhyay's case, the strong sensorial feeling-with is carried across senses in ways that more clearly make apparent what Brian Massumi would call a relational, or virtual body, a body of 'pure variability' activated in the sensing.[29] With Clark, the same force of relation is felt, but to register, the actual proximity of touch is added to the mix. That said, there is also in Clark's poem the sense of the activation of an emergent relation, a feeling-with that exceeds the actuality of the hands-on of touch. As with Mukhopadhyay, there is a sense of a more-than that accompanies the actual body, composing with the sensation that moves through that body.

A touch is here foregrounded, I want to suggest, that is synaesthetic, felt-across and with. Synaesthetic because

[28] Ralph Savarese. 'More Than a Thing to Ignore: An Interview with Tito Rajarshi Mukhopadhyay'. *Disability Studies Quarterly* 30, no.1 (2010) DOI: https://doi.org/10.18061/dsq.v30i1.1056

[29] Brian Massumi. 'The Art of the Relational Body: From Mirror-Touch to the Virtual Body'. In *Mirror-Touch: Thresholds of Empathy With Art*, ed. Daria Martin (Oxford: Oxford University Press, 2017), 201–202.

it carries the more-than of sense. If synaesthesia is the making-felt of experience as emergent across a field of relation that is itself infrasensing, and what is activated in both Clark and Mukhopadhyay's words is the feeling-with of experience itself, these are synaesthetic experiences. This may be no surprise in relation to Mukhopadhyay, who has written extensively about his synaesthesia.[30] But it might be a surprise to consider that someone who can neither see nor hear sees-hears with the world's touching.

Listen again: 'All things living and dead cry out to me / when I touch them,' writes Clark. A hearing in a touch. 'My wife again asks me / how did I know just where and how / to caress her.' A seeing in a touch. And even more than that. A feeling toward a seeing-hearing touch, a knowing with the world in the relation. A virtual body felt and activated. In Massumi's words: 'Every "single" sense experience is the envelopment in a dominant mode of appearance of an "infinitesimal" (virtual) continuation of other-sense experiences. Every perception is a composition of the full spectrum of experience, "practically" appearing as if it were disparate and disconnected from the continuum.'[31] Synaethesia is this experience intensified.

In 'The Art of the Relational Body: From Mirror-Touch to the Virtual Body', Massumi writes: 'Synaesthetes do not add a deviation from the normal path of development.

---

[30] See Tito Mukhopadhyay. *How Can I Talk If My Lips Don't Move: Inside My Autistic Mind* (New York: Arcade Publishing, 2011). There are several passages in this book that expand on Mukhopadhyay's synaesthesia, including the description of a woman's voice 'that tasted like a tamarind pickle' (p.110) and a man's voice that 'transformed into a long apple green and yellow strings' (p. 200).

[31] Brian Massumi. 'The Art of the Relational Body', 195.

They just prune the same developmental path less fully'.[32] To understand this process philosophical approach to sensation, it is necessary to begin with the fullness of experience and to see modes of narrowing or subtraction – such as consciousness – for what they are. Consciousness, as Alfred North Whitehead states, is the 'acme of emphasis'.[33] It is the reduction from the welter of potential of what can be named, organised, categorised. But it never comes completely denuded. With all consciousness comes the tremor of what evades it, of what exceeds it. This is what I call the more-than. Synaesthesia is the more-than of sense, which is already always in excess of what can be quantified experimentally or otherwise.

The feeling-with of the world is never experienced consciously in all of its fullness. A certain parsing – or pruning, in Massumi's terms – is always necessary in order to subtract from the welter and distinguish one sensation or perception from another. This is not detrimental to experience: experience grows from the cuts that propel it in new directions. To parse is absolutely necessary. The question is, as Massumi also asks, what kind of parsing is at stake? And under what conditions? Massumi speaks in this context of 'artful perception'. 'If a perception is a composition, there is an artfulness to it'.[34] When Mukhopadhyay writes 'I may select a fraction of the environment – say, "that shadow of a chair" or "that door hinge over there" – and grow my opinions and ideas around it' he is creating artful

---

32 Brian Massumi. 'The Art of the Relational Body', 194.

33 Alfred N. Whitehead. *Adventures of Ideas* (New York: Free Press, 1967), 182.

34 Brian Massumi. 'The Art of the Relational Body', 196.

conditions for perceptual experience. The 'artful' here suggests not that Mukhopadhyay makes an artwork of perception, but that he composes with the wealth of potential in perception as he experiences it in order to extract its most lively expression. This is artfulness: the effects created through a moving-with of experience that alters the conditions of existence. Mukhopadhyay explains: 'This creates a defense system for my over-stimulated visual sense organ. Maybe poetry happens to grow around these things.' By finding artful modes of subtraction, he creates the conditions for expression, which in his case, means poetic writing. How might non-synaesthetes parse more artfully?

In Clark's *Clamor*, we also hear artfulness. 'I can be too eager to listen: The scar here on my thumb is a gift from a cracked bowl that begged to be broken.' A feeling-with the world is everywhere present, not as a frustration, but as a gift that brings to expression new ways of knowin-Cracked bowls feel their way into the urgency of a touch.

The touching evoked here is of two tonalities. It is both the touching of the hands-on feeling of the world, and the incipient touch the world calls forth. It is both the being in the world of feeling, and the feeling-with of the world emerging. In Mukhopadhyay we hear this through the personification of the oxygen, a personification which is not a making-human of the oxygen, but a more-than-human becoming-oxygen. What is heard here is the molecules struggling to counter their disappearance, the effects of this disappearance on the environment, and on those who most need it, the humans. All at once, each level of experience overlaps, the incipiency of one affecting the coming-into-actualisation of the other. If mirror-touch synaesthesia, or sight-touch synaesthesia, is about feeling-with, these are two examples of it, it seems to me, neither of which directly require either touch or vision.

Why call it mirror-touch synaesthesia, then? With Brian Massumi, I would agree that the nomenclature is deeply misleading. Building on research on mirror neurons – neurons that fire when an action is observed –[35] the problem with mirror-touch synaesthesia is that it seems incapable of imagining a world that begins with a feeling-with, a world that begins in the relational middle, in the virtual body. As such, it carries the same implied bias of much work on mirror neurons, 'that our perception is fundamentally a passive reception of an image constituting a private representation of the world, which, under normal conditions, is then cognitively corrected to purify it of illusions of perspective and other unthinking errors'.[36] In addition, the assumption that we ever perceive along single sensory routes is deeply erroneous:

> What normally pass for mono-sense experiences are, in fact, cross-modal fusions presented in a dominant sense. For example, to see the shape and texture of the object is to perceive, in vision, its potential feel in the hand. To feel that potential touch is to see the potential kinaesthetic experience of walking towards

[35] A more complete definition is as follows: 'A mirror neuron is a neuron that fires both when an animal acts and when the animal observes the same action performed by another. Thus, the neuron "mirrors" the behaviour of the other, as though the observer were itself acting'. https://en.wikipedia.org/wiki/Mirror_neuron.

[36] Brian Massumi. 'The Art of the Relational Body', 192.

> the object. [...] It is well known that object vision cannot develop without movement. [...] Every 'single' sense experience is the envelopment in a dominant mode of appearance of an 'infinitesimal' (virtual) continuation of other-sense experiences. Every perception is a composition of the full spectrum of experience, 'practically' appearing as if it were disparate and disconnected from the continuum.[37]

Senses are felt on a continuum in an amodal register. The world is felt across registers of sensation that bathe our bodies in complexity, a co-composition of world-bodying that changes the environment and the bodies composed by it at every turn.

John Lee Clark proposes the concept of distantism to counter the tendencies at the heart of these assumptions. Distantism, defined by Clark as the tendency to privilege mediation over direct perception, is what allows the neurotypical worldview to dominate, what allows the body to be parsed from its environment, and what enables a worldview that DeafBlind experience – to speak of just one discounted form of experience – is no experience at all. Whether we are speaking of the necessity to frame our academic knowledge based on objective data, or whether as DeafBlind people our engagement with the world is considered by others to be impossible without the mediation of a sighted intervenor, or whether we are expected to diminish our experience of the world as autistics by limiting our sensory experiences in order to 'pass,' or whether our black, brown or indigenous bodies are expected to be less threatening by moving to rhythms (including

---

[37] Ibid., 194.

rhythms of thought) neurotypical (and the list goes on), we are engaging in distantism.

For Clark, distantism promotes the impossibility of a DeafBlind feeling-with the world. In this limit-case of distantism, a lived experience of feeling-felt is denied. Clark writes: 'Researching our community's history, I see that we have always been tactile. But hearing and sighted people have always attempted to keep our tactilehoods in check. We've always been denied access to some of the most basic human rights. What should we call this force of suppression? I propose to call it distantism.'[38]

There is no distantism in the relational body. That is to say, distantism is not a quality of bodying: bodying is never parsable from the world with which it co-composes. 'If one brings one's perception to the edge of release and inhabits the resurgent complexity, has one acted upon experience—or released oneself to be acted upon by it?'.[39] Perception on the edge is always already with the world in its unfolding. This withness, as mentioned above, can never be articulated in its fullness, but the feeling of it remains with us nonetheless. It is this feeling that moves in the lines of Clark and Mukhopadhyay's poetry, in the rhythm of the more-than-saying their feeling-with makes felt. Distantism is not how we perceive, it is how perception is imposed on us. It is how it is framed by Empathy Quotient tests. It is how it is made intelligible by baseline beliefs about the homogeneity of experience neurotypically parsed.

---

[38] John Lee Clark. 'Distantism' https://johnleeclark.tumblr.com

[39] Brian Massumi. 'The Art of the Relational Body', 196.

This has spacetime effects. In his piece 'My Dream House: Some Thoughts on a DeafBlind Space,' Clark writes:

> Now I'm going to discuss something very particular and perhaps difficult for non-DeafBlind people to fully grasp, so bear with me as I try to explain it. You know the saying 'Out of sight, out of mind'? Well, for DeafBlind people everything that's out of sight remains in the mind's eye. We can relate to what Gauguin once said: 'I shut my eyes in order to see.' This is why DeafBlind vision is often better than eyesight—we know where everything is and see them through walls, through doors, through drawer doors, through anything in front or under or below them. They aren't hidden. The bad news is that we also see, or imagine that we see, everything that's behind the walls, under the fridge, inside the gap between the floor and the bottom of the cabinet under the sink.[40]

DeafBlind vision is topological. It is not restrained to the imposition of Cartesian perspective. Perception moves with the world, creating a lively image of its composition and altering that image, while retaining its complexity, through coming into contact with it. This account of DeafBlind spacetime is analogous to the account of the body-world continuum being put forward here. Bodies are not limited to their envelopes – they are extensive, moving-with the world in its transformation. Think of how the oxygen moves in Mukhopadhyay's account. There too, space is topological. To move with the world

[40] John Lee Clark. My Dream House: Some Thoughts on a DeafBlind Space, http://visionlossresources.org/blog/dbsm/my-dream-house-some-thoughts-on-a-deafblind-space

is to have bodied, and to have bodied is to have worlded. The world grows in the bodying.[41]

Qualities of experience overlap. There is no distance. Everything has an effect. Everything makes a difference. A body is this quality of multisense overlap in incipient contact with an infinity of sense potentials. These sense potentials are not located in a discrete sense, or in an object. They cannot be distilled to an ear or an eye, and cannot be located in a table or a marigold. They are always between, amodal, operating as thresholds of sensation that carry intensities themselves carried in the feeling. Following Lucy Blackman (see fn.64, p. 187), and her emphasis on the verb 'carrying' as a way of reminding ourselves that everything is always in movement, we might speak of feelings carrying the edge of consciousness, feelings not fully subtracted, not fully known-as-such, but nonetheless active and transformative, their effects lively, the bodying recomposed in the relation.

Massumi writes: 'A determinate experiential form origamies into relief when an actual movement cuts its patterning and orientation into the vibratory intensity of the virtual body, drawing out a determinate stand-out

[41] For a very interesting account of Deaf space with a particular focus on the dorsal, see Robert Sirvage's TEDx talk at Gallaudet entitled 'An Insight from DeafSpace' https://www.youtube.com/watch?v=EPTrOO6EYCY. In this video presentation, he described the relational movement of signing Deaf couples walking together to demonstrate that their communication includes an attention to the incipient movement all around them. This is more than simple protection (watching someone's space and making sure they are safe). This is included in the communication itself. It is at the heart of the ethos of Deaf communication.

expression of the potential it enfolds'.[42] The virtual body is the topological shape feeling takes when it moves with the world. 'The closest geometrical approximation to the hyperorder of the virtual body is not the extensive grid defined by the Cartesian coordinates. It is topological. Topology is the geometry of continuous deformation'.[43]

Bodying, always topological, is regularly projected onto Cartesian coordinates, the Cartesian coordinates in turn back-gridded onto it. If they weren't, Clark wouldn't need a Dream House and it wouldn't be necessary to continuously emphasise how the body is not limited to the form it most visibly takes. To give the body the shape of an outline is to impose distantism on the body. Having done that, the further imposition of Cartesian coordinates on the geometries in which we live and move is an easy second operation. If we are a limited spacetime, a bounded envelope, if we are already coordinated by a template that organises us, why wouldn't we create architectures that support that very kind of body schema? And in that architecture, in those worlds, wouldn't it make sense that we should restrict our sensing to the coordinates it privileges? Of course, no architecture is fully capable of organising a body, but as Clark emphasises, when you are DeafBlind, it can come close to negotiating for you the measure of your movement experience.

Clark's Dream House and Mukhopadhyay's account of the near-oxygenless mine remind us that the only people who take Cartesian coordinates and neurotypical

---

[42] Brian Massumi. 'The Art of the Relational Body', 201.

[43] Ibid., 202.

limitations for granted are those who most easily fit in the category where the senses are nicely pruned and existence is organised according to preimposed restrictions. I am not saying that DeafBlind folks are neurodiverse in the sense of neurologically divergent. Some may well be, but I wouldn't want to generalise across a heterogeneous population. What I am saying is that their lived experience of topological spacetime and the effects it has on their bodying make them squarely non-neurotypical. It is time, perhaps, to think of another term that carries the force of the non-neurotypical without including the 'neuro' as the marker of its difference. Because even autistics, who are most definitely neurodivergent, are diverse in an infinity of ways that expand from the neurological. This is why I use the adjective neurodiverse – to remind us that we need a concept for a diversity within diversity that isn't measured by the standard of typicality. A diversity in diversity is one that senses fully and differentially, that lives and participates in a world still defining itself according to measures not yet in place. It includes populations historically excluded from the matrix of the human: neurodiverse life, DeafBlind life, black life, indigenous life, feminist life, trans life. It includes modes of life-living that exceed the human, that feel the more-than human world not as other but as with.

In the mid 2000s, a group of DeafBlind activists began to invent and share a mode of communication that would allow them to take back control of their own complex fields of sensation and to collectively invent new ones. The hope, as Clark articulates it, was be to be able to move from a distantist engagement with touch to a metatactile one. He writes:

> [A] response I often get when I interact with people [is] [h]ow did I know that their shoulder needed a massage, or that they were hungry or sad, or a spot on their arm was itchy? The owners of pets I meet are also amazed. Almost immediately I've found their pets' sweet spots. 'That's right! She loves that. But how did you know?' I wasn't conscious of it. It was natural. So natural, in fact, that I didn't have a name for it, this skill that goes beyond just feeling texture, heft, shape, and temperature. I'd like to call it metatactile knowledge.[44]

This 'skill that goes beyond just feeling texture, heft, shape, and temperature' sounds a lot like the feeling-with Mukhopadhyay describes as the feeling-being of oxygen in the miners' space.[45] The becoming-oxygen of the more-than-human is the way Mukhopadhyay enters into the touching of the environment. It is how he feels-with the texture, heft, shape and temperature of that singular ecology.

A modality that moves beyond but includes the hands-on gesture of touch, metatactile knowledge is the act of reaching-toward experience, allowing all co-composing bodily senses – including the kinaesthetic, the proprioceptive, the vestibular – to connect to the incipiencies of

---

[44] John Lee Clark. 'Metatactile Knowledge'. https://johnleeclark.tumblr.com/post/130321809778/metatactile-knowledge

[45] This is also a responsibility-before, a modality of touch I discussed more thoroughly in *Politics of Touch*. Touch, in this way of living, is the emergent quality of the relation as it unfolds. This is different from a responsibility-for, which still suggests a hierarchy of interaction. I discuss this more at length in 'Waltzing the Limit,' in *Always More Than One*.

a welling environment. Encouraging the welling environment to 'grow around him,' as Mukhopadhyay might say, enables the necessary parsing while facilitating the richest possible experience of sensation, or feeling-with. I say feeling-with to foreground the Whiteheadian notion of feeling which also does its work without cognition and cannot be reduced to a human experience. 'Consciousness presupposes experience, and not experience consciousness'.[46] In a philosophy of pure feeling (as opposed to one of pure reason), the world is alive with feeling, and it is this feeling that moves through us, creating the lures that orient our experience.

When Clark speaks of the bowl asking to be touched he is resisting giving touch a primarily human inflection. To sense for him is to feel-with in the Whiteheadian manner, to be in experience, affected by it. This is metatactile sensing, to connect to the quality of an encounter as much as to the actual shape of the surface with which one comes into contact, to feel *with* the encounter, coming into contact with the complexity of relations the encounter calls forth.

Clark suggests that metatactile knowledge is a 'protactile' mode of touch. The ProTactile movement celebrates the metatactile: it honours all kinds of tactility, including, I would hazard, the shaping of experience through the force of the relational, or virtual body. Foregrounding the importance for communication of a direct perception of relation, ProTactile encourages DeafBlind people and anyone who communicates with them to engage

[46] Alfred N. Whitehead. *Process and Reality* (New York: Macmillan, 1985), 53.

in continuous physical touch. This continued contact, they argue, allows them to finally become autonomous in their communication by being more attuned to the nuances of the nonlinguistic aspects of communication. Bringing out the full potential of TASL [Tactile American Sign Language], and allowing, as becomes necessary, for TASL to depart from the habits of VASL [Visual American Sign Language], which remains the mother tongue of many in the DeafBlind community, ProTactile is as much a linguistic as a cultural movement. Claiming experience according to their own complex registers of sense, ProTactile teachers and students emphasise that it's high time for the DeafBlind to be teaching the DeafBlind.[47] As Christine Roschaert describes it, ProTactile 'broadens the spectrum of communication of the Deafblind outside of the standard Tactile with (American or any other international) Sign Language and several other manual methods.'[48]

ProTactile does not limit itself to a set of preexisting coordinates. It is not a system of gestures or touches. It is not a grid that can be used generally across myriad situations: 'we want to emphasize that PT is not a set list of symbols with associated meanings, like "touch signals"', Jelica Nuccio, the founder of ProTactile explains. ProTactile is a linguistic-cultural paradigm, and an ethos. 'ProTactile

---

[47] John Lee Clark writes: 'There are distantist modes of touch and there are protactile modes of touch. A distantist cannot truly teach or empower our children to live and learn as tactile people. Yet the field of education of DeafBlind children has never included us as teachers. Why is that?' https://johnleeclark.tumblr.com

[48] Christine Roschaert. Tactile the World (blog), https://tactilethe world.wordpress.com, 2013.

philosophy is not just about "accessing" communication; it affects all areas of life, including DeafBlind culture, politics, empowerment and language.'[49] Based on the strong belief, also prevalent in the Deaf community, that separating language and culture is an impossibility, ProTactile brings into action tendencies of listening and speaking that best address the singularity of DeafBlind experience. A mode of encounter grown from within the culture, ProTactile is a call for the DeafBlind community to reject distantism and embrace the incipiency of feeling of a touch that reaches toward experience in the making.

Jelica Nuccio and AJ Granda describe the ethos of ProTactile this way: 'The purpose of ProTactile philosophy is to support DeafBlind culture, language, interpersonal relationships, [and] politics.'[50] While touch has always played an important role in DeafBlind culture, and much communication already moves through touch,[51] the modality of touch foregrounded through intervenors tends toward distantism: 'We can see in the record how distantism set in, and how hearing and sighted people wanted things to look right. It didn't look good when we went around "groping in the dark." It didn't look good for

---

[49] Jelica Nuccio and A.J. Granda. Welcome to Protactile: The DeafBlind Way (vlog #5). protactile.org, March 2016.

[50] Ibid.

[51] For an account of ProTactile from an ethnographic perspective, see Terra Edwards, 'Bridging the Gap Between DeafBlind Minds: Interactional and Social Foundations of Intention Attribution in the Seattle DeafBlind Community', *Frontiers in Psychology* 6 (2017) DOI: https://doi.org/10.3389/fpsyg.2015.01497. On Touch Signals, Haptic Communication and Back Channeling, see https://nationaldb.org/library/page/2588. See also https://www.facebook.com/ntfdbi/posts/841440079290709

us to cluster together and have too much fun. Education meant we had to sit behind a desk.'[52] With the intervenor, the practice is to create a communicational model that mediates touch. Touch is necessary, it is understood, but only at certain stages of the (mediated) encounter. 'But when we go exploring or when we just exist, sighted and hearing people rush in to intervene. Can they help us? Please don't touch. They will be happy to describe it to us. They will guide us. No, they will get it for us. It's much easier that way. Hello! My name is Katie and I'm your Intervenor!'[53]

For someone outside the DeafBlind community who cannot understand sign language, a proTactile video provides little to no information-as-content. I cannot understand the details of what is being said. What I can perceive, however, is the force of relation: bodies are actively listening and composing together. The conversation has a shape, and that shape feels dynamic. A vitality affect is felt in the watching. Communication has clearly taken on an emergent quality, activating the virtual body of sensation in the encounter.

Vitality affects, as described by Daniel Stern, are emergent attunements felt in the relation. Stern speaks of an overlap of movement, time, force, space and intention/directionality as being at the heart of all vitality affects, or what he also calls vitality 'forms'.[54] These five elements

---

[52] John Lee Clark. https://johnleeclark.tumblr.com

[53] Ibid.

[54] Daniel N. Stern. *Forms of Vitality: Exploring Dynamic Experience in Psychology, the Arts, Psychotherapy, and Development* (Oxford: Oxford University Press, 2010), 4.

must not be seen to work in isolation. Together they form a Gestalt, and that Gestalt has affective tone. Describing vitality affects, Stern speaks of:

> the force, speed, and flow of a gesture; the timing and stress of a spoken phrase or even a word; the way one breaks into a smile or the time course of decomposing the smile; the manner of shifting position in a chair; the time course of lifting the eyebrows when interested and the duration of their lift; the shift and flight of a gaze; and the rush or tumble of thoughts. These are examples of the dynamic forms and dynamic experiences of everyday life. The scale is small, but that is where we live, and it makes up the matrix of experiencing other people and feeling their vitality.[55]

Vitality affects are:

> the felt experience of force – in movement – with a temporal contour, and a sense of aliveness, of going somewhere. They do not belong to any particular content. They are more form than content. They concern the 'How,' the manner, and the style, not the 'What' or the 'Why'.[56]

ProTactile is a recognition that DeafBlind communication carries its own singular vitality affect, and that this needs to be valued. One aspect of this singularity is the emphasis on movement. Without sight and hearing to facilitate connection to the world, DeafBlind people have to connect more deeply to their kinesthetic and vestibular senses. They do this by doing what we all do: they move.

---

55 Ibid., 6.
56 Ibid., 8.

In a description of ProTactile communication in process, Clark emphasises the role movement plays. In *Where I Stand*, he writes:

> As a DeafBlind person, standing for me is almost never about being still or in one place. Waiting for a bus, I would move without realizing it. My way of standing by moving around gives me more information about where I am. I'm taking in the scene, being present in the world, and prodding things a bit, exploring. And when two DeafBlind people talk to each other while standing, they always move around so that, after a while, they're standing where the other person was. Later on, they'd be back to their former positions, having circled around each other. This phenomenon is the result of each person shifting to the left to listen to the other person tactilely in a more comfortable way, hand following hand at a certain angle. I would always find myself emerging from an engrossing conversation standing in a different place.[57]

Movement gives experience shape. Speaking about the primacy of movement in experience, Stern writes:

> [D]ynamic changes [...] occur constantly. Our respirations rise and fall over a cycle that repeats every three or four seconds. Our bodies are in almost constant motion: we move our mouth, twitch, touch our face, make small adjustments in head position and orientation, alter our facial expression, shift the direction of our gaze, adjust the muscular tone of our body position, whether standing, sitting, or lying (if awake). These processes go on even when not visible

[57] John Lee Clark. *Where I Stand: On the Signing Community and My DeafBlind Experience* (Minneapolis: Handtype Press, 2014) Kindle Edition. Loc. 116-120.

> from the outside. Gestures and larger acts unfold in time. They change fluidly once an act has started. We can be conscious of any of this, or it can remain in peripheral awareness. In addition, with every movement there is proprioception, conscious or not.[58]

How to well the chaos? 'How do we not implode into the intensity, lost in the infinite virtual folds of potential experience?', Massumi asks. His answer: 'through movement. Every movement makes a cut—it brings certain elements of experience into relief, origamiing the continuum on the fly'.[59] Movement is primary: it is through movement that incipient sensation catches the world's tendencies and moves into them, altering them in the passage.

Making movement primary by itself shatters distantism, for distantism requires position. It requires pre-choreographed placeholders that have already been given value, that have already been signalled as worthy of attention. This is why distantism is so central to the template of neurotypicality: it allows the value of experience to be mapped in advance. And this is why neurodiverse experience is so threatening: because it makes felt what would otherwise remain backgrounded, and gives it value, thereby reinventing the very concept of value. New ways of living proliferate, and with them come new ways of knowing.

Movement is everywhere in the literature on ProTactile, itself called a movement. For too long, DeafBlind communication tended to be watered down to the most

---

[58] Daniel N. Stern. *Forms of Vitality*, 9.

[59] Brian Massumi. 'The Art of the Relational Body', 199.

atrophied of communicational models: third party interpretation. Not only was this slow, it lost the quality of the vitality affect of the communicational swarm in the stagnancy of the ordered back-and-forth. Little could be shared in the making. This mode of communication was closer to reporting than conversation. With ProTactile comes a liveliness in communication that allows the vitality affect of the conversation to be felt by all. This results in 'a true sense of empowerment' (Granda).[60] As Nuccio says: 'Deafhood[61] involves so many things – ASL, culture, who you are, your identity – that is exactly what PT is.'[62] This is not to say that facilitators are never necessary: 'I am not saying that we don't need sighted assistants. After all, we do live in a distantist society, and we should avail ourselves of distance-information readers. However, the way our SSP services are performed can be smothering. That's why a key concern of the Protactile movement is autonomy.'[63] When intervenors become ProTactile, they shift from mediators to facilitators, facilitators here understood in the sense given to them by autistics such as

---

[60] Jelica Nuccio and A.J. Granda. Welcome to Protactile, 2016.

[61] On the Deafhood foundation website (www.deafhood.org), Deafhood is defined in the following way: Deafhood 'is a way of gathering together and framing what we already know of Deaf culture, life, politics, etc. The framing process itself reveals ways in which we can move 'beyond' present Deaf cultural limitations resulting from the colonialism of Sign Language Peoples (SLP).' The concept was developed by Paddy Ladd in 1993.

[62] Jelica Nuccio and aj granda. Welcome to Protactile: The DeafBlind Way (vlog #3). protactile.org, March 2016.

[63] John Lee Clark https://johnleeclark.tumblr.com

Lucy Blackman,[64] who emphasises that communication is relational at its core. Facilitation is important in all life situations, not to mediate experience but to co-compose techniques that move beyond the insistence, in our neoliberal economy, on individuality-above-all. Metatactility, after all, is a collective action, an aliveness with the world that acknowledges the interpenetrating registers of experience.

Metatactile modes of touching put the dynamic shape back into DeafBlind communication: they make the vitality of the exchange felt to all who participate. This shape is continuously composing itself, as is the case in all communication. Reinventing what it might mean to communicate is key to this practice, and this includes communication with the more-than, engagement with what else the world carries, and what else a body-world relation can be.

There is much to learn from ProTactile's engagement with touch as an ethos that troubles distantism. The neurotypical template moves at the pace of distantism, opting for mediation at every turn. Working with a pre-existing matrix, it organises, categorises, prioritises, grids, excludes. Justifying forms of knowledge acquisition, modes of self-presentation, moral categories, it shapes the contours of education. It also organises the vocabulary of sensation, of perception, of experience. When Suzi Guimond writes – 'the world of deaf-blindness is far from a dead one. The world is constantly full of vibrations and smells

---

[64] See Lucy Blackman, *Carrying Autism, Feeling Language* (Self-published, 2013).

and changes in temperature and air pressure. Many people seem to believe that without ears and eyes, the world becomes unmoving and still, but this couldn't be farther from the truth' – she is speaking about a value-system predicated on neurotypical understandings of sensation. She is underscoring the ways in which the categorising of experience in advance through neurotypical codes limits our capacity to imagine experience beyond the spatiality of distantism. Organising bodies by limiting the wealth of sensation fosters a systematic account of experience that supports the kind of classification that marks many of us as less-than human and keeps us from receiving (or inventing) the opportunities we need to thrive.

ProTactile *immediates* experience.[65] Moving-with experience in the making, the intervenor-as-mediator no longer has a role to play. Experience is lived, from the edges in. 'The formative relation of co-implication in the same event is the changing ground of experience. If the virtual body can be said to represent anything, it is this relationality of the life of the body' (Massumi 2017: 204). ProTactile is a reaching-toward the world that makes felt how the world is already poised to meet the encounter, the relational body of communication alive with the force of the touch that will give it dynamic shape. For what occurs in the encounter of emergent communication can never be reduced to two enclosed, pre-constituted selves, one active, one passive. Nor is the encounter only human. Or only interactive. 'Society is not companionship or

[65] For a sustained encounter with the concept of immediation, see Erin Manning et al. series *Immediations* (Open Humanities Press).

friendly association with others; it's companionship or friendly association without others, in the absence of the other, in the exhaustion of relational individuality, in consent not to be a single being'. The 'consent not to be a single being', in Édouard Glissant's resonant words (in Moten 2016),[66] is a call to a synaesthesia that honours the more-than of sense that includes the force of metatactility and vibrates with worlds verging toward consciousness. Not distantist, but not proximist either. In the field of minor sociality where relational bodies compose with the force of the incipiency of a touching beyond touch, ProTactile proposes a reaching-toward that touches experience in the making.

References

Aspiegrrl. 'Autism and Angels'. Available at: https://aspiegrrl.wordpress.com/tag/sensory-integration-disorder (14 December 2011).

Baron-Cohen, Simon et al. 'Savant Memory in a Man with Colour Form-Number Synaesthesia and Asperger Syndrome'. *Journal of Consciousness Studies* 14, nos.9–10 (2007): 237–51.

Baron-Cohen, Simon et al. 'Mirror-Touch Synaesthesia is Not Associated with Heightened Empathy, and Can Occur with Autism'. PLoS ONE 11(8) (2016): e0160543. DOI: https://doi.org/10.1371/journal.pone.0160543.

Blackman, Lucy. *Carrying Autism, Feeling Language*. Self-published, 2013.

Buxton, Liz. 'Experience: I See Words as Colours'. *The Guardian*, 19 August 2016. https://www.theguardian.com/lifeandstyle/2016/aug/19/experience-i-see-words-as-colours

[66] Fred Moten. Bobby Lee's Hands. Organise Your Own (blog), 5 December 2016. https://organizeyourown.wordpress.com

Cioffi, Maria C., James W. Moore and Michael J. Banissy. 'What Can Mirror-Touch Synaesthesia Tell us about the Sense of Agency'. *Frontiers in Human Neuroscience* 8 (2014): 256 DOI: https://doi.org/10.3389/fnhum.2014.00256.

Clark, John Lee. *Where I Stand: On the Signing Community and My DeafBlind Experience.* Minneapolis: Handtype Press, 2014.

Clark, John Lee. 'Distantism', Notes from a DeafBlind Writer, 2017. https://johnleeclark.tumblr.com/post/163762970913/distantism

Halberstadt, Amy G. et al. 'Preservice Teachers' Racialized Emotion Recognition, Anger Bias, and Hostility Attributions'. *Contemporary Educational Psychology* 54 (2018): 125–138.

Jewanski, Jörg, Sean A. Day, and Jamie Ward. 'A Colorful Albino: The First Documented Case of Synaesthesia, by Georg Tobias Ludwig Sachs in 1812'. *Journal of the History of the Neurosciences* 18(3) (2009): 293-303. DOI: https://doi.org/10.1080/09647040802431946

Maister, Lare, Michael J. Banissy, and Manos Tsakiris. 'Mirror-touch Synaesthesia Changes Representations of Self-identity'. *Neuropsychologia* 51, no.5 (2013): 802–808.

Manning, Erin. *Politics of Touch: Sense, Movement, Sovereignty.* Minneapolis, MN: University of Minnesota Press, 2007.

Manning, Erin. *Always More Than One: Individuation's Dance.* Durham, NC: Duke University Press, 2013.

Manning, Erin and Brian Massumi. *Thought in the Act: Passages in the Ecology of Experience.* Minneapolis, MN: Minnesota University Press, 2014.

Massumi, Brian. 'The Art of the Relational Body: From Mirror-Touch to the Virtual Body'. In *Mirror-Touch: Thresholds of Empathy with Art*, edited by Daria Martin. Oxford: Oxford University Press, 2017.

Massumi, Brian. 'The Thinking-Feeling of What Happens'. *Inflexions: A Journal for Research-Creation* 1 (2008). http://inflexions.org/n1_The-Thinking-Feeling-of-What-Happens-by-Brian-Massumi.pdf

Maurer, Daphne and Catherine J. Mondloch. 'Neonatal Synesthesia: A Reevaluation'. In *The World of Newborn*, edited by Daphne Maurer and Charles Maurer. New York: Basic Books, 1988.

Moten, Fred. Bobby Lee's Hands. Organise Your Own (blog), 5 December 2016. https://organizeyourown.wordpress.com/2016/12/05/bobby-lees-hands-by-fred-moten/

Mottron, Laurent et al. 'Veridical Mapping in the Development of Exceptional Autistic Abilities'. *Neuroscience & Biobehavioral Reviews* 37, no.2 (2013): 209–228.

Mottron, Laurent et al. 'Enhanced Perceptual Functioning in Autism: An Update and Eight Principles of Autistic Perception'. *Journal of Autism and Developmental Disorders* 36, no.1 (2006): 27–43.

Mukhopadhyay, Tito. *How Can I Talk If My Lips Don't Move: Inside My Autistic Mind*. New York: Arcade Publishing, 2011.

Mukhopadhyay, Tito. *The Mind Tree: A Miraculous Child Breaks the Silence of Autism*. New York: Riverhead Books, 2007.

Nuccio, Jelica and aj granda. Welcome to Protactile: The DeafBlind Way (vlog #3). protactile.org, 2016. http://www.protactile.org/2016/03/pro-tactile-vlog-3.html

Nuccio, Jelica and aj granda. Welcome to Protactile: The DeafBlind Way (vlog #5), 2016. http://www.protactile.org/2016/03/pro-tactile-vlog-5_14.html

Roschaert, Christine. Pro-Tactile: The DeafBlind Way!!! Tactile the World (blog) 2013. https://tactiletheworld.wordpress.com/2013/02/18/pro-tactile-the-deafblind-way/

Savarese, David J. 'Passive Plants'. *The Iowa Review* 47(1) (2017). https://iowareview.org/from-the-issue/volume-47-issue-1-spring-2017/passive-plants.

Savarese, Ralph. 'Toward a Postcolonial Neurology: Autism, Tito Mukhopadhyay, and a New Geo-Poetics of the Body'. *Journal of Literary and Cultural Disability Studies* 4, no.3 (2010): 273–289.

Savarese, Ralph. 'More Than a Thing to Ignore: An Interview with Tito Rajarshi Mukhopadhyay'. *Disability Studies Quarterly* 30, no.1 (2010). DOI: https://doi.org/10.18061/dsq.v30i1.1056.

Savarese, Ralph. *See It Feelingly: Classic Novels, Autistic Readers and the Schooling of a No-Good English Professor*. Durham: Duke University Press, 2018.

Savarese, Ralph. 'Reading Fiction with Temple Grandin: Yes, people with autism can understand literature'. *Salon*, 2 September 2018. https://www.salon.com/2018/09/02/reading-fiction-with-temple-grandin-yes-autistic-people-can-understand-literature/

Stern, Daniel N. *Forms of Vitality: Exploring Dynamic Experience in Psychology, the Arts, Psychotherapy, and Development*. Oxford: Oxford University Press, 2010.

Whitehead, Alfred N. *Adventures of Ideas*. New York: Free Press, 1967.

Whitehead, Alfred N. *Process and Reality*. New York: Macmillan, 1985.

Wynter, Sylvia. 'No Humans Involved, An Open Letter to my Colleagues'. *Forum N. H. I.: Knowledge for the 21st Century* (*Knowledge on Trial*) 1, no.1 (1994).

Yergeau, Melanie. *Authoring Autism: On Rhetoric and Neurological Queerness*. Durham: Duke University Press, 2017.

The Illicit Touch: Theorising Narratives of Abused Human Skin

Nicole Nyffenegger

Skin is the largest sensory organ of the human body. It touches the world around it and it feels the world touching back. The outside world's touch is often non-directed, allowing the recipients to subjectively evaluate the ensuing sensations, such as, for example, those caused by a brush of the lift doors. Directed touch, in contrast, objectifies the recipients. A loving touch makes them objects of adoration; a hateful touch makes them objects of disdain. The objectification is taken to extremes with the specific kind of directed touch that is at the centre of my project here. It is the one that violates the boundaries of what a given society considers to be morally, ethically or legally right: an illicit touch. When perpetrators touch human skin in such a way, they counteract norms in order to lay claim to the lived bodies of individuals.

Their boundary-transgressing touch marks those individuals as weak, inferior, subhuman. An exploration of such illicit touch, however, shows that 'what is right' is relative and unstable as ever. To those who touch illicitly, there is always their own right, their own justification for doing so. It is construed as emerging naturally from their race, their gender or their social status. In denial of the fluidity that enabled its very nascence, this right is even conceived as stable enough to be documented on the skins of the victims, in the form of visible and (or so the perpetrators like to think) permanent marks. However, these marks, the traces of the illicit touch, are anything but permanent and are instead met by counter-inscriptions and narrative appropriations that once again shift and reframe 'what is right'. The narratives of abused and marked skins in which our culture abounds, I argue here, are key to understanding the manifold valences of touch in connection with norms, normativity and law.

I start from two 'boxes' into which I gather such narratives. One box is about books that are bound in human skin instead of animal-derived leather, the other box is concerns Auschwitz number tattoos. In the first case, individual bookbinders crossed the boundaries of what twenty-first century European and American societies (and probably the bookbinders' contemporaries, whose responses we lack) consider to be right. This becomes evident in the shared abjection of those who narratively engage with such books. In the second case, a regime purposely crossed those same boundaries in order to objectify and dehumanise its victims. But the victims, their descendants, and generations of writers have narratively challenged the perpetrators' supposed right to do so. By telling their own stories about the marks it left on the victims' skins, they have reframed the Nazi regime's illicit touch as such. The narratives in the two boxes stem from autobiographical accounts, fiction, film, news reports, blog posts and court documentation. I happily allow myself to abandon the stance of academic detachment inside the boxes, adding my own narratives of encounters with abused skin to the others. There can be no aiming at completeness, neither inside nor outside the boxes, where I propose a number of theoretical entry points for discussing those narratives. Both my selections of those entry points and of the narratives are but fragments towards a theory of the ways in which skin, touch and law connect.

Box I: Books Bound in Human Skin

Sometime around 1900, medical doctor and bibliophile Ludovic Bouland of Strasbourg (1839-1932) apparently thought he had every right and a good reason to bind a small book in his private collection in human skin. On this winter morning in 2012, as I inspect the volume that is now *Closed Stores EPB Bindings 14* of the Wellcome Library in London, the white cotton gloves available in the rare materials reading room seem to me to acquire an additional function. Usually meant to protect a delicate object from the touch of its readers, they now protect me from feeling the book's unusual binding. Without the gloves, I would be forced to perform an illicit touch, mimicking Bouland's boundary-transgressing objectification of this specific piece of human skin. I wonder about the unceremonious way in which the librarian has just handed me the small brown box: does she even know what this is? What about the other three readers in the room: how would they react if I now told them what this is? And what about myself? Inadvertently, I find myself taking notes not about the object in front of me but about my reaction to it.

Michelle Lovric fictionalises her encounter with the same volume in her novel *Book of Human Skin.*[1] In her 'Historical Notes,' she explains that narrator Gianni Boccole's reactions to finding a book bound in human skin in his master's collection are based on her own reactions when examining the volume at the Wellcome Library. The servant Gianni, clumsy in his language and manners but not in his emotions, expresses his horror as follows: 'In what way was I fit to touch sich a thing? In what way was I fit to touch anyone else, now that I had toucht that filthy thing? Is anyone insent what touches a book of humane leather?'[2] In contrast to Gianni and Lovric, I am not particularly disgusted by the human leather. On the contrary, I am irritated to find that the book looks, feels, smells and sounds just like the many leather-bound books I have touched before, all of which, of course, were bound in the processed skin of dead animals. It makes me wonder whether Gianni's question should be rephrased: 'Is anyone innocent that touches a book of leather?' Is not our own seemingly innocent touch of any leather-bound book part and parcel of the ongoing carnage of our fellow creatures? How have we human animals come to think of our skins as different while, when it comes down to it, our skins are tangible proof of our own animality?

---

1 Michelle Lovric. *The Book of Human Skin* (London: Bloomsbury, 2010).

2 Ibid., 146.

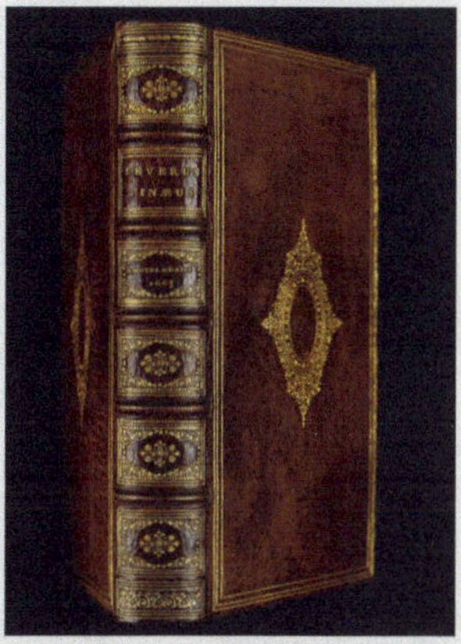

Figure 1A. *Closed Stores EPB Bindings 14.* 'S. Pinaeus, De integritatis et corruptionis virginum...' Credit: Wellcome Collection.

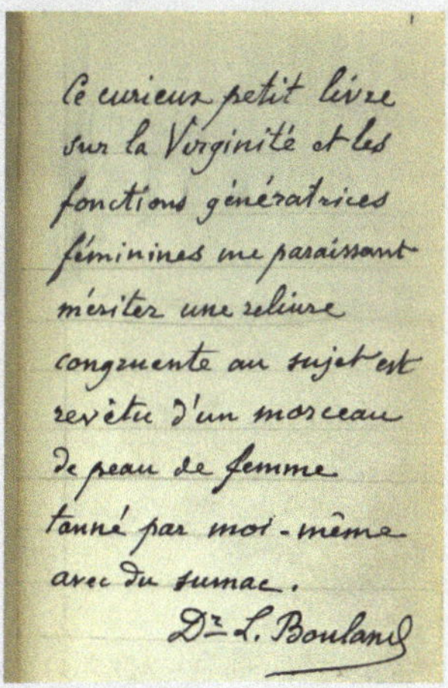

Ce curieux petit livre
sur la Virginité et les
fonctions génératrices
féminines me paraissant
mériter une reliure
congruente au sujet est
revêtu d'un morceau
de peau de femme
tanné par moi-même
avec du sumac.
Dr L. Bouland

Figure 1B. Bouland's note in *Closed Stores EPB Bindings 14.* 'S. Pinaeus, De integritatis et corruptionis virginum...' Credit: Wellcome Collection.

What does disgust me is the handwritten note that Bouland rather irreverently glued into the then 250 years old volume to explain that he found the book an appropriate binding consisting of a piece of female skin tanned by himself.[3] The hand is a quick and sloppy one, the piece of paper not cut specifically to fit the size of the book's printed pages.[4] The note reads: 'This curious little book on the Virginity and the female generative functions seemed to me to merit a binding congruent to the subject is [sic] bound in a piece of woman's skin tanned by myself with sumac. Dr L. Bouland.'[5]

There is a striking incongruity between Bouland's objectification of the woman's skin, the skin's removal, tanning and use as bookbinding, and the jovial tone he adopts in reporting it. To refer to the volume as 'this curious little book' belittles both it and the transgressive nature of its production. To focus on the specific technique of tanning suggests that this is no more than a harmless little experiment. The academic title in front of Bouland's signature presents him as the medical doctor in the exclusive position of obtaining

[3] Annabel Geddes, founder of the London Dungeon, bought the book as a possible exhibit in 1979; the Wellcome Trust acquired it from her in 2001. John Symons, 'Ce Curieux Petit Livre', Wellcome Trust *News and Features*, 2001.

[4] Michelle Lovric comments in a personal communication that she was also 'offended by Bouland choosing such cheerful carnival coloured marbling for his endpapers'.

[5] *'Ce curieux petit livre sur la Virginité et les fonctions génératrices féminines me paraissont mériter une reliure congruente au sujet est [sic] revêtu d'un morceau de peau de femme tanné par moi-même avec du sumac. Dr. L. Bouland'*, my translation.

human skin for his bibliophile interests.[6] Apparently, Bouland's social and professional standing enabled him to think of his illicit touch as a justified one.

Together with the book's human-skin binding and the note, the contents of the volume bring to the fore a number of farther-reaching gender issues. Printed in Amsterdam in 1663, the book contains five medical treatises on virginity, female diseases, pregnancy and childbirth dating from the sixteenth and seventeenth centuries.[7] The five treatises were all written by men and in Latin. Latin was upheld as the exclusive language of the male-dominated medical profession, thus effectively barring most women from access to medical book-knowledge about their own bodies. Men controlled that knowledge and, by extension, women's bodies. This may well be why, 250 years later, Bouland's obvious choice for his anthropodermic bibliopegy was a woman's rather than a man's skin. Bouland's note throws these connections of medicine and gender into sharp relief: a male medical doctor with a name and a title obtains the skin of an unnamed woman. Bouland's irreverence and the fact that this woman's skin was available to medical students for experiments clearly outside the medical curriculum sug-

---

[6] Paul Combes in 1910 relates that he personally saw the book and learnt that Bouland had acquired the skin during his medical studies in France. Paul Combes. 'Peau Humaine Tannée', *Intérmediaire des chercheurs et curieux* LXII, 30 October 1910. gallica.bnf.fr/ark:/12148/bpt6k73420v/f337.image, 661–662.

[7] Séverin Pineau. *De integritatis & corruptionis virginum notis: graviditate item & partu naturali mulierum, opuscula*; Luigi Bonacciuoli. *Enneas muliebris*; Felix Platter. *De origine partium, earumque in utero conformatione*; Pierre Gassendi. *De septo cordis pervio, observatio*; Melchioris Sebizii. *De notis virginitatis.*

gest that her body was an unclaimed one, that she was probably a woman on her own and of low social status. In clear contrast stands the social and professional status of the medical doctor that was almost exclusively accessible to men. Such a gender-based power structure is symptomatic of a patriarchal society, in which the female body is always already inscribed by its cultural construction.[8]

Have you seen this? Another one! – a short, hurried email from a friend on 6 June 2014 with a link to the latest news: 'Harvard University book bound in human skin.' 'Reader warning: Harvard experts say book is bound in human skin.'[9] Heather Cole had just published the findings of Harvard conservators in a Houghton Library blog. Having ruled out the possibility that the binding was primate skin from great apes or gibbons, she reported, 'they are 99% confident that the binding is of human origin.'[10] CNN

8 See e.g., Susan Bordo. *The Unbearable Weight: Feminism, Western Culture, and the Body* (Oakland: University of California Press, 2003), 41. Also: Judith Butler. 'Foucault and the Paradox of Bodily Inscriptions', *The Journal of Philosophy* 86, no. 11 (1989): 601–607; Judith Butler. *Gender Trouble: Feminism and the Subversion of Identity* (New York: Routledge, 1990); Elizabeth Grosz. 'Inscriptions and Body-Maps: Representations and the Corporeal', in *Feminine, Masculine and Representation*, ed. Anne Cranny-Francis and Terry Threadgold (Sydney: Allen and Unwin, 1990).

9 'Harvard University Book Bound in Human Skin', *BBC News*, 5 June 2014, accessed 1 March 2018, http://www.bbc.com/news/world-us-canada-27721571; Jethro Mullen. 'Reader Warning: Harvard Experts Say Book is Bound with Human Skin', *CNN*, 5 June 2014, accessed 1 March 2018, http://edition.cnn.com/2014/06/05/us/harvard-book-human-skin/index.html.

10 Heather Cole. 'The Science of Anthropodermic Binding', *Houghton Library Blog*, 4 June 2014, accessed 6 April 2018, http://blogs.law.harvard.edu/houghton/2014/06/04/caveat-lecter/, n.p.

headed their online report with the trigger warning 'It's reading matter not for the faint of heart.' The headlines, as well as my friend's email, prove that to US Americans and Western Europeans in 2014, a human-skin book-binding was clearly far away from what they considered to be right. However, many of the reports followed Cole's suggestion that the book 'serves as a reminder that such practices were at one time considered acceptable.'[11] Quite to the contrary, the Harvard volume shows the opposite: I was both shocked and somehow relieved to realise that none other than Ludovic Bouland was the binder of the Harvard volume, too.

Figure 2A. *Des destinées de l'ame.* FC8.H8177.879dc, Houghton Library, Harvard University. Credit: Houghton Library Blog.

[11] Ibid., n.p.

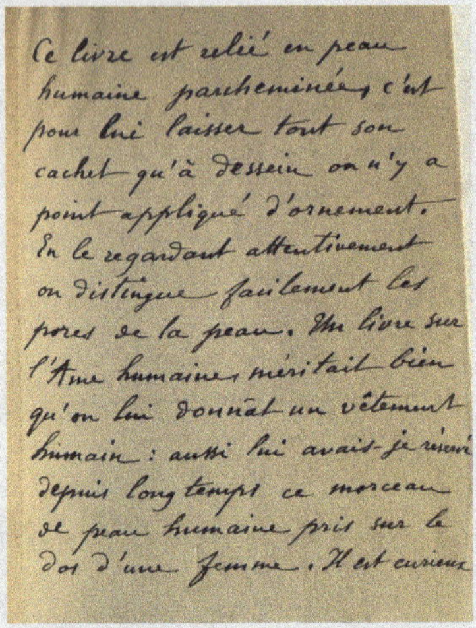
Ce livre est relié en peau
humaine parcheminée, c'est
pour lui laisser tout son
cachet qu'à dessein on n'y a
point appliqué d'ornement.
En le regardant attentivement
on distingue facilement les
pores de la peau. Un livre sur
l'Ame humaine méritait bien
qu'on lui donnât un vêtement
humain : aussi lui avais-je réservé
depuis longtemps ce morceau
de peau humaine pris sur le
dos d'une femme. Il est curieux

Figure 2B. Bouland's note in Des *destinées de l'ame* (front). FC8. H8177.879dc, Houghton Library, Harvard University. Credit: Houghton Library Blog.

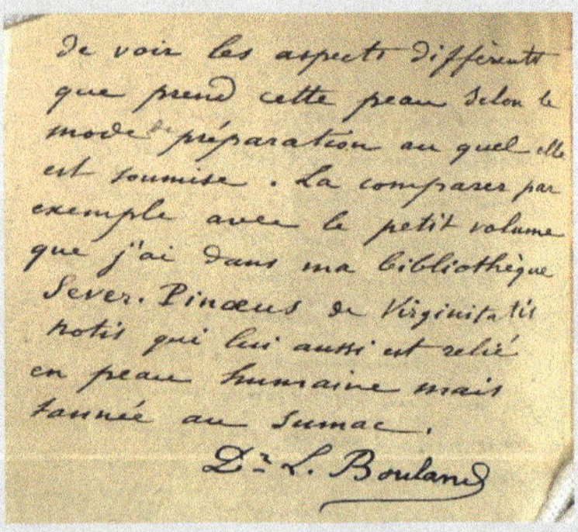
de voir les aspects différents
que prend cette peau selon le
mode de préparation auquel elle
est soumise. La comparer par
exemple avec le petit volume
que j'ai dans ma bibliothèque
Sever. Pinaeus de Virginitatis
notis qui lui aussi est relié
en peau humaine mais
tannée au Sumac.
Dr L. Bouland

Figure 2C. Bouland's note in *Des destinées de l'ame* (back). FC8. H8177.879dc, Houghton Library, Harvard University. Credit: Houghton Library Blog.

Author Arsène Houssaye had personally given this copy of his *Des destinées de l'ame* to Bouland, who thought that this book on the soul, too, 'deserved to have a human clothing'. In addition, he points out, he had reserved this specific piece of skin 'taken from a woman's back' for a long time.[12] A memorandum inserted by J. B. Stetson states that the skin was taken from the unclaimed body of a woman who died of a stroke in a French mental hospital.[13] The tag 'mental hospital', when I first read it, provided a split-second of relief, followed swiftly by the shock of realising that I had just dehumanised the unnamed woman due to her status as mentally 'abnormal'. I am myself guilty of shifting the boundaries of 'what is right'. So is Bouland. His note in this volume looks familiar: the hand is sloppy, the tone jovial, and again, he is more concerned with the differing effects of diverse tanning processes (he references today's Wellcome volume for comparison) than with his endeavour possibly violating any boundaries.[14]

Two of the very few books that are proven to be bound in human skin (while other claims have recently been

[12] '*Un livre sur l'Ame humaine méritait bien qu'on lui donnait un vêtement humain: aussi lui avais-je réservé depuis longtemps ce morceau de peau humaine pris sur le dos d'une femme*'. My translation.

[13] Object description in the Harvard library catalogue, http://id.lib.harvard.edu/aleph/005786452/catalog (accessed 23 April 2018).

[14] 'It is interesting to see the different appearances this skin takes depending on the method of preparation it is submitted to. Compare it for example with the little volume I have in my library, Sever. Pinaeus de Virginitates notis which is also bound in human skin but tanned with sumac' – '*Il est curieux de voir les aspects différents que prend cette peau selon le mode de preparation au quelle elle est soumise. La comparer par example avec le petit volume que j'ai dans ma bibliothèque, Sever. Pinaeus de Virginitates notis qui lue aussi est relié en peau humaine mais tannée au sumac*', my translation.

refuted[15]) were bound by the same person. This problematises Cole's claim that human-skin bookbinding was 'at one time considered acceptable'.[16] If at all, such a claim is only tenable with additional explanations of the kind I have tried to provide here, namely that the acceptability of anthropodermic bibliopegy greatly depends on whose touch objectifies whose skin. Bouland's gender and status, weighed against the inferior gender and status of the unnamed women, seem to have given him enough justification. The fact that many news reports included the information about the unclaimed female body from the mental hospital without tracing it back to its source – Cole does not refer to the relevant library catalogue entry in her blog post[17] – suggests that such a provenance seems not only likely in accordance with feminist criticism but that it also has the potential to relativise the illicit touch to

---

15 Connor provides an overview of older findings, including potentially fictional ones. Steven Connor. *The Book of Skin* (London: Reaktion, 2004), 42–46. Several books that were long believed to be bound in human skin have in recent years been proven to have animal-leather bindings. Gerald Chaudron. '"It's Not Human!" Another Example of Anthropodermic Bibliopegy Discredited', *RBM: A Journal of Rare Books, Manuscripts, and Cultural Heritage*, 18, no. 1 (2017): 26–36, accessed 3 April 2018, DOI: https://doi.org/10.5860/rbm.18.1.26; Karen Beck. '852 RARE: Old Books, New Technologies, and "The Human Skin Book" at HLS', *Et Seq: The Blog of the Harvard Law School Library*, 3 April 2014, accessed 1 March 2018, http://etseq.law.harvard.edu/2014/04/852-rare-old-books-new-technologies-and-the-human-skin-book-at-hls/.

16 Cole, 'Science of Anthropodermic Binding', n.p.

17 Heather Cole. 'Bound in Human Skin', *Houghton Library Blog*, 24 May 2013, accessed 6 April 2018, http://blogs.harvard.edu/houghton/2013/05/24/bound-in-human-skin/.

some extent, because it allows a conceptualisation of the woman as not fully human.[18]

The same mechanisms are at work with a number of other books proven or alleged to be bound in human skin, because the skin used is that of executed criminals. To make use of that skin is but a consistent extension into death of one person's legal right to lay claim to another person's lived body.[19] Posthumously, the criminals are further degraded by the dehumanisation that is inherent in the treatment of their skin in ways that are normally reserved for animals. The degradation is heightened by ridicule when the criminals' skins are used as a binding for their own trial records or life-narratives.[20] What,

---

18 E.g. Heather Saul. 'Harvard Scientists Confirm Arsène Houssaye Book is Bound in Human Skin', *The Independent*, 5 June 2014, accessed 1 April 2018, https://www.independent.co.uk/arts-entertainment/books/harvard-scientists-confirm-ars-ne-houssaye-book-is-bound-in-human-skin-9493448.html; Eliana Dockterman. 'This Harvard University Library Book Is Bound in Human Skin', *Time*, 6 June 2014, accessed 1 April 2018, http://time.com/2835499/this-harvard-university-library-book-is-bound-in-human-skin/.

19 The gruesome list of abused skin in Nazi concentration camps that Czech inmate Dr Franz Blaha provided at the Nuremberg trials ('saddles, riding breeches, gloves, house slippers, and ladies' handbags') does not contain a book, but the principles of abused skin are the same as the ones outlined here: 'Nuremberg Trial Proceedings Vol. 5: Thirty-Second Day'. Friday 11 January 1946, 170. *The Avalon Project*, accessed 29 April 2018, http://avalon.law.yale.edu/imt/01-11-46.asp. I approach the Nazis' illicit touch through the Auschwitz number tattoos in the second part of this contribution.

20 Connor and Thompson list several examples. Connor. *The Book of Skin*, 42–45; Lawrence S. Thompson. *Religatum De Pelle Humana* (Hamden: Archon Books: 1949), 137. The Bristol Archives, for instance, hold a volume that contains documents on the murder case of Eliza Balsum as well as of the trial and execution of her murderer John Horwood. The bookbinding made of Horwood's skin is embossed with the comment 'Cutis Vera Johannis Horwood'. Fay Curtis. 'The

after all, could a court official expect from those he showed such a book but amused remarks about how witty a punishment this bookbinding is? Behind the ridicule, however, lies a society's need to reinstate law and order. The criminal literally becomes an object that is ridiculously easy to handle, that cannot escape the touch of those who are in the right according to this society's moral, ethical and legal codes. In a similar vein, Steven Connor claims: 'Normally, it is the legal document that is binding upon the bodies it concerns; here, the body's own binding seems to underwrite and circumscribe the power of the official record'.[21] Reactions between morbid fascination and revulsion, however, also characterise books bound in human skin as abject, as something that, according to Julia Kristeva, 'disturbs identity, system, order'.[22] Binding books in human skin, the diverse narratives in the box show, is not usually considered right. Doing it in the name of justice, however, as is the case with the criminals' skins, can shift 'what is right' because a crime itself is likewise abject as 'it draws attention to the fragility of the law'.[23] To punish one abject deed (the crime) by another (the bookbinding) is to fight fire with fire. The crime, in this logic, justifies the abuse of the

John Horwood Book', *Bristol's Free Museums and Historic Houses* (blog), 17 April 2014, accessed 6 April 2018, https://www.bristolmuseums.org.uk/blog/archives/john-horwood-book/.

21 Connor. *Book of Skin*, 43.

22 Kristeva. *Powers of Horror* (New York: Columbia University Press, 1982), 4.

23 Ibid., 4.

criminal's skin and the otherwise illicit touch is thus reframed as a legitimate one.

Not all books bound in human skin, however, bespeak irreverence for another human being. Some on the contrary testify to a 'loving' and yet illicit touch. Lawrence Thompson documents cases of men and women who explicitly wished their skins to be turned into parchment or bookbinding for the continued use of their loved ones.[24] In this case, it is the subject's desire to be flayed that is abject in that it requires another to cross the boundaries of 'what is right'. As such, it is a request for the ultimate labour of love.

> In Peter Greenaway's 1996 film *The Pillow Book*,[25] a publisher has the body of his deceased male lover exhumed and has his skin, including hands, feet and lips, turned into a book. Subsequently, he obsessively touches and kisses the pages of this book and wraps himself into the fold-out pages. The living skin itself seems to have invited its transformation, since it was previously inscribed by the now dead man's female lover, an author with the habit of presenting her works to publishers on the skins of living men. Through the illicit touch by which he has turned his lover's skin into parchment, the publisher has managed to obtain an embodiment of everything he loves. Man, literature, book, skin, parchment, have all merged into one object he will keep touching illicitly in his fetishistic desire.

[24] Thompson. *Religatum De Pelle Humana*, 144–145.

[25] Peter Greenaway, dir. *The Pillow Book*, produced by Terry Glinwood et al. (1996).

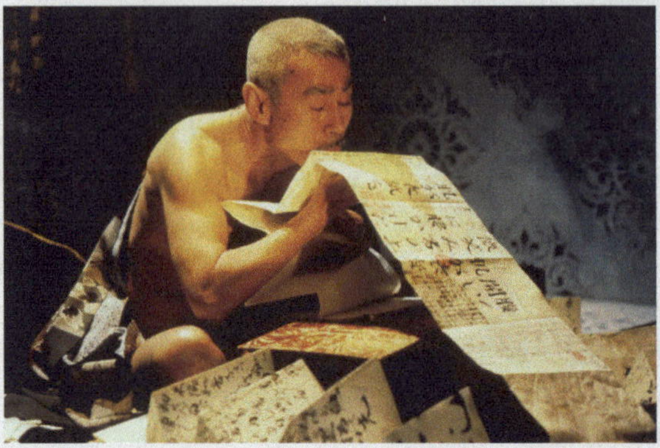

Figure 3. Still image from *The Book of Human Skin*. Credit: Moviestore collection Ltd/Alamy Stock Photo.

A fetishistic desire is also what Lovric's *Book of Human Skin* presents as the cause of protagonist Minguillo Fasan's passion for anthropodermic bibliopegy. Having grown up as a child who was so abominable that everybody in his household, including his mother, denied him all physical touch, he later starts collecting books bound in human skin. Both the initial acts of flaying, tanning and binding the books and Minguillo's subsequent caresses of the volumes cross the boundaries of what is considered right by the novel's late eighteenth-century Venetian society. The formerly lived bodies of humans are doubly objectified, first when they are made to envelop books and later when they become the defenceless objects of Minguillo's repeated illicit touch.

Fetishistic desire can only be surmised in the case of Bouland and his books bound in human skin, but the power issues at stake remain the same as with the two fictional fetishists. Behind the illicit touch that precedes (and sometimes follows) human-skin bookbinding lies a desire to objectify a lived body. Material, tangible, workable surface that it is, skin invites its abuse as bookbinding in ways that the 'deep body'[26] does not. It is possible that Bouland objectified the two unnamed women's skins to the point at which they were just one of many material options to indulge in the fashion of 'sympathetic bibliopegy', which saw collectors between the eighteenth and the early twentieth century envelope their volumes in materials that suited the book's content (e.g. books on glazing in glass, on woollen mills in wool, Rudyard Kipling's *Jungle Book* in zebra skin, and Charles Darwin's works in that of monkeys).[27]

Other perpetrators pursue their desire to possess and dominate the body of another human by literally marking the human skin. The emerging field of skin studies has recently shifted the focus towards skin as the surface on which relations to others are inscribed both metaphorically and physically.[28] This allows for new theoretical perspectives which I propose to explore in the following section, provided for example by tattoo and body modification theories[29] or by human-animal studies, both of

---

26 MacKendrick. *Word Made Skin*, 7.

27 Lawrence S. Thompson. *Bibliologia Comica or Humorous Aspects of the Caparisoning and Conservation of Books* (Hamden: Archon Books, 1968), 15–40.

28 E.g. Karmen MacKendrick. *Word Made Skin: Figuring Language at the Surface of Flesh* (New York: Fordham University Press, 2004); Nicole Nyffenegger and Katrin Rupp. Introduction to *Writing on Skin in the Age of Chaucer* (Berlin and Boston: De Gruyter, 2018); Didier Anzieu. *Le Moi-Peau* (Paris: BORDAS), 39–40.

29 Victoria Pitts-Taylor. *In the Flesh: The Cultural Politics of Body Modification* (New York: Palgrave Macmillan, 2003); Margo DeMello. *Bodies of Inscription: A Cultural History of the Modern Tattoo Community* (Durham: Duke University Press, 2000); Margo DeMello. *Body Studies: An Introduction* (London: Routledge, 2014); Jane

which offer entry points for approaching the dehumanisation of the victims of the illicit touch.[30]

Box II: The Auschwitz Number Tattoos

How are we to approach these metonyms for the atrocities committed against Jewish women, men and children by the Nazi regime? Deeply distressed by her readings on WWII, the protagonist of Emily Prager's novel *Eve's Tattoo*, a writer living in New York in the 1990s, thinks to have found a way.[31] For her fortieth birthday, she has herself tattooed with the number of an unknown female Auschwitz victim whose picture she has found. In view of the gradual disappearance of the last generation of Holocaust survivors, she construes her tattoo as 'sacred' and as an act of keeping 'that event' alive.[32] Her friends swiftly diagnose some sort of midlife crisis. Eve, by contrast, specifies: 'To me, this tattoo is about the fate of women. The tattoo will help me find out about it.'[33] She thus reframes her aging body as an entry point to an understanding of the fates of women under the Nazi regime. Eve's lack of knowledge about her own tattoo, however, becomes an embarrassment when she meets an Auschwitz survivor who not only reads her tattoo like a text but also sarcastically comments on her obvious lack of the actual experience: 'So … you came to the kemp in 'forty-four about when Primo Levi came. Late in the war. Perhaps that's how you survived.'[34]

Caplan. Introduction to *Written on the Body: The Tattoo in European and American History* (Princeton: Princeton University Press, 2000).

30 E.g. Charles Patterson. *Eternal Treblinka: Our Treatment of Animals and the Holocaust* (New York: Lantern Books, 2002).

31 Emily Prager. *Eve's Tattoo* (London: Chatto & Windus, 1991).

32 Ibid., 11–12.

33 Ibid., 12.

34 Ibid., 144.

While Eve does not choose the tattoo light-heartedly, she makes the mistake of conceiving of it primarily in the modern Western sense, as a voluntary mark. For her, the tattoo is a way to 'write oneself.'[35] A woman's self-willed tattoo, according to the feminist reclaiming discourse, can function to reclaim the body from its 'victimization and objectification in patriarchal culture', especially if it violates standard beauty norms as Eve's tattoo undoubtedly does.[36] The tattoo in this case functions as a 'counter-strategic reinscription'[37] of the always already inscribed female body, in the case of Eve as a body that is ageing, menopausal and childless. 'I am forty today … I don't have children. I want to give someone life. I'm giving Eva life', she says about the number tattoo that was once also the number of the unnamed woman she chooses to call Eva, in an attempt to style herself as the alter ego of the victim.[38]

Eve's tattoo is empowering to her because it is a self-chosen one, while the exact opposite is the case for the Auschwitz number tattoos. They, in contrast, stand in a long tradition of punitive and ownership marks throughout European history, from runaway Roman slaves, to adulterers or criminals in the Middle Ages, to British army deserters, to the French galley slaves of the

---

[35] DeMello. *Bodies of Inscription*, 12.
[36] Pitts-Taylor. *In the Flesh*, 49.
[37] Grosz. 'Inscriptions and Body-Maps', 64.
[38] Prager. *Eve's Tattoo*, 17; see also Rob Baum, '"And Thou Shalt Bind Them as a Sign upon Thy Hand": *Eve's Tattoo* and the Holocaust Consumer', *Shofar: An Interdisciplinary Journal of Jewish Studies* 28, no. 2 (2010): 116–138.

nineteenth century.[39] These punitive and ownership tattoos are the marks of what we would perceive as an illicit touch, that the perpetrators, however, would have construed as justified through the purportedly inferior status of the slaves, sinners and criminals. In a circular logic, the Jews' constructed inferiority enabled the Nazi administration to justify their claim on the bodies of their victims and to inscribe that claim on their skins; the number tattoos, in turn, helped them further dehumanise the Jews and facilitated their objectification for those involved in their exploitation and killing.

Primo Levi describes in *If This Is a Man* the moment of the tattooing in Auschwitz as a baptism, and the number as his new name: 'My number is 174517; we have been baptized, we will carry the tattoo on our left arm until we die … and for many days, while the habits of freedom still led me to look for the time on my wristwatch, my new name ironically appeared instead, a number tattooed in bluish characters under the skin.'[40] The replacement of the wristwatch by the number tattoo is rife with symbolism: the subject that was once free to organise his time by looking at his own watch has become an object, dispossessed of both valuables and freedom. Almost thirty years later, in *The Drowned and the Saved*, Levi theorised this

[39] DeMello. *Body Studies*, 247–251; Susan Benson. 'Inscriptions of the Self: Reflections on Tattooing and Piercing in Contemporary Euro-America'. In *Written on the Body: The Tattoo in European and American History*, ed. Jane Caplan (Princeton: Princeton University Press, 2000), 234–254; Mark Gustafson. 'The Tattoo in the Later Roman Empire and Beyond'. In ibid., 17–31.

[40] Primo Levi. *Survival in Auschwitz*, trans. Stuart Woolf (New York et al.: Simon & Schuster, 1996 [1947]). 27. *Survival in Auschwitz* is the US title of *If This is a Man*.

process further: 'The operation was not very painful and lasted no more than a minute, but it was traumatic. Its symbolic meaning was clear to everyone: this is an indelible mark, you will never leave here; this is the mark with which slaves are branded and cattle sent to the slaughter, and that is what you have become. You no longer have a name; this is your new name. The violence of the tattoo was gratuitous, an end in itself, pure offence: were the three canvas numbers sewed to pants, jackets, and winter coat not enough? No, they were not enough: something more was needed, a nonverbal message, so that the innocent would feel his sentence written on his flesh.'[41]

The degradation to slaves and cattle culminates in the dismissal of a previous identity ('you no longer have a name'). Whatever identity he once had has been palimpsestically overwritten by the perpetrators' inscription on his skin. They have made him into a number, an entity that can be moved around, changed and erased. To Orthodox Jews, the moment of tattooing must have been even more traumatic because it violated Mosaic Law. Since the prohibition of tattooing in Leviticus 19:28 was commonly interpreted as a way to distinguish Jews from barbarians,[42] the Nazis' transgressive touch forced the newly tattooed Jews into the role of barbarian, with which came the fear of losing the right to a

---

[41] Primo Levi. *The Drowned and the Saved*, trans. Raymond Rosenthal (New York et al.: Simon & Schuster, 2017 [1986]), 104–105.

[42] Levi. *The Drowned and the Saved*, 105.

Jewish burial.[43] The mechanisms at work here are similar to our treatment of animals, scholars in human-animal studies have claimed.[44] While the abuse and eating of animals constructs the human,[45] the dehumanisation of the victims reversely enabled the perpetrators to construct them as animals. Consequently, the perpetrators not only saw themselves in the right, they also sought to confirm and stablise this constructed subhuman status of their victims by permanently marking them: 'this is an indelible mark, you will never leave here.'

Levi reminds his readers that this message of the number tattoos was felt physically long after the sting of the needle. In a passage in which he reflects on the differing treatment of political prisoners as opposed to Jewish prisoners, he relates that in moments of obvious inequity the Jews 'felt the tattoo burn like a wound.'[46] The minor momentary pain ('it was not very painful') is perpetuated and intensified by the highly symbolic presence of the tattoo exactly because it is perceived as the mark left by an illicit touch ('so that the innocent would feel his sentence written on his flesh').

---

43 See also the explanations of Rabbi Benjaminson on chabad.org. The fear that a tattooed person cannot be buried in a Jewish cemetery is still very present. Chani Benjaminson, 'Can a person with a tattoo be buried in a Jewish cemetery?', *Chabad.org*, accessed 1 April 2018, https://www.chabad.org/library/article_cdo/aid/533444/jewish/Can-a-person-with-a-tattoo-be-buried-in-a-Jewish-cemetery.htm.

44 Patterson. *Eternal Treblinka.*

45 E.g. Karl Steel. *How to Make a Human: Animals and Violence in the Middle Ages* (Columbus: Ohio State University Press, 2011).

46 Levi. *The Drowned and the Saved*, 90.

The moment of tattooing and of 'becoming a number' is presented as such a decisive one in numerous survival narratives that it almost appears to have become a literary motif. Ulrike Landfester suggests that the singling out of this specific moment as a threshold experience, which 'metonymically prefigures the horrors of things to follow', is owed to the fact that the new, abhorrent realities of life in the camp that come after this moment are impossible to express in words.[47] The importance this moment is thus given in so many narratives stands in stark contrast to the fact that the number tattoos seem not to have been of any specific legal relevance during the Nuremberg trials.[48]

I have proposed elsewhere to think of tattoos as having a multi-layered spatial and temporal existence.[49] A tattoo is more than a mark on skin. It begins its existence in a virtual form, as a thought that later becomes a plan. Once it is etched in the skin and becomes visible, it starts to signify. The process of decoding requires readings through others, which are subjective, or explanations by the tattooed person, which likewise are formed by narrative choices. Such a tattoo narrative, however, not only evolves from the tattoo, but in turn also shapes the tattoo; without the narrative, the tattoo would not signify in the same way.[50] Finally, the tattoo also has a performative

[47] Ulrike Landfester. *Stichworte: Tätowierung und europäische Schriftkultur* (Berlin: Matthes & Seitz, 2012), 255–357, 360.

[48] Ibid.

[49] Nicole Nyffenegger. 'Saint Margaret's Tattoos: Empowering Marks on White Skin', *Exemplaria* 25, no. 4 (2013): 267–283.

[50] DeMello. *Bodies of Inscription,* 12.

quality, when it is shown or hidden, when it is combined with a specific gesture or sound. The tattoo, in other words, is made up of diverse virtual, visual, narrative and performative realisations.[51] Together, they form the layers that make the tattoo. The meaning of Eve's tattoo, for example, is what she relates it to be. Since she tells several different tattoo narratives about it, at different moments and in different places, the tattoo consists of these diverse temporal and spatial layers.

This concept of the tattoo's multilayered spatial and temporal existence is applicable also to tattooing in Auschwitz, which started in 1941 when the number of prisoners increased rapidly and the death rate was high. With the introduction of the practice of stripping the dead, identification numbers sewn onto clothes became useless. The Nazi camp adminstrations replaced them by numbers permanently etched in the skin in order to identify the bodies of those who had previously been registered.[52] But while they thus clearly struggled to make the tattooing reflect their own constantly shifting categorisations of their prisoners,[53] the tattooed victims already began to read and interpret the tattoos in ways the Nazi regime could not have foreseen.

---

[51] I first proposed this theory based on the specifically medievalist concept of textuality that Paul Zumthor has called *mouvance*. Paul Zumthor. *Speaking of the Middle Ages* (Lincoln: University of Nebraska Press, 1986), 96.

[52] *Holocaust Encyclopedia*, s.v. 'Tattoos and Numbers: The System of Identifying Prisoners at Auschwitz', accessed 1 April, 2018, https://www.ushmm.org/wlc/en/article.php?ModuleId=10007056.

[53] Levi. *The Drowned and the Saved*, 100, 104.

The websites of Yad Vashem and the United States Holocaust Memorial Museum provide a heart-breaking wealth of documentation, including historical footage, photos and personal reports on the tattoos made in Auschwitz. In the early years, only those deemed fit for labour were tattooed, while the others were killed immediately. Jakob Frenkiel describes how the tattoo, consequently, became his chance for survival: 'The day after we arrived [in Auschwitz], my brother Chaim and I were lined up with kids and old people. I asked a prisoner what was going to happen to us. He pointed to the chimneys. 'Tomorrow the smoke will be from you.' He said if we could get a number tattooed on our arms, we'd be put to work instead of being killed. We sneaked to the latrine, then escaped through a back door and lined up with the men getting tattoos.'[54] In this cynical way, the tattoo already became a symbol of survival at this early stage. In the prisoners' readings of the tattoos, low numbers also incited respect from the other prisoners because they symbolised having managed to survive for a relatively long time.[55]

Similarly, Szlamach Radoszynski reports that he reinterpreted his number as a symbol for life: 'Day after day my job [in Auschwitz] was to shovel dirt over discarded, still-smoldering ashes of cremated victims. I kept wondering whether I, too, would end up the same. But I was sustained by the fact that the number tattooed on my arm -#128232- added up to 18, the Jewish mystical

[54] *Holocaust Encyclopedia*, s.v. 'Jakob Frenkiel', accessed 1 April 2018, https://www.ushmm.org/wlc/en/idcard.php?ModuleId=10006316.

[55] Jodi Rudoren. 'Proudly bearing elders' scars, their skins "never forget"', *New York Times*, 30 September 2012, accessed 3 July 2014, http://www.nytimes.com/2012/10/01/world/middleeast/with-tattoos-young-israelis-bear-holocaust-scars-of-relatives.html?pagewanted=all&_r=0; Levi, *The Drowned and the Saved*, 28.

symbol for life.'[56] An anonymous commentary on chabad.org dating from 2017 presents the same narrative as their mother's appropriation of the mark: 'she added the numbers up and realized that with this deplorable and demonic action by the Nazis, it was a sign from Hashem that she was going to live through the death camps.'[57]

Ruth Klüger, in *Still Alive: A Holocaust Girlhood Remembered*, describes such reinterpretations as a symptom of utter despair: 'Thanks to the dog tag under my skin, I was suddenly so aware of the enormity, the monstrosity, really, of my situation that I felt a kind of glee about it. I was living through something that was worth witnessing ... It tells you something about how beaten down and stripped of a sense of self I already was that I thus invented for myself a future based on the experience of the most abysmal humiliation yet, a future where precisely that abyss would appear honorable ... We'll be witnesses, we thought, meaning there'll come a future when this will be over, and the number will be a piece of incontrovertible evidence.'[58]

These first interpretative and narrative appropriations show the inherent instability of meaning of the supposedly indelible mark on skin. The tattoos had certainly not been devised as symbols of hope but they were reinterpreted as such, either in a literal sense (when the tattoo

[56] *Holocaust Encyclopedia*, s.v. 'Szlamach Radoszynski', accessed 1 April 2018, https://www.ushmm.org/wlc/en/idcard.php?ModuleId=10006723.

[57] Yisroel Cotlar. 'Honor a Holocaust Victim by Tattooing Her Number?' *Chabad.org*, accessed 1 April 2018, https://www.chabad.org/library/article_cdo/aid/1739170/jewish/Honor-a-Holocaust-Victim-by-Tattooing-Her-Number.htm.

[58] Ruth Klüger. *Still Alive: A Holocaust Girlhood Remembered* (New York: Feminist Press at the University of New York, 2001), 98.

meant suitability for labour) or in a metaphorical sense (a number adding up to the Jewish symbol for life). The plural existence of this latter narrative attests to the multi-layered temporal and spatial existence of both tattoo and tattoo narrative. In Klüger's account, finally, the number symbolises the hope of its own reinterpretation in the future. The number tattoos were, however, not only met by such narrative appropriations but also by actual counter-tattoos etched in the skin of victims.

Stanislawa Leszczynska spent two years as a midwife-prisoner in Auschwitz-Birkenau. She describes the cruelty towards mothers and their newborn babies, the killings of newborns and, as of 1945, the abduction of blue-eyed children for 'Germanisation.' Jewish babies were tattooed with the identification numbers of their mothers right after birth and drowned in a barrel. The mothers were then made to witness the body being 'thrown out of the block and torn to pieces by rats.'[59] As for the non-Jewish, blue-eyed children that were selected for 'denationalization' (Leszczynska refers to 'several hundred'), the midwives used a counter-tattoo to increase the chances that mother and child could one day be reunited: 'With the intention to create possibilities that these babies may in the future be returned to their mothers, we organized a way of marking these babies with a tattoo, that would not arouse the suspicion of the SS-men. Due to this many mothers were hopeful that one day they may find their lost child.'[60]

[59] The International Auschwitz Committee. *Nazi Medicine: Doctors, Victims, and Medicine in Auschwitz* (New York: Howard Fertig, 1986), 189.

[60] The International Auschwitz Committee. *Nazi Medicine*, 190.

The absurdity of tattooing newborn babies before killing them shows that towards the end of the war, the camp authorities had given up any logic in favour of pure cruelty. For the women witnessing the tattooing and murder of the newborns, it must have been evident that a tattoo no longer increased their chances of survival, as it may have done in the earlier years. The fact that the babies were not given their own number but that of their mothers further dehumanised both mother and child. The child and the mother were made a monstrosity of two bodies with one identity. However, as with the counter-tattoos described above, there was a very small minority of Auschwitz tattoos that were meant to inspire hope. The illicit touch of the perpetrator, in this case, was identified as such and counteracted by the same means but with the reverse aim. Similarly, Holocaust survivor Eva Kor describes the moment of her tattooing as a chance of fighting the imminent illicit touch by biting one of the Nazi officers.

In a text originally published on the question-and-answer site *Quora* in December 2014, Kor describes the moment as follows: 'I decided I was going to fight. I was not going to let them touch me. I didn't really know how much it would hurt, but it wasn't the tattoo that bothered me as much as my thought, *What right do they have to do anything to me physically?* And maybe it was my only way to make a stand against what had been happening to me all day long. When it was my turn, I began to really carry on … The women were holding me down by my head and legs and arms and one of the Nazis grabbed my arm. The only thing I could do was bite. I don't even know how I managed to do that because they tried to keep me flat.

> But I snapped up and bit his arm ... From the way I was raised, to bite someone was so crude that I had to block it out of my mind to preserve who I thought I was ... Many survivors, when they read my account, they say there is no way anyone could get away with biting a Nazi. That was probably true. But I was not a regular prisoner - I was a "Mengele Twin".[61]

Kor frames her act of resistance along the lines of the 'writing back' paradigm posited by postcolonial studies, according to which the suppressed resist by subverting the colonisers' discourse. Hers is a biting back, a claim of another's body which not only transgresses the boundaries of what the Nazi officer would have defined as right but also the boundaries of what she herself defined as right. The illicit touch she is herself forced to administer in order to counteract the perpetrator's illicit touch becomes a threat to her own identity: 'to bite someone was so crude that I had to block it out of my mind to preserve who I thought I was'.

Personal accounts of survivors attest to the various ways of coping with the mark of the Nazis' illicit touch after the war. One of the first and visually perhaps most impressive acts of appropriation was, however, a performative one, of showing rather than of speaking about the number tattoo.

---

[61] Eva Kor, reply to 'What do Holocaust survivors think of their tattoos?,' *Quora*, 23 December 2014, https://www.quora.com/What-do-Holocaust-survivors-think-of-their-tattoos.

The gesture of rolling up the sleeve and presenting the outstretched arm to the photographer has become iconic by now, when the last generation of Auschwitz survivors can be seen identifying themselves as victims in photos that resemble the ones taken only days after the liberation of the concentration camps.

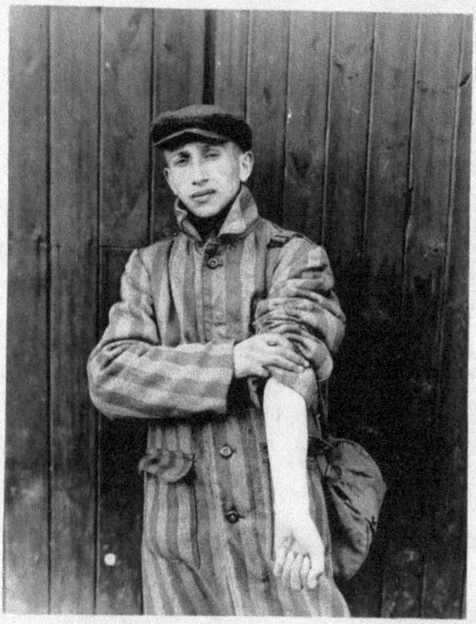

Figure 4. A survivor of the Buchenwald concentration camp displays his tattooed arm. Credit: United States Holocaust Memorial Museum, courtesy of Stanley Moroknek. Reproduced by permission from the United States Holocaust Memorial Museum.

The meaning of the gesture has, however, expanded since it was first performed. While it stood for survival then, it additionally stands today for regained agency, for the freedom of making choices. Primo Levi reflects on how his performance of showing or hiding the number tattoo changed depending on whether his audience was curious or incredulous: 'At a distance of forty years, my tattoo has become a part of my body. I don't glory in it, but I am not ashamed of it either; I do not display and do not hide it. I show it unwillingly to those who ask out of pure curiosity; readily and in anger to those who say they are incredulous. Often young people ask me why I didn't have it erased, and this surprises me: Why should I? There are not many of us in the world to bear this witness.'[62]

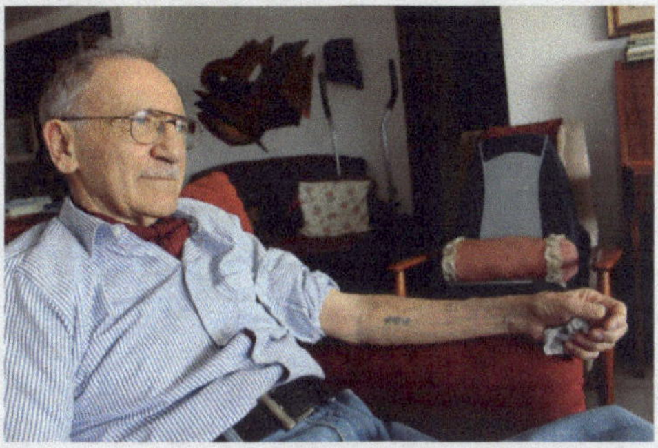

Figure 5. Auschwitz Survivor Yeshiyahu Folman. Originally published in 'Auschwitz Concentration Camp Tattoo Shared by Father and Son' *Public Radio International (PRI)*, 19 April 2012. Reproduced by permission from Daniel Estrin.

The appropriation of the Auschwitz number tattoos has continued until today in narratives, whenever victims speak or write about their experiences of living with them. Their narratives of how they got the tattoo and of what it means to them reshape the tattoo. Some of the narratives suggest that the questions of whether to show

[62] Levi. *The Drowned and the Saved*, 105.

the tattoos or not, whether to get them removed or not, whether to speak about them or not, matter less than the fact that the victims, once objectified by the number, have by now regained the agency to make these choices.

Ruth Klüger writes that she was happy to be able to say about her tattoo whatever she wanted, even to claim that it was her boyfriend's phone number: 'When I was a waitress, guests often asked what number that was. It made me laugh that they did not know … I occasionally said that it was the phone number of my boyfriend. He is lucky, said one guest … I was free to say what I wanted, that made me happy.'[63]

The 2012 film *Numbered* traces such tattoo narratives of Auschwitz survivors. It also presents yet another act of appropriation and reinterpretation of the number tattoo that is taking place in today's Israel. In view of the imminent disappearance of the last generation of Holocaust survivors, young Israelis have begun to have their grandparents' number tattoos etched in their own skins as a token of remembrance. They see the tattoos as a new approach to a repetitive discourse.[64]

It is an ongoing debate whether or not the grandchildren of Holocaust survivors have the right to appropriate these tattoos in such a way, and whether or not they have more right to do so than those who cannot claim a

[63] My translation into English (the English translation quoted elsewhere in this article cuts this passage) from Ruth Klüger, *weiter leben: Eine Jugend* (Göttingen: Wallstein Verlag, 2008), 207.

[64] Rudoren. 'Proudly Bearing Elders' Scars'; Dana Doron and Uriel Sinai, dirs., *Numbered*, produced by kNow Productions (2012); Eliran Rubin. 'Passing on Holocaust Tattoos', *DeutschlandWelle*, 28 November 2012, accessed 3 July 2014, http://www.dw.de/passing-on-holocaust-tattoos/a-16397305.

direct connection to the Holocaust, such as performance artist David Blaine or the fictional Eve in Prager's novel.[65] Prager presents her protagonist's attempt at appropriation as a failed one, although it is exactly the artificiality of the connection that allows Eve to tell, not one single narrative, but many, all of which are based on her thorough reading of women's fates under the Nazi regime.

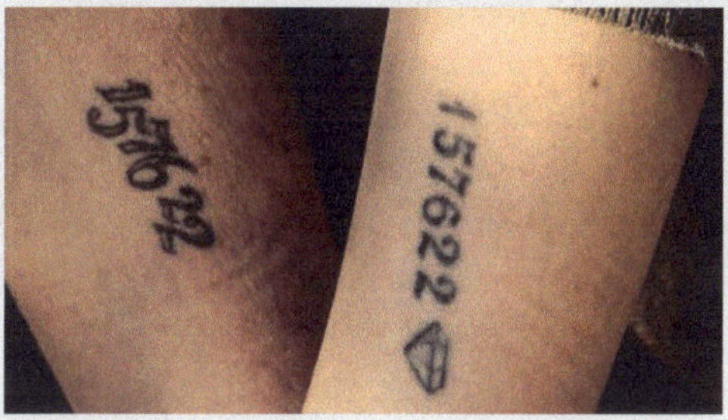

Figure 6. The forearms of the young Israelis Jona Diamant and Eli Sagir. Originally published in 'KZ-Nummer als Tattoo' *Frankfurter Rundschau*, 2 February 2013. Reproduced by permission from Rico Grimm.

As the debate concerning such appropriations continues, further narratives complicate any simplistic equation of permanent marks with stable meanings: Klüger comments that she found it strange 'that the armpits of the SS were also decorated with tattoos. The same procedure for honor and shame, if one chose to choose these perspectives.'[66] Footage in the BBC series *Auschwitz*

[65] E.g. Rudoren. 'Proudly Bearing Elders' Scars'; WENN, 'Blaine Reveals Secret Of Holocaust Tattoo', Contact Music, 2 September 2003, accessed 1 April 2018, http://www.contactmusic.com/david-blaine/news/blaine-reveals-secret-of-holocaust-tattoo

[66] Klüger. *Still Alive*, 98.

shows that what Klüger in her childhood still identified as the SS symbol of honor turned against those bearing this mark after the liberation of the camps. Russian soldiers can be seen making half-naked Germans walk in line with raised arms so they can search for what have now become marks testifying to their crimes.[67]

The tattooed SS men are one of the rare examples in which the illicit touch is originally a 'loving' one along the lines of the fetishist desire discussed above. The bodies of those deemed especially gifted were claimed for the Reich by the mark. These tattoos too, had an unstable meaning and were reinterpreted after the war. The Jewish victims' tattoos, to the present day, are shaped and reshaped in tattoo narratives. By way of numerous acts of appropriation and counter-inscription, these tattoos have come to stand metonymically for the horrors inflicted on the victims and for the Nazi regime's illicit touch. Instead of standing in for the dehumanised victims as intended by the perpetrators, they now, in Levi's words, stand for 'what man's presumption made of man in Auschwitz.'[68]

The illicit touch, which I have here approached through abused and marked human skin, is not a thing of the past. The narratives that are an integral part of the abused skin, both in the case of books bound in human skin and in the case of the Auschwitz tattoos, reach into our present time. They inform our thinking about more recent cases

[67] *Auschwitz: The Nazis and 'The Final Solution'*, directed by Laurence Rees and Catherine Tatge, aired 11 January 2005, on BBC Two.

[68] Levi. *Survival in Auschwitz*, 55.

in which an illicit touch has aimed at objectifying the lived bodies of others. In 2019, as the #MeToo movement is still gaining impetus, we see the same mechanisms at work. Powerful white men in the recent past thought themselves in the right when they not only touched others transgressively, but openly boasted about the act. Like Bouland, they did it in a jovial tone aimed at justifying their deeds as harmless pastimes, and like him, some of them have not faced any consequences for their illicit touch.[69]

References

Anzieu, Didier. *Le Moi-Peau*. Paris: BORDAS, 1985.

Baum, Rob. '"And Thou Shalt Bind Them as a Sign upon Thy Hand": *Eve's Tattoo* and the Holocaust Consumer'. *Shofar: An Interdisciplinary Journal of Jewish Studies* 28, no. 2 (2010): 116–138.

Beck, Karen. '852 RARE: Old Books, New Technologies, and 'The Human Skin Book' at HLS'. *Et Seq: The Blog of the Harvard Law School Library*. 3 April 2014. Accessed 1 March 2018. http://etseq.law.harvard.edu/2014/04/852-rare-old-books-new-technologies-and-the-human-skin-book-at-hls/.

Benjaminson, Chani. 'Can a person with a tattoo be buried in a Jewish cemetery?' *Chabad.org*. Accessed 1 April 2018. https://www.chabad.org/library/article_cdo/aid/533444/jewish/Can-a-person-with-a-tattoo-be-buried-in-a-Jewish-cemetery.htm.

[69] I thank Michelle Lovric for her support of this project at different stages and for drawing my attention to these instances of illicit touch in the recent past. I also thank Annette Kern-Stähler, Zoë Lehmann Imfeld, Rory Critten, Kathrin Scheuchzer for their comments on earlier versions of this article and Lara Portmann for her great work. Special thanks also go to my two anonymous readers for their invaluable suggestions.

Benson, Susan. 'Inscriptions of the Self: Reflections on Tattooing and Piercing in Contemporary Euro-America.' In *Written on the Body: The Tattoo in European and American History*, edited by Jane Caplan, 234–254. Princeton, NJ: Princeton University Press, 2000.

Bordo, Susan. *The Unbearable Weight: Feminism, Western Culture, and the Body*. 2nd ed. Oakland, CA: University of California Press, 2003.

Butler, Judith. *Gender Trouble: Feminism and the Subversion of Identity*. Thinking Gender. New York: Routledge, 1990.

Butler, Judith. 'Foucault and the Paradox of Bodily Inscriptions.' *The Journal of Philosophy* 86, no. 11 (1989): 601–607.

Caplan, Jane. Introduction to *Written on the Body: The Tattoo in European and American History*, xi-xxiii. Princeton: Princeton University Press, 2000.

Chaudron, Gerald. '"It's Not Human!": Another Example of Anthropodermic Bibliopegy Discredited.' *RBM: A Journal of Rare Books, Manuscripts, and Cultural Heritage* 18, no. 1 (2017): 26–36. Accessed 3 April 2018. DOI: https://doi.org/10.5860/rbm.18.1.26.

Cole, Heather. 'Bound in Human Skin.' *Houghton Library Blog*, 24 May 2013. Accessed 6 April 2018. http://blogs.harvard.edu/houghton/2013/05/24/bound-in-human-skin/.

Cole, Heather. 'The Science of Anthropodermic Binding.' *Houghton Library Blog*, 4 June 2014. Accessed 6 April 2018. http://blogs.law.harvard.edu/houghton/2014/06/04/caveat-lecter/.

Combes, Paul. 'Peau Humaine Tannée.' *Intérmediaire des chercheurs et curieux*, LXII, 30 October 1910: 661–662. Accessed 1 April 2018. gallica.bnf.fr/ark:/12148/bpt6k73420v/f337.image.

Connor, Steven. *The Book of Skin*. London: Reaktion, 2004.

Cotlar, Yisroel. 'Honor a Holocaust Victim by Tattooing Her Number?' *Chabad.org*. Accessed 1 April 2018. https://www.chabad.org/library/article_cdo/aid/1739170/jewish/Honor-a-Holocaust-Victim-by-Tattooing-Her-Number.htm.

Curtis, Fay. 'The John Horwood Book'. *Bristol's Free Museums and Historic Houses* (blog), 17 April 2014. Accessed 6 April 2018. https://www.bristolmuseums.org.uk/blog/archives/john-horwood-book/.

DeMello, Margo. *Bodies of Inscription: A Cultural History of the Modern Tattoo Community*. Durham: Duke University Press, 2000.

DeMello, Margo. *Body Studies: An Introduction*. London: Routledge, 2014.

Dockterman, Eliana. 'This Harvard University Library Book Is Bound in Human Skin'. *Time*, 6 June 2014. Accessed 1 April 2018. http://time.com/2835499/this-harvard-university-library-book-is-bound-in-human-skin/.

Doron, Dana, and Uriel Sinai, dirs. *Numbered*. 2012. Produced by kNow Productions.

Estrin, Daniel. 'Auschwitz Concentration Camp Tattoo Shared by Father and Son'. *Public Radio International (PRI)*, 19 April 2012. Accessed 2 November 2018. https://www.pri.org/stories/2012-04-19/auschwitz-concentration-camp-tattoo-shared-father-and-son.

Greenaway, Peter, dir. *The Pillow Book*. 1996. Produced by Terry Glinwood et al.

Grimm, Rico. 'KZ-Nummer als Tattoo'. *Frankfurter Rundschau*, 2 February 2013. Accessed 2 November 2018. http://www.fr.de/politik/holocaust-kz-nummer-als-tattoo-a-756135.

Grosz, Elizabeth. 'Inscriptions and Body-Maps: Representations and the Corporeal'. In *Feminine, Masculine and Representation*, edited by Anne Cranny-Francis and Terry Threadgold, 62–74. Sidney: Allen and Unwin, 1990.

Gustafson, Mark. 'The Tattoo in the Later Roman Empire and Beyond'. In *Written on the Body: The Tattoo in European and American History*, edited by Jane Caplan, 17–31. Princeton: Princeton University Press, 2000.

'Harvard University Book Bound in Human Skin'. *BBC News*, 5 June 2014. Accessed 1 March 2018. http://www.bbc.com/news/world-us-canada-27721571.

Holocaust Encyclopedia. United States Holocaust Memorial Museum. Accessed 7 July 2014. https://encyclopedia.ushmm.org/.

International Auschwitz Committee, The. *Nazi Medicine: Doctors, Victims and Medicine in Auschwitz*. New York: Howard Fertig, 1986.

Klüger, Ruth. *Still Alive: A Holocaust Girlhood Remembered*. New York: Feminist Press at the University of New York, 2002. Originally published as *weiter leben: Eine Jugend* (Göttingen: Wallstein Verlag, 1992).

Klüger, Ruth. *weiter leben: Eine Jugend*. Göttingen: Wallstein Verlag, 2008.

Kor, Eva. 2014. Reply to 'What do Holocaust survivors think of their tattoos?' *Quora*, 23 December 2014. https://www.quora.com/What-do-Holocaust-survivors-think-of-their-tattoos.

Kristeva, Julia. *Powers of Horror: An Essay on Abjection*. European Perspectives. New York: Columbia University Press, 1982.

Landfester, Ulrike. *Stichworte: Tätowierung und europäische Schriftkultur*. Berlin: Matthes & Seitz, 2012.

Levi, Primo. *Survival in Auschwitz*. Translated by Stuart Woolf. Including 'A Conversation with Primo Levi by Philip Roth'. New York et al.: Simon & Schuster, 1996. Originally published as *Se questo è un uomo* (Turin: De Silva, 1947).

Levi, Primo. *The Drowned and the Saved*. Translated by Raymond Rosenthal. New York et al.: Simon & Schuster, 2017. Originally published as *I sommersi e i salvati* (Turin: Einaudi, 1986).

Lovric, Michelle. *The Book of Human Skin*. London: Bloomsbury, 2010.

MacKendrick, Karmen. *Word Made Skin: Figuring Language at the Surface of Flesh*. New York: Fordham University Press, 2004.

Mullen, Jethro. 'Reader Warning: Harvard Experts Say Book is Bound with Human Skin'. *CNN*, 5 June 2014. Accessed 1 March 2018. http://edition.cnn.com/2014/06/05/us/harvard-book-human-skin/index.html.

Nyffenegger, Nicole. 'Saint Margaret's Tattoos: Empowering Marks on White Skin'. *Exemplaria* 25, no. 4 (2013): 267–283.

Nyffenegger, Nicole, and Katrin Rupp. Introduction to *Writing on Skin in the Age of Chaucer*, 1–15. Berlin and Boston: De Gruyter, 2018.

Patterson, Charles, *Eternal Treblinka: Our Treatment of Animals and the Holocaust*. New York: Lantern Books, 2002.

Pitts-Taylor, Victoria. *In the Flesh: The Cultural Politics of Body Modification*. New York: Palgrave Macmillan, 2003.

Prager, Emily. *Eve's Tattoo*. London: Chatto & Windus, 1991.

Rees, Laurence, and Catherine Tatge, dirs. *Auschwitz: The Nazis and The 'Final Solution.'* Six-episode series. 2005. Produced by the BBC.

Rubin, Eliran. 'Passing on Holocaust Tattoos'. *Deutschland Welle*, 28 November 2012. Accessed 3 July 2014. http://www.dw.de/passing-on-holocaust-tattoos/a-16397305.

Rudoren, Jodi. 'Proudly Bearing Elders' Scars, Their Skin Says "Never Forget"'. *New York Times*, 30 September 2012. Accessed 3 July 2014. http://www.nytimes.com/2012/10/01/world/middleeast/with-tattoos-young-israelis-bear-holocaust-scars-of-relatives.html?pagewanted=all&_r=0.

Saul, Heather. 'Harvard Scientists Confirm Arsène Houssaye Book is Bound in Human Skin'. *The Independent*, 5 June 2014. Accessed 1 April 2018. https://www.independent.co.uk/arts-entertainment/books/harvard-scientists-confirm-ars-ne-houssaye-book-is-bound-in-human-skin-9493448.html.

Steel, Karl. *How to Make a Human: Animals and Violence in the Middle Ages*. Columbus, OH: Ohio State University Press, 2011.

Symons, John. '"Ce Curieux Petit Livre"'. Wellcome Trust *News and Features*. 2001. Accessed 1 March 2012. https://web.archive.org/web/20101012013620/https://wellcome.ac.uk/News/2001/Features/WTX024047.htm

Thompson, Lawrence S. *Religatum De Pelle Humana*. University of Kentucky Libraries Occasional Contributions, vol. 6. Hamden, CT: Archon Books, 1949.

Thompson, Lawrence S. *Bibliologia Comica or Humorous Aspects of the Caparisoning and Conservation of Books*. Hamden, CT: Archon Books, 1968.

United States Holocaust Memorial Museum. Accessed 7 July 2014. https://www.ushmm.org/.

WENN. 'Blaine Reveals Secret Of Holocaust Tattoo'. Contact Music, 2 September 2003. Accessed 1 April 2018. http://www.contactmusic.com/david-blaine/news/blaine-reveals-secret-of-holocaust-tattoo.

Yad Vashem – The World Holocaust Remembrance Center. Accessed 7 July 2014. https://yadvashem.org/.

Zumthor, Paul. *Speaking of the Middle Ages*. Lincoln, NE: University of Nebraska Press, 1986.

Surface/Touch

B.A. Zanditon

1. Making Rubbings

> *A rubbing is a reproduction of the texture of a surface created by placing a piece of paper or similar material over the subject and then rubbing the paper with something to deposit marks ...*[1] *The Surrealists introduced this technique into art: Max Ernst made rubbings of textures he found evocative and played with them to create new images. He called it frottage.*[2] *Frottage may (also) refer to: sexual rubbing; non-penetrative sex ...*[3]

Making a rubbing is intimate; even transgressive.

I have been asked to think about my rubbings in relation to institutional power. I am intrigued. I sniff at the words like a dog. In the introduction to 'Law and the Senses' *See*,

---

1 https://en.wikipedia.org/wiki/Rubbing retrieved 12 June 2018

2 https://en.wikipedia.org/wiki/Surrealist_techniques#Frottage retrieved 12 June 2018

3 https://en.wikipedia.org/wiki/Frottage retrieved 12 June 2018

the editors state, 'capitalism relentlessly crafts our sensorial immersion into hyperaesthetic atmospheres, mirrored by art's ongoing fetishisation of site-specific sensoriality'.[4] Is this what I do? Fetishise site-specific sensoriality? I feel uncomfortable and put the phrase into Google. Amongst the offered related links is 'list of kinks wiki'. I don't want to be accused of fetishising site-specific sensoriality; fetishising implies doing it for its own sake, for its own pleasure, and that feels self-indulgent. But my feeling that making rubbings of surface textures is somehow 'weird' is precisely connected to a discomfort with not understanding why I feel a compulsion to do this. I'm not at ease with self-indulgence. I have a look at Pallasmaa's *The Eyes of the Skin*[5] and discover that I live in an oracularcentric culture. Perhaps rubbings are less weird or fetishistic than an act of rebellion against the hegemony of the eye.

My work is about both touch and the eye. My eye touches. I feel the surface with my eye. My eye feels the texture. But, my eye is mine. It is private. Whatever goes from the external world through the optic nerve to my brain is personal to me. You will never see what I see. And it's locked up inside my head. And when I die, it will die with me. But, if I make a rubbing, I am making something out there in the 'real world'. We can both look at it. We can talk about what it is. We can wonder what it might mean. It's a building. How was it made? What materials? Who was responsible for that finish? Making rubbings of

[4] Andrea Pavoni et al., eds, *See*. (London: University of Westminster Press, 2018).

[5] Juhani Pallasmaa. *The Eyes of the Skin: Architecture and the Senses*. Chichester: Wiley-Academy, 2005.

the Queen Elizabeth Hall and Hayward Gallery[6] took me to the London Metropolitan Archive where I found the architects' and structural engineers' drawings and learned that these were translated by carpenters into the three-dimensional formwork that held the concrete. Those buildings were, in effect, hand-made.[7] What does this tell us about institutional power?

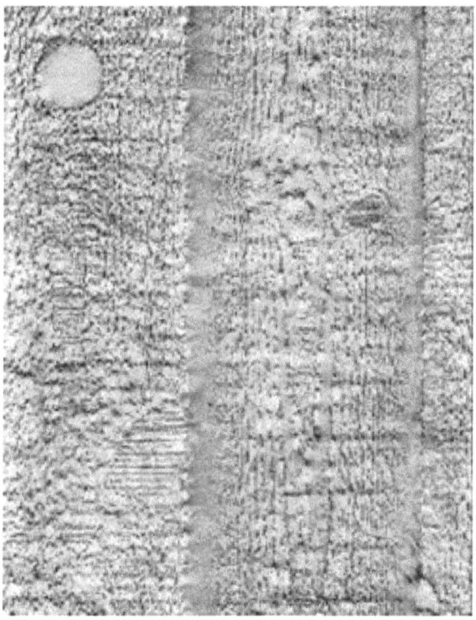

In situ cast concrete, Hayward Gallery, showing texture of soft wood grain shuttering, 2015

[6] In Autumn 2015 I was given permission to make rubbings in and around these buildings.

[7] For an account of how these buildings were made, see *The Art of Concrete: Building the South Bank Arts Centre*, https://www.westminster.ac.uk/sites/default/public-files/general-documents/southbank-pamphlet.pdf from the series, 'Constructing Post-War Britain, Building Workers' Stories 1950-1970'.

Touch: my fingers' ends tingle typing the word. In 2018 I was invited to run a workshop at the Queen Elizabeth Hall where people would be allowed to make their own rubbings. One visitor, a partially sighted man who had come with his young daughter, sat down to make a rubbing. I went over to talk with him. 'I can't see this', he said, pointing at the paper with its graphite marks, 'but when I touch the surface I feel what the rubbing reveals to you'. Another visitor came back to tell me she'd been walking around the site observing its surfaces for the first time. Touch helps us to see.

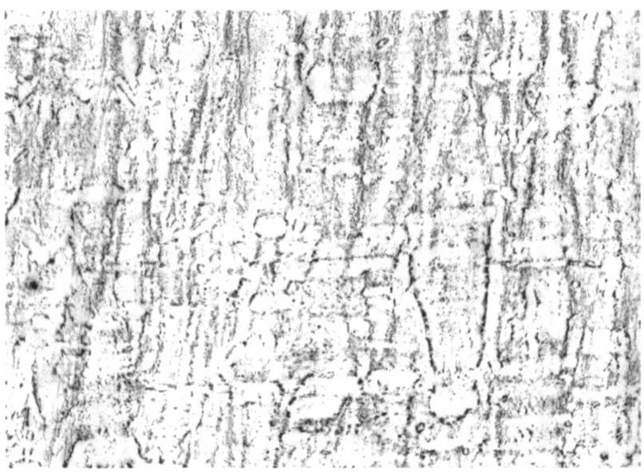

Texture of the Hornbeam trunk. This richness is not visible to the naked eye. 2018

The workshop offered participants the unusual opportunity to work in uncontested space.[8] But making a rubbing,

[8] Uncontested because consent was given as a precondition of running the workshop.

a like for like representation of surface, is rarely neutral. The making raises questions: does one have the right, in a city, to engage with surfaces? Is making a rubbing an act of trespass? Are there any property issues? A rubbing doesn't damage the surface, but would a security person know that? A rubbing is nothing. An impression. A trace. It has no agency. It helps no one. It offers only an expectation. Sometimes it functions as evidence; sometimes it makes an attractive image: 'Look', it says, 'you didn't notice how lovely I am, did you?' Rubbings are conditional, speculative, exploratory. It is their enactment that endows them with agency. In the moment of their making, the enactor's relationship to the space, the surface, the act, is where our interest lies.

2. Inventory of Rubbings

The more I try to answer these questions, the more I think I'm the wrong person to answer them. The method I will follow feels a bit like reverse engineering. In trying to figure out an answer I look back at the rubbings I've done.

I've been surprised to find that as soon as I started studying art formally, about 12 years ago, I started making rubbings. My rubbings were made in public spaces: a drain cover on a pavement, for example, or of inanimate objects, or in institutional space where I felt I needed to ask for permission. Sometimes, though, I'd do a rubbing quickly and surreptitiously: the tiles in the loo at the new extension to the Tate Modern; or the concrete wall surface in the loos at the Building Centre in Store Street.

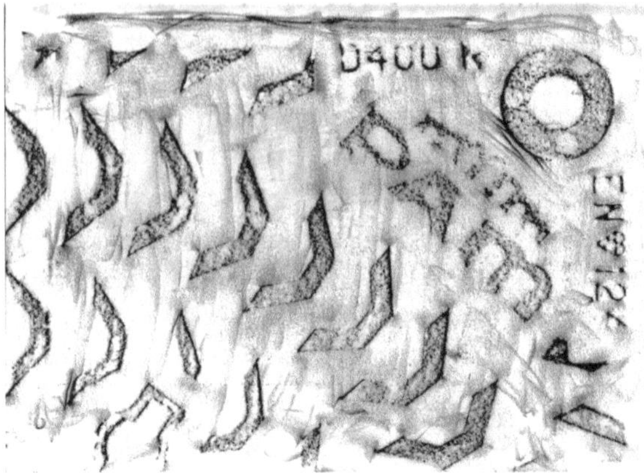

Drain cover, partial rubbing, Hercules Road, 2007

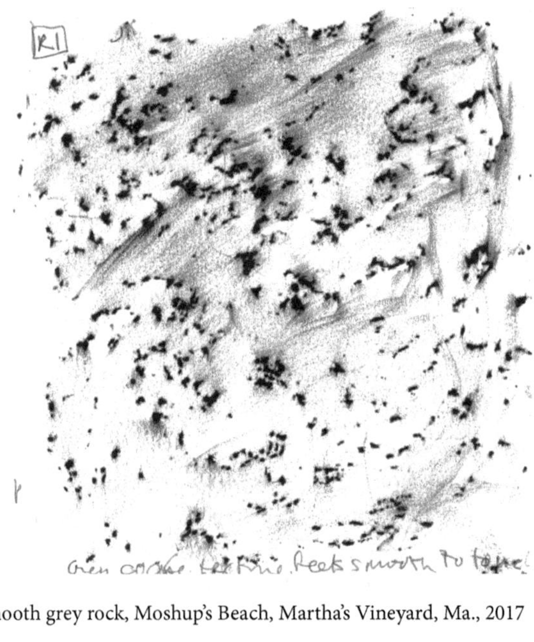

Smooth grey rock, Moshup's Beach, Martha's Vineyard, Ma., 2017

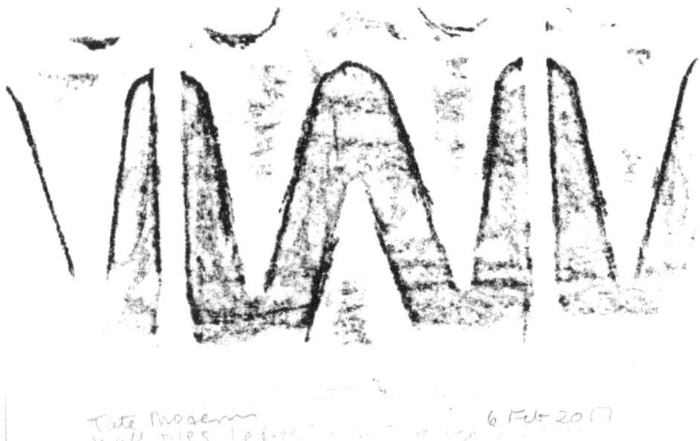

Wall tiling, toilets, Blavatsky Building, Tate Modern, 2017

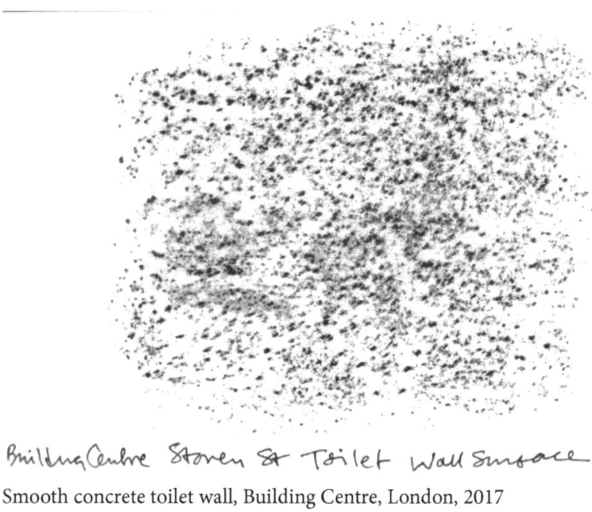

Smooth concrete toilet wall, Building Centre, London, 2017

I wondered whether my discomfort with making rubbings in any but the most uncontested spaces (pavement drain covers, for example) was in any way a gendered response. Would a man feel he had to ask permission? My approach to rubbings has largely been opportunistic. I have used the technique to provide me with information, as a way to record surface, to capture texture, as aide-memoire. Rubbings are often engagement with place. With the Southbank project, the rubbings drew me into the architecture and became a post hoc map of the buildings' construction. Rubbings are always about institutional power: why else would making a rubbing feel furtive? Every rubbing belongs somewhere: in a public space, or on private property. Regardless of its provenance there is always a responsible body and, therefore, someone who might take exception to the intrusion of touch.

3. Site Specific Investigations

I work with site. The Brushing Room, Chelsea College of Art, 2011, comprised a graphite rubbing on a wall, picking out the faint shadow of an archway that had long ago been removed. The site had once been at the top of a staircase in what had been the Royal Army Medical College and was shown, on old plans, as The Brushing Room. Officers' outer clothing would be removed and brushed down so that they could enter their living quarters without trailing dust and grime. It seemed fitting that, in making my work, I brushed the surface of this architectural feature with graphite: adding a layer of dust in a place that, historically, had been dedicated to its removal. The configuration of the room in which I found the arch bore no obvious relation to the original architecture.

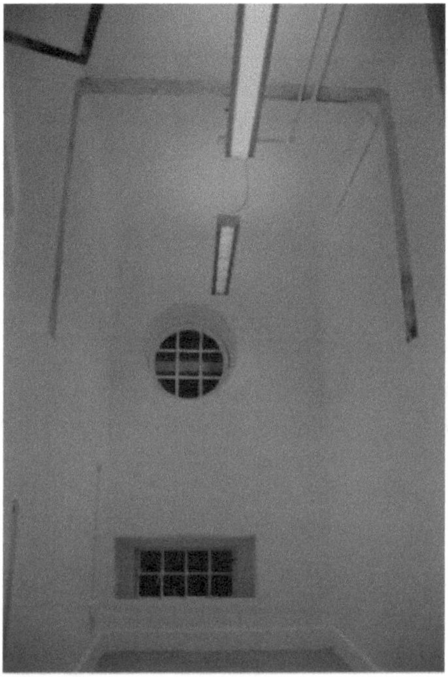

The Brushing Room, Chelsea College of Art, 2011

Wall mapping, Project Room, Chelsea College of Art, 2011. The history of an institution can be read in the marks on its walls. I booked a project room only to discover that the previous occupant, while carefully slapping polyfilla over all the holes they'd made, had forgotten to smooth it down, leaving lumpy rows along either wall. I made a careful atlas of these marks – taking rubbings and mapping them on a grid. This was one of a number of projects I did meticulously, recording signs of previous occupation. It was a forensic examination.

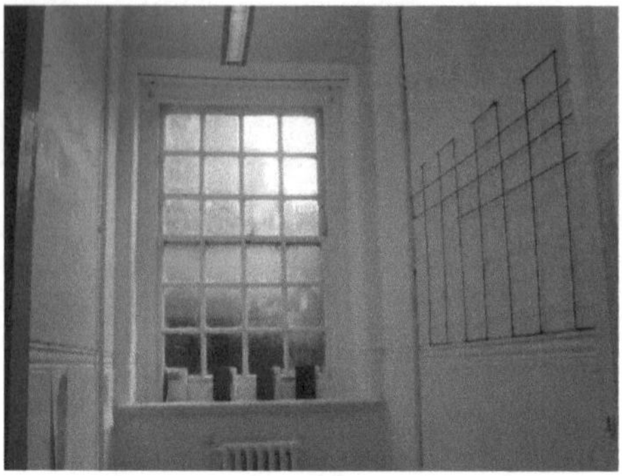

Wall Mapping, Project Room, Chelsea College of Art, 2011

On the windowsill are four notebooks containing original rubbings of the marks on the two walls. The right-hand wall shows the gridding from which I made maps. Below is a graphic representation of the wall.

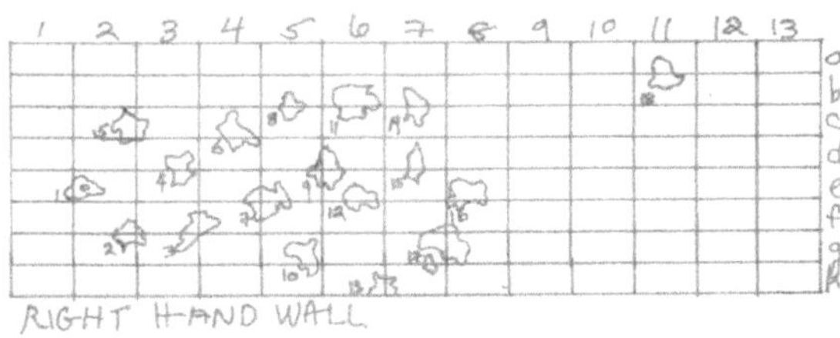

Wall Mapping. Map of wall, Project Room, Chelsea College of Art, 2011

Museums project

Since 2013, I have been documenting visits to museums in Greater London. Museums raise all kinds of issues around institutional power: how did they start and who started them, how are they housed (a purpose-built edifice?), where did the collection come from? How representative of the subject is it? It struck me more forcibly each time that any collection is random – that the British Museum, for example, is full of what was found, of what was left when civilisations crumbled, and what was taken and chosen for display. Museums validate their collections by displaying them as if they are definitive, and they are famously places where one is enjoined not to touch.

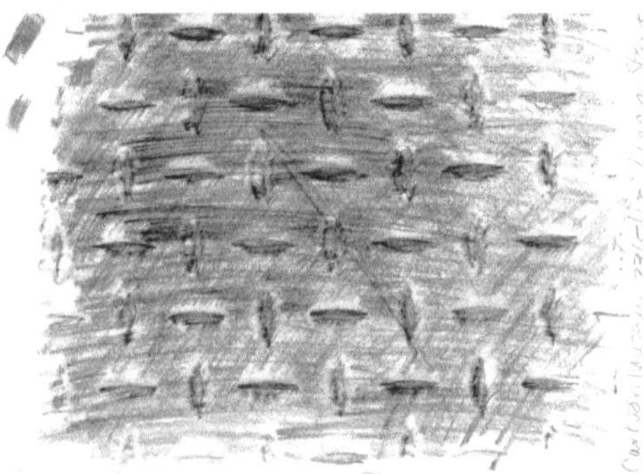

Stair lino, Cartoon Museum, London, 2013

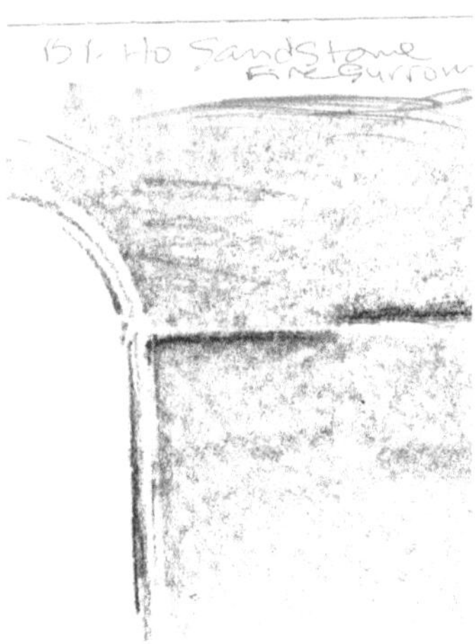

Sandstone fireplace, Benjamin Franklin House, London, Undated

London Transport Museum, partial step plate of Tube carriage, 2013

Sketch books

Looking through my sketch books, I realise that I have always been unconsciously aware of institutional power's raising the question of whether and when to ask permission, and an anxiety not to be caught. I would not have felt the same about photography or sketching, only rarely feeling the need to ask permission to do those. I turn to Pallasmaa again:

> The eye is the organ of distance and separation, whereas touch is the sense of nearness, intimacy and affection. The eye surveys, controls and investigates, whereas touch approaches and caresses. [9]

Until you make a rubbing, you can't know what it will tell you. I like to make rubbings because I like to touch.

[9] Juhani Pallasmaa. *The Eyes of the Skin: Architecture and the Senses.* Chichester: Wiley-Academy, 2005, 46.

I was asked (correspondence with editor) 'to think of the normativity/regularity of your work in relation to the surfaces you are rubbing and what institutional power they represent', and the answer is they are always in relation to power. Touch always has the potential to be transgressive, and my approach to where, when, and how I make rubbings has always been, albeit subconsciously, dictated by that understanding.

And then I remember that there is a project I've wanted to do for a long time and I've not known how to go about it and it is precisely because it is about institutional power. I would like to make rubbings of the thresholds of each of the Cambridge colleges, but institutional thresholds are forbidding and you need to be invited to cross them. I got to know Cambridge when I did site-based projects there in 2014/15.[10] I never engaged with the University and became increasingly aware of how much it dominates the landscape and how other it is. But it used to be different. I have *The City of Cambridge Official Guide*,[11] issued by 'Authority' of the Council of the City of Cambridge, Guildhall, Cambridge. It is undated but contains a Rag Week photo dated 1959 and an advertisement for a school giving term dates for 1961. It offers a walk through Cambridge which would be hard to negotiate in 2018. On page 88, for example, we are strolling around Trinity: 'We now come to Nevile's Court … Make your way to the far right-hand corner of the Court, to the flight of stairs

[10] http://www.zanditon.com/thresholds/all.htm

[11] E. Cave (ed.) *The City of Cambridge Official Guide*. (Croydon: Home Publishing, n.d./1961).

leading to the entrance to the library. Open to visitors in the afternoons'. This is not a walk one could undertake today. Though whether in 1960 I could have made rubbings without permission, I do not know.

I make rubbings out of curiosity – how will this look? how will this feel? – institutions invite conformity; not the open-ended curious gaze.

References

E. Cave (ed.) *The City of Cambridge Official Guide*. Croydon: Home Publishing, 1961.

Juhani Pallasmaa. *The Eyes of the Skin: Architecture and the Senses*. Chichester: Wiley-Academy, 2005.

Andrea Pavoni et al., eds, *See*. London: University of Westminster Press, 2018.

Appendix: Rubbings Inventory: Table of rubbings found in a sample of sketch books from 2007–2017

Rubbings Inventory – Sketchbooks, 2007-2017

Surface Details			Location Details			Date	Permissions	
Description	Natural World	Built Environment	Description	Public Realm	Private Property		Yes	No
Street furniture: bench support nearest to bridge facing south		X	Public seating area, Riverside, MI6 Building, Vauxhall	X		31.01.07		X
Street furniture: lamp standard third from bridge facing north		X	Thames Path, MI6 Building, Vauxhall	X		31.01.07		X
3 textured surfaces		X	Parade Ground, Chelsea College of Art		X	13-15.06.07		X
Partial rubbing (upper right corner) of access/manhole cover		X	North side, Hercules Road, Lambeth	X		30.07.07		X

Surface Details			Location Details			Date	Permissions	
Description	Natural World	Built Environment	Description	Public Realm	Private Property		Yes	No
Rubber matting over hole in pavement		X	Lambeth Palace Road on approach to bridge opposite Lambeth Palace	X		30.07.07		X
Audio speaker surface; visitors are given a stethoscope to press against this to listen to audio descriptions		X	Florence Nightingale Museum, Guys and St Thomas' Hospital Trust		X	11.01.13	X	
Textured lino on stairs		X	Cartoon Museum, London		X	23.05.13	X	
Embossed Chubb maker marks on door of room safe		X	Cartoon Museum, London		X	23.05.13	X	

Metal grille work on the inside lid of an iron chest, c.1700, oldest piece of furniture in Bank		X	Bank of England Museum		X	19.06.13	X	
Wooden step with brass lettering; step onto a District and Circle Line tube carriage c. 1960s		X	London Transport Museum, Covent Garden		X	14.11.13	X	
Top of wooden balustrade handrail overlooking the dinosaur in the front entrance		X	Natural History Museum, Kensington		X	24.11.14		X
Sandstone fireplace surround		X	Benjamin Franklin House, Charing Cross		X	Undated (2015?)	X	
Latex casts of screw cut open to reveal 360-degree surface		NA	Studio		NA	17.03.15	NA	

Surface Details			Location Details			Date	Permissions	
Description	Natural World	Built Environment	Description	Public Realm	Private Property		Yes	No
Side of plastic gear wheel - Found object		NA	Studio		NA	17.04.15	NA	
Breeze block wall: Tyvek test rubbings x 2		NA	Studio		NA	30.04.15	NA	
Metal grill table surface		X	Hyde Park near Marble Arch, open air cafe		X	25.10.15		X
Eroded fragment of oyster shell	X		Moshup's Beach, Aquinnah, Martha's Vineyard		X	29.06.15		X
Pink granite boulder	X		Great Rock Bight, Chilmark, Martha's Vineyard		X	30.06.15		X

Embossed identification marks on unidentified metal objects; part of testing equipment		X	Kirkaldy Testing Museum, Southwark		X	Undated, 2016	X	
Polished concrete surface, toilet cubicle wall		X	Building Centre, Store Street		X	30.11.2016		X
Wall tiles, toilet cubicle		X	Tate Modern, Blavatnik Building		X	06.02.17		X
Various exposed surfaces, multi-level building site		X	Southbank Place, Waterloo		X	29.03.17	X	
Coarse textured boulder, smooth to touch	X		Moshup's Beach, Aquinnah, Martha's Vineyard		X	22.06.17		X
Chestnuts, x2: concave and convex sides	X		Wanstead Flats, Wanstead	X		26.09.17		X

Remains of a Fall

Tolis Tatolas

Senses are physiological functions that provide humans with perceptual data. Sensors create stimulations that travel to the central nervous system (brain) through the sensory pathway, which controls most of the activities of the body by processing, integrating, and coordinating the information it receives. It is commonly accepted that, out of all five traditional senses, vision plays a leading role in the neurophysiological procedure of perception. Think of the oft-used phrase 'to get the whole picture', which indicates that someone wants to understand the overall state of a situation. Which sense, then, comes second in the hierarchy? What happens when someone loses the ability to see – or, when someone walks in a room during night-time and the lights are suddenly turned off? In all cases, everyone will extend their hands by reflex in order to sense the space though touch, if vision is not available.

This series of photographic works presents remains of old, derelict residential buildings. Many of their structural elements are exposed on partition walls, or are shared with the adjoining buildings. They emerge from within the buildings' interiors and masonry: built-in bookcases, ceramic tiles, indoor pebbledash and coloured wall coatings, wallpapers, decorative plaster ornaments, iron protruding from reinforced concrete, electrical switches, parts of plumbing fittings, taps, and bricks. These act as pieces of a puzzle that impel the observer to link them up and to compose an image of the past. In this procedure, memory is of great importance. The buildings have been demolished either by natural causes, such as earthquakes or physical decay, or through human intervention, in the name of urban regeneration.

Despite the fact that the representations in the works can be 'seen', for they are produced through the medium of photography, they can nevertheless also indirectly stimulate the sense of touch. The most prominent feature of these works is the variety of textures of the surfaces. These are so powerful that they also invoke touch in an imaginary, synaesthetic way. Through their richness, what would have initially been flat surfaces seem to physically protrude from their two-dimensionality to occupy space, and to form what appear to be three-dimensional structures. This impression endows these surfaces with a kind of sculptural quality. A large number of colours and a variety of materials found on the walls, as well as the play of light, add more detail, leading to a sharper result. These surfaces can, then, be thought of as 'urban palimpsests', which contain layers of important historical information about a city: an ever-changing environment. They have the power to trigger memory. They also become a pool from which collected data of the past can be drawn, so that future pathways can be designed for cities.

We are currently undergoing a period in which every day is a little fest of a continuous technological revolution. We constantly 'eye-witness' extraordinary changes in technology and overuse them in our daily lives. Meanwhile, however, touch has replaced the former main means of communication, such as speech and handwriting. This reflects the high priority given to, and the cultural significance of, touch. Moreover, the dramatic climate changes that impact the global population and the widespread socio-political and financial crises, combined with the posthuman direction of thinking, highlight an urgent necessity. It becomes imperative that we carry out a meticulous study of normativity as it relates to a high-performance culture. The habits based through which society functions seem to have shifted from the 'anaesthetic' arena of common sense towards a field in which human senses interconnect. Human and the city are joined in a way that creates a hybrid: a large scale post-organism, which is reproduced in a *sui generis* way.

In these photographic works the surfaces of the building remains have become exposed through human intervention in the overwhelming majority of cases. They are reminiscent of an auto-immune disease, during which the organism itself attacks and rejects its own parts. They resemble an urban atopic dermatitis, where buildings are vanishing because of, mainly, human activity, but also environmental damage. The remains of fallen buildings simultaneously stimulate the senses of vision and touch and stand there to keep memory alive, as parts of a sequential transition, physical or imaginary. They become an allegory that recounts, in a nuanced way, the dynamics of the changes taking place in the constantly evolving operations of performance culture.

This aligns with the fact that senses are by default in a dynamic state. Senses are capable of perceiving the social environment as part of an organism in the ever-rotating wheel of evolution. They thus gain new potential and features through which to react to a host of stimulations in a perpetually changing world. As such, they can be said to transcend the limits of biology and philosophy, and become central to socio-cultural structures. The recent change in the hierarchy of senses, as we have hitherto known it, whereby touch does not follow vision, but seems to be its extension, its complement, or even its prerequisite, pays testimony to that. The haptic now plays a leading role in the urban normative, with a host of repercussions. As the sense primarily associated with privacy it is ambivalent in its potential: it can also be considered as the most affective, and as the most intrusive. This ambivalence becomes even more interesting when these two qualities of the haptic are juxtaposed, alternated, or even combined. It is at this juncture that, in a similar vein to bodily reactions to the haptic, photographs of buildings with their rich textures resulting from a variety of human intentions may serve as an interesting allegory of the contemporary double-edged sensorial experience of the city.

The new normativity, then, can be felt and better understood. Vision meets touch meets layers of history meets the contemporary flux in a constant reconfiguration. It is then that we can, perhaps, dream of law-making processes that respond exactly to this complex web of relationships, illustrated by the buildings in these photographs and the wealth of visual-haptic experiences that these point to.

Project: Remains of a Fall

Medium

Archival pigment print on museum grade fine art paper-Signed, titled, dated and numbered in ink on verso Limited Edition of 3 +1AP

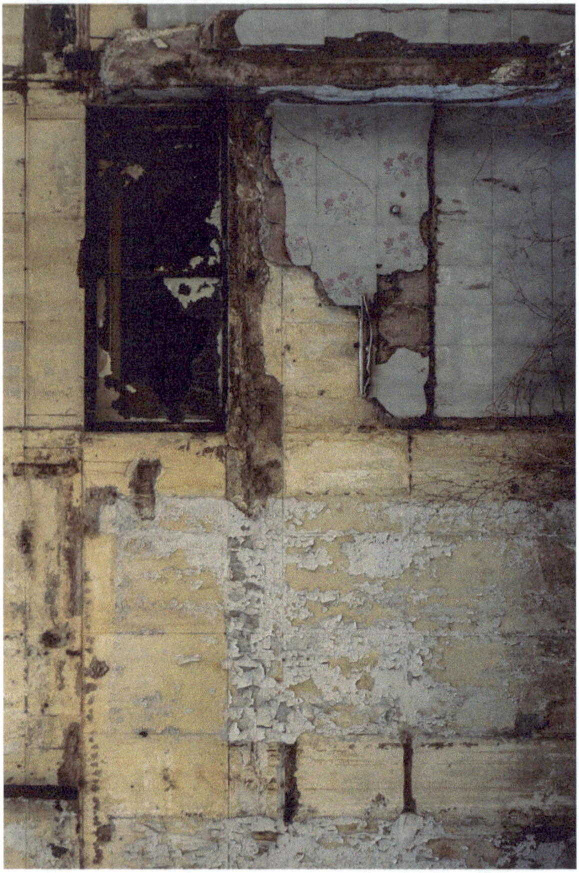

Untitled, 2017 / 80×120cm

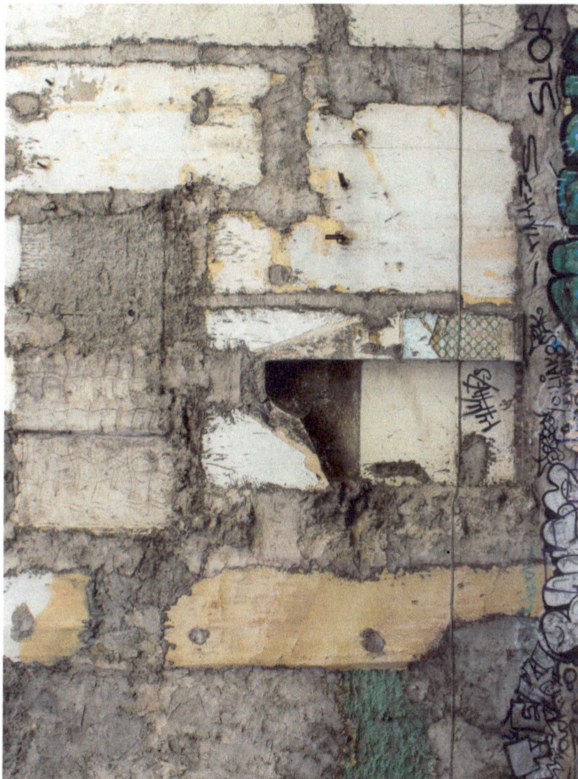

Untitled, 2018 / 80×120cm

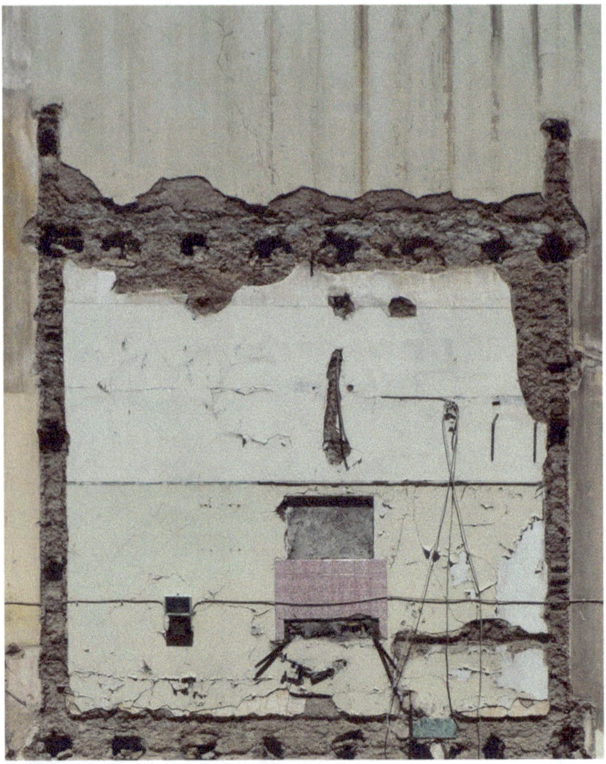

Untitled, 2018 / 80×120cm

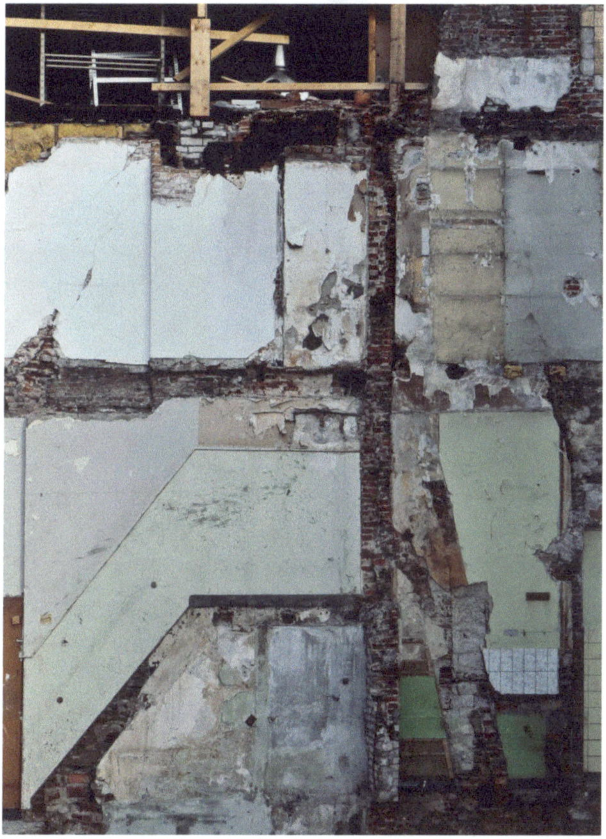

Untitled, 2016 / 110×80cm

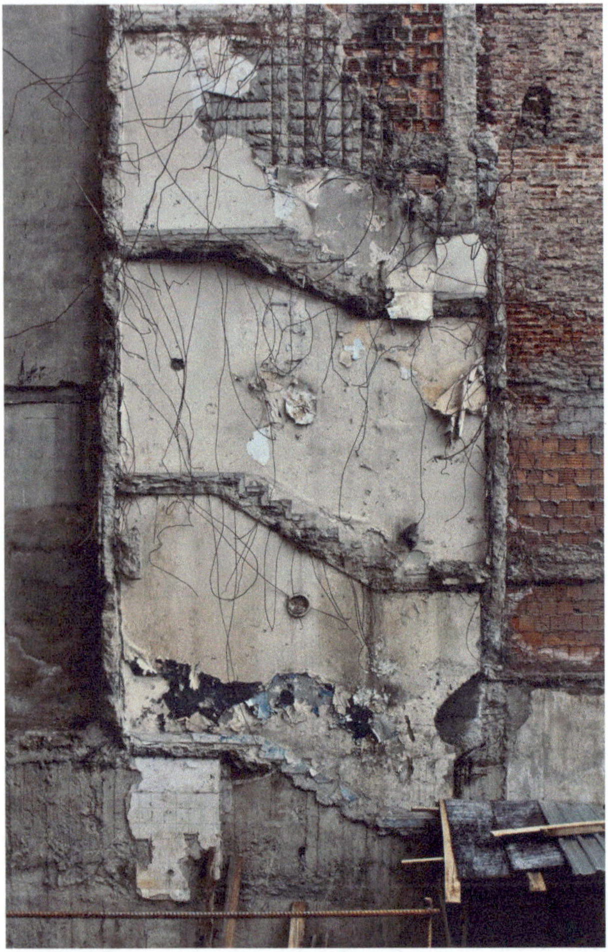

Untitled, 2015 / 125×80cm

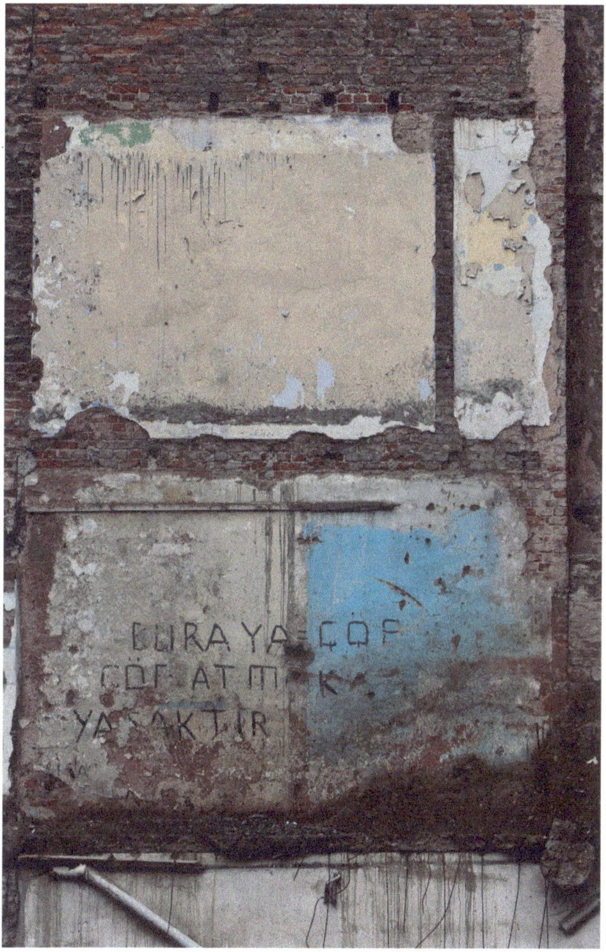

Untitled, 2015 / 125×80cm

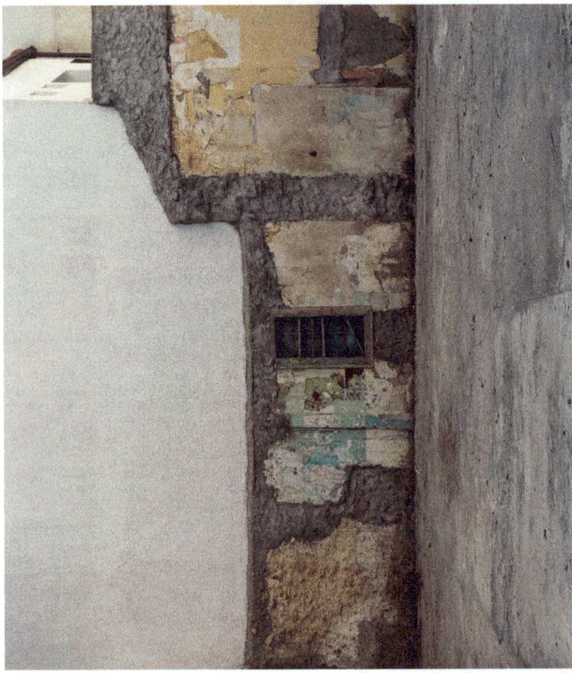

Untitled, 2012 / 80×92cm

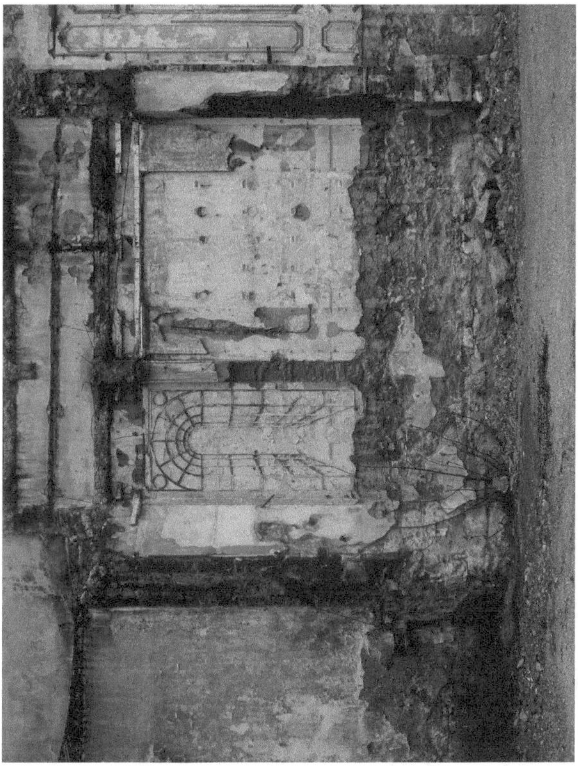

Untitled, 2011 / 80×105cm

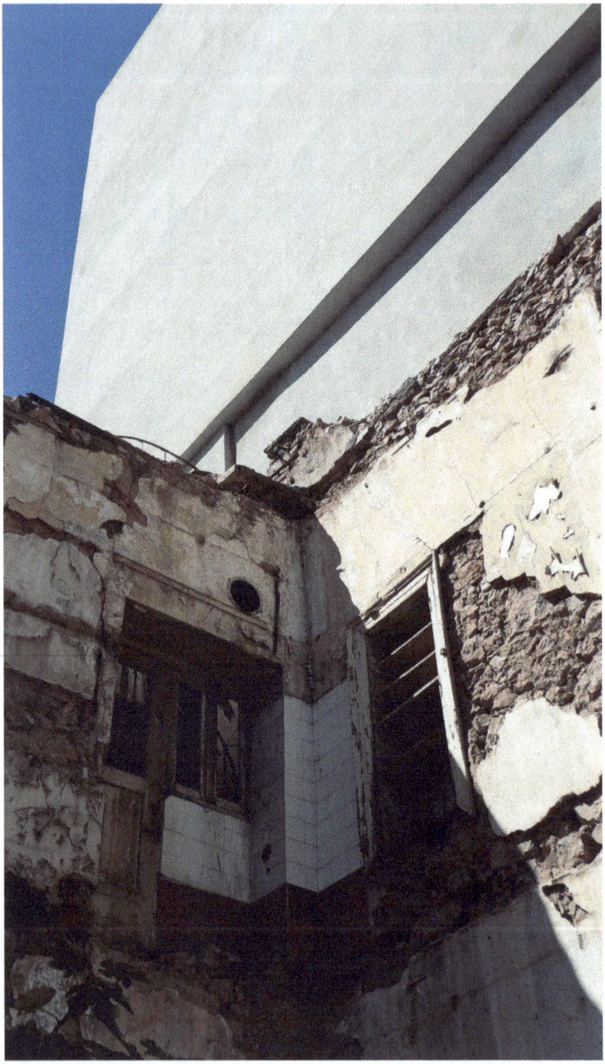

Untitled, 2012 / 140×80cm

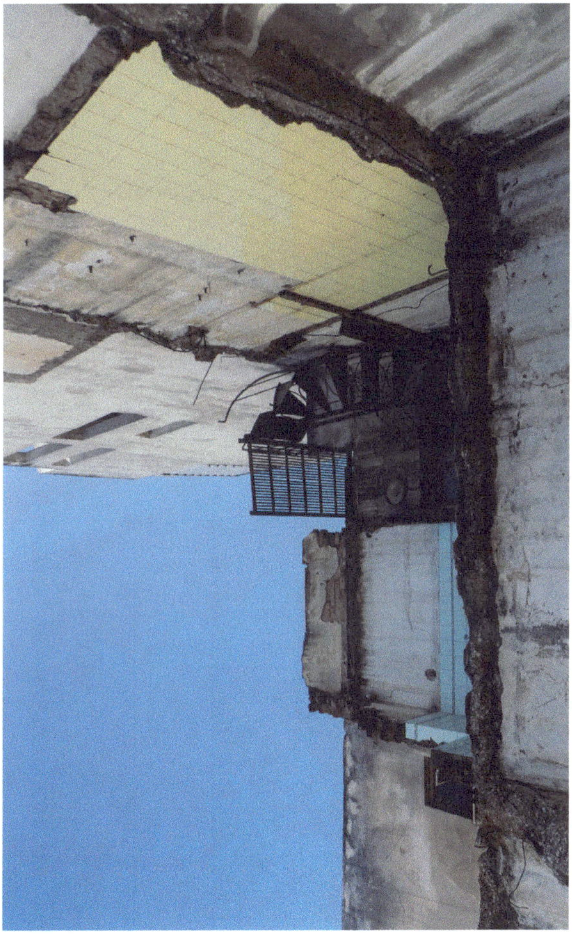

Untitled, 2012 / 80×130cm

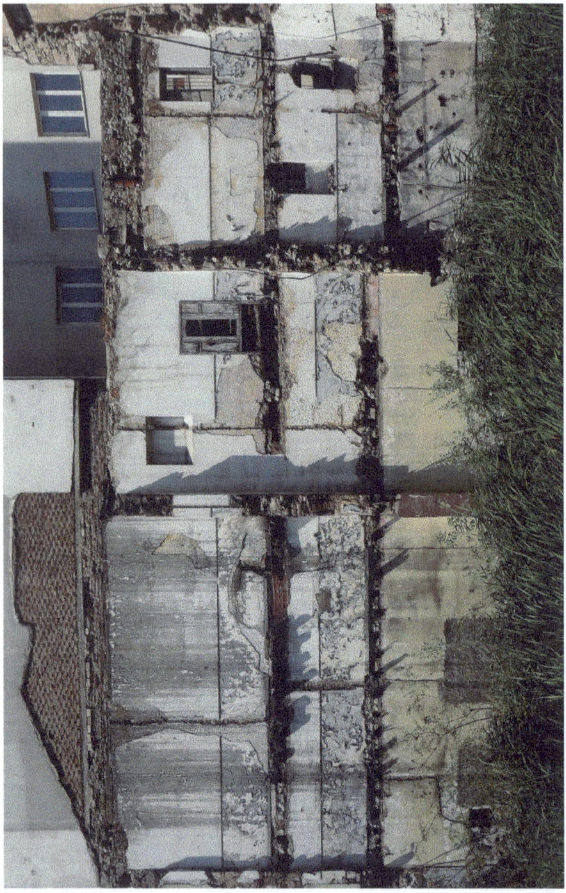

Untitled, 2011 / 80×125cm

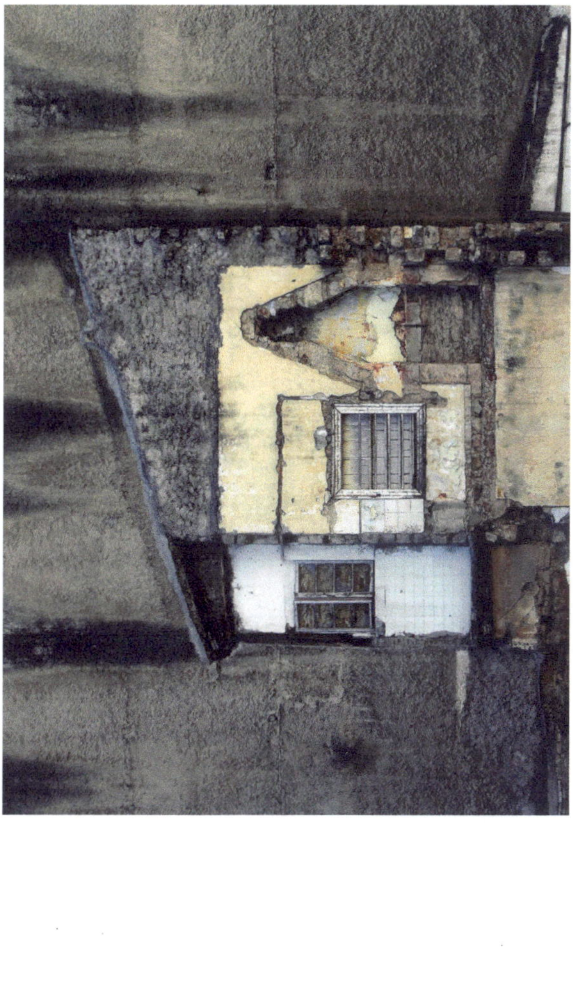

Untitled, 2012 / 80×110cm

The Contributors

Dr Jan Hogan is an artist and writer engaged in place-based research. Her work revolves around the materiality and sensitivity of paper and its agency in recording traces of events between human and nonhuman entities and forces. Jan is the Head of the Art Discipline at the School of Creative Arts and Media, University of Tasmania, Australia. Jan's research is interdisciplinary in its focus on social and ecological justice in settler colonial environments.

Professor Erin Manning is a professor in the Faculty of Fine Arts at Concordia University (Montreal, Canada). She is also the founder of SenseLab (www.senselab.ca), a laboratory that explores the intersections between art practice and philosophy through the matrix of the sensing body in movement. Current art projects are focused around the concept of minor gestures in relation to colour and movement. Art exhibitions include the Sydney and Moscow Biennales, Glasshouse (New York), Vancouver Art Museum, McCord Museum (Montreal) and House of World Cultures (Berlin) and Galateca Gallery (Bucharest). Publications include *For a Pragmatics of the Useless*, *The Minor Gesture* (2016), *Always More Than One: Individuation's Dance* (2013), *Relationscapes: Movement, Art, Philosophy* (2009) and, with Brian Massumi, *Thought in the Act: Passages in the Ecology of Experience* (2014).

Dr Nicole Nyffenegger is a Senior Lecturer in Medieval and Early Modern Literature and Culture at the University of Bern, Switzerland. She currently works on the textuality of marked skin in medieval and early modern literature and has in this context published an article on 'Saint Margaret's Tattoos' (2013) and a co-edited volume entitled *Writing on Skin in the Age of Chaucer* (2018) to which she contributed a chapter on blushing and paling. Further publications and research foci include discourses of the (gendered, wounded, violated) human body, gender and performance, authorship in medieval historiography, margins and marginality, and cultural conflict and identity.

Professor Naomi Segal is a Visiting Professor at Birkbeck, University of London. She has published 18 books and 97 articles on comparative literature, cultural studies, gender, psychoanalysis and the body. Her most recent monographs are *Consensuality: Didier Anzieu, Gender and the Sense of Touch* (2009) and *André Gide: Pederasty and Pedagogy* (1998). She is an Academic Associate of the British Psychoanalytical Society, Chevalier dans l'Ordre des Palmes académiques, a Member of the Academia Europaea, and an Honorary Fellow of Queens' College Cambridge and the Institute of Modern Languages Research.

Dr Moritz von Stetten has studied sociology, philosophy and politics in Heidelberg (Germany) and Manchester (UK). In 2018, he completed his dissertation at the a.r.t.e.s. graduate school and the institute of media culture and theatre in Cologne. It deals with the critical reception and processing of Niklas Luhmann's system theory in the international and interdisciplinary academic discourse. Now his research focuses on the sociology of mental illness, medical sociology, sociology of the body, affect theory and phenomenology.

Tolis Tatolas lives and works in Athens as a spatial designer and visual artist. He received a BA (Hons) (2008) in interior design from the Vakalo College of Art-Design/University of Derby and a BSc (Hons) (2002) in biology from the Aristotle University of Thessaloniki. He has had eight solo shows and participated in 21 group shows in Greece, the UK and Austria. He has written the book *Animals in the Homeric Ages* (2005) and has contributed to the edited volume *Science and Technology in Homeric Epics* (2008). Texts and artworks by him have been published in the Greek and international press. In the frame of his artistic activity he has curated the sets and costumes of works by Greek and international playwrights in Athens (Megaron – The Athens Concert Hall, Aggelon Vima etc.). Works of his are part of private collections in Greece and abroad (USA, UK, France, Canada, and Czech Republic). He has been a member of the Chamber of Fine Arts of Greece since 2014. Tatolas' artistic interests focus on geometry and abstraction and on how these can reflect ideas and conditions, and create and communicate feelings in a way similar to representational art. Creatively, he employs a holistic approach to aesthetics, within a framework of unity of all arts.

B.A. Zanditon (b. 1944) is a visual artist and writer living and working in London. Originally from the United States, she took a Fine Art Degree from Chelsea College of Art and Design as a mature student in 2011. Her work frequently takes an archival approach to documenting site.

The Editors

Dr Caterina Nirta is Senior Lecturer at the University of Roehampton, UK. Her research interests revolve around the body, space and time. She is the author of *Marginal Bodies, Trans Utopias* (2017).

Dr Danilo Mandic is Lecturer in Law at the University of Westminster. His research focuses on copyright law and its relation to technology. His other research interests comprise sound studies, art and law, and media studies.

Dr Andrea Pavoni is Post-doctoral Fellow at DINAMIA'CET, ISCTE – Instituto Universitário de Lisboa, Portugal. He completed his PhD at the University of Westminster, London, in 2013. His research explores the relation between materiality and normativity from various transdisciplinary angles. He is the author of *Controlling Urban Events: Law Ethics and the Material* (2018).

Professor Andreas Philippopoulos-Mihalopoulos LLB, LLM, PhD, is Professor of Law & Theory at the University of Westminster, and Director of the Westminster Law & Theory Lab. He is the author of *Absent Environments* (2007), *Niklas Luhmann: Law, Justice, Society* (2010), and *Spatial Justice: Body, Lawscape, Atmosphere* (2014), as well as editor of several books. His interests are typically interdisciplinary, including space, corporeality, new materialism and philosophy.

The Westminster Law & Theory Lab is a research lab based at the University of Westminster, experimenting with collapses between law and other disciplines, such as geography, religion, anthropology, art theory, political theory and so on.

Index